THE TEACHER AND THE CHILD DEVELOPMENT

THE TEACHER AND THE CHILD DEVELOPMENT

SURESH DUTT

ANMOL PUBLICATIONS PVT. LTD.
NEW DELHI - 110 002 (INDIA)

ANMOL PUBLICATIONS PVT. LTD.
4374/4B, Ansari Road, Daryaganj
New Delhi - 110 002
Ph.: 23261597, 23278000
Visit us at: www.anmolpublications.com

The Teacher and The Child Development

ISBN 81-7488-780-6

PRINTED IN INDIA

Published by J.L. Kumar for Anmol Publications Pvt. Ltd., New Delhi - 110 002 and Printed at Mehra Offset Press, Delhi.

Contents

Preface

Wordsworthian saying 'Child is the father of man' will ever remain relevant. Making of a nation depends on the sound development of children. For formation of civilized, cultured and happy society, we have to educate and train our children properly. As such 'Child Psychology' is the basis which is to be thoroughly researched and understood.

Amidst plenty of literature available on child psychology, the present work is unique which embodies latest research and developments in the field.

Volumewise organization of the work is: The Child and Personality Development; Moral Values in Child Development; Understanding Children; Behaviour Modification and Child Development; Teacher and the Child Development; Experiments in Teaching for Child Development; Curriculum and Child Development; and Teaching Methods and Child Development.

This encyclopaedia will prove a veritable mine of information for students, researchers, academics in the field of psychology and education. Besides this, administrators, policy planners, psychologists, and psychiatrists will also find this most useful and informative.

S. D.

1

Ideas for Teacher Education

The education of teachers, is undergoing criticism and revision. The members of the profession of education throughout its ranks are concerned with their own qualifications and are co-operating in many efforts to improve their preparation and to assure better initial preparation for those now entering upon the work of teaching. Parents are taking a lively interest in the questions of what kind of education is best for their own families and how to secure the services of teachers who are equipped to provide such education. Lay leaders called upon to take part in establishing and maintaining the schools are raising important questions with respect to the purposes of schools, the efficiency and value of present school programs, and the best means of enabling education to keep pace with the expanding educational needs of today. These developments necessarily have special significance for teacher education.

From this ferment in teacher education construction suggestions are emerging. Changes are taking place, some the result of criticism and some the result of other social factors, such as the shortage of manpower for all leadership occupations in a time of population growth and increased opportunity. Professional leaders Teacher education are earnestly trying to guide these changes wisely. This Book has set forth policies and grants recommended for teacher-education institutions. While there will continue to be differences of view as to the merits of such recommendations, they are already receiving serious attention in many quarters.

A program of development for teacher education such as is presented in this volume, is no mere accumulation of specific proposals for change. Its orientation toward the future is based upon an analysis of what is desirable in the future, with due regard to what has served well in the past and what is cherished in the present. It is based upon a body of ideas as to the significance of teacher education and the relation of the education of the teacher to the attainment of desirable values in the life of the people in future years. It is well that these central and controlling ideas become explicit, in order that they, along with the specific proposals that flow from them, may be examined and evaluated. The purpose of the present chapter is therefore to set forth this body of central ideas and to indicate how they have had a part in the thinking of the writers of the whole volume.

TEACHER EDUCATION INFLUENCES PUBLIC POLICY

In a general way educational systems, particularly those conducted at public expense, have always been partially justified in terms of their contribution to the public welfare. Likewise the teacher has always been seen as performing a public function through the educational program. Nationalism in Western political history has generally involved some form of supporting educational program, and frequently teachers have been selected and trained to give expression to that program. With the development of the scientific outlook and political democracy, however, the concept of free schools came to embody the purpose of education for free citizenship and independent civic judgment. Such free schools came to require teachers who showed no political partisanship in the classroom and who possessed no doctrinal or dogmatic limitations upon their powers of thinking and of teaching people to exercise their civic birthrights of freedom. Public policy in free society came to require schools and teachers to guarantee the security of such a society.

Recent years have brought a heightened awareness of the significance of the education of teachers in this respect. The profession of education senses its needs and opportunities in contributing to the realization of the goals of democratic life.

A substantial part of the general public recognizes that through public education democratic communities exist and advance. Teacher education is increasingly seen as a vital ingredient of the process of achieving freedom through public education.

Perhaps the best evidence of this view of the relation of education and social and cultural development today is to be found in the large amount of public interest, criticism, and discussion directed toward schools and school programs, as well as toward teachers and teaching methods.

It would be a mistake to suppose that Americans are unanimous in this respect. Voices are heard demanding that schools stay out of the business of directly shaping the development of citizens and leave it to the disciplines of learning in the common branches of knowledge to produce their own effects in due time upon the civic behavior of people.

Other voices complain that education, at least at certain times and places, has misunderstood the intentions of the founding fathers and fostered types of social development that are, for one reason or another, undesirable.

The very controversial character of civic education is a sign of its great importance. If teacher education is to be viewed as a means of developing the most fundamental potentialities of community life, the issues in this connection must be thought through by teachers and teachers must be free to think them through, without interference from any source. The program of teacher education must be designed accordingly.

EDUCATION IS FOR THE INDIVIDUAL PERSON

The heart of the idea of a free society is the dignity and worth of the individual person. If that ideal is to be achieved, it will only be achieved through the support of a surrounding culture—a body of beliefs, values, and ways of everyday behavior—which is directed toward this goal. Different cultures create different persons. The very humanity of man is defined by his place in a cultural complex which sets certain expectations of him and sponsors certain specific ways of perceiving and molding him.

Education in the United States and under similar national cultures elsewhere in the world is increasingly developing a concept of the individual who may be able to safeguard and extend the life of freedom. Political and social issues involving governments, armies, churches, prime ministers, farmers, bankers, and many other power structures and symbols thrust themselves forward in every day's news. These issues represent conflicts of values held by men. Their resolution depends primarily upon the kinds of men involved and in some cases may seal the fate of freedom for an age. If schools and communities can create men of principle and good will, men whose action is based upon understanding, deliberation, and intelligence, and men skilled in working with each other, there can be hope for the eradication of the prospect of struggle to death and annihilation on this planet. No less a purpose is worthy of the program of teacher education today.

What are the crucial attributes of a program calculated to serve such a purpose? In the first place, it will be an integral program based upon the fact that changes in human behavior are changes in the unitary person, rather than changes supposed to have been induced in one or more discrete parts of a human personality. Schools and colleges have too long and too frequently operated as if it were possible to train a muscle or a frontal lobe of an individual without being concerned with the rest of him. Too often educational programs have assumed that a particular brand of knowledge can be assimilated and mastered or a particular intellectual skill developed, such as mathematical thinking or aesthetic appreciation, without reference to the total functioning of the personality with its shifting controls of fear, confidence, drive, loyalty, and the like. Thus a teaching program to be effective, must be built as one fabric whose distinctive quality and value reside in all of the threads together, rather than in any one color or accent of design viewed as if it were alone. Not only does each particular educational activity of the student have a vital setting in which it finds its significance, but the program of an educational institution is to be evaluated in terms of its total effect upon the student. A program may not be judged to be good in terms of the fact that instruction in a certain subject is offered or a particular procedure is followed or a particular requirement is set. An educational program is necessarily a composite of formal and informal activities on the part of the student. It is to be conceived as a co-operative and single undertaking on the part of those who have charge of it and work in it, frequently including members of the general community who do not see their primary function as education, but who nevertheless have a valuable educational contribution to make.

In the second place, a teacher-education program to support a free society has clear objectives in terms of persons who behave or respond in certain ways, who can do certain things, and who exert certain kinds of influence upon others. The program is designed to produce a certain kind of human product, rather than merely to conduct a tour through certain marked territory for students, letting them make whatever interpretations and draw whatever conclusions they please. This is one of the most delicate and difficult conditions to be met in education, for it involves the very issue of freedom itself. Shall a student have true freedom to learn without being subject to the selective judgments of his teachers as to what he should learn? When the question is asked this way it answers itself: His freedom shall not be limited by his teachers! Freedom to learn, however, implies opportunity to learn and such opportunity is provided in some necessary degree by teachers. Thus some selection from the world of educational possibilities is inevitable and it should be made with a view to developing in the student the intelligence required for responsible freedom. A free man does not come into being automatically; he achieves his freedom by deliberate and purposeful effort in which he is aided by wise teachers.

It is perhaps anomalous that at a time when communication is so far advanced and group action is so crucial in the world at large, educational specialists should be arriving at a new awareness of the old and seemingly trite observation that education is a total process of change in individual people. The professional teacher deals with the process of bringing about changes of this nature. The final evaluation of the educational program as a whole must be in terms of individual persons acting singly and in their group relations. Teacher education must be so conceived if the general educational enterprise is to come to possess such validity.

There is a comprehensive and practical though searching test of education for the profession of teaching. It lies in the competent and successful performance of the individual as a teacher. The whole process of such professional education, including its general, personal, and strictly technical elements, should therefore contribute to the end in view. It should be continuously guided in terms of the developing student becoming a teacher.

Much has been made in this book of the "student personnel" concept or point of view. Essentially this concept is one to animate the work of every person who contributes to the professional education of the teacher. Special student personnel services of an institution contribute to the intelligent appraisal and discovery of the needs and possibilities of individual students. They will fall far short of effectively safeguarding the individual student, however, if they are expected to accomplish their purpose alone. They require the support of all other parts of the program of the institution in the same way that they support that whole program. No student who is lost to his instructors as an individual person struggling on his own toward maturity and competency can be recovered securely by the administration of some mysterious institutional medicine called student personnel service. The spread of this student personnel point of view among members of teacher education staffs has been wide and rapid in recent years. While the zeal of those who have perfected and introduced specialized services has sometimes been misunderstood, the total program of teacher education is now so developing in its regard for the individual student that there can be no basis for lack of harmony in the pursuit of this objective in the future. There is but one basic objective for all to seek, namely, the development of the competent teacher.

EDUCATION FOR FREEDOM IS AN EXPERIMENT

Those who were born around the turn of this century in the United States lived out their childhood and a part of their youth in a restlessly expanding and hard working economy but in a fairly comfortable ideological climate. The moral position of free government seemed good, since human slavery had been abolished and revolution from tyranny had been demonstrated to be desirable and possible, even if it had not yet been accomplished in every possible location. There was little doubt in the minds of ordinary Americans that the onward march of the idea of civic freedom would reach its goal in a matter of time.

What a rude awakening has been wrought by two world wars, the industrial and technological eradication of geographical distance, and the emergence of a vast, new, and precarious balance of power among governments! Even the mammoth strength of the United States of America has at times been challenged to show its intellectual and spiritual claims to hegemony. Its economic and military potentials seem insufficient guarantees of the survival of the idea and practice of human freedom for which this country has been a brilliant symbol in the modern world. Freedom was not so secure as we thought, it is not secure today, nor can its further attainment by any means be assured. Men can try to secure their freedoms, but not known formula will either certainly gain them or guarantee their preservation under all circumstances. The quests for the free life in the community and, indeed, in the individual himself must necessarily involve experimentation, from which, it is hoped, some things may be learned to guide others in the future.

There is no call to disregard the substantial gains man has made in the long, slow struggle for freedom—from ignorance, from hunger and disease, and from enslavement to others. There is no denying that education has played a part in promoting that struggle, as well as in preparing men to use and to safeguard such freedom as they have gained. The goal is far from attained, however, and education cannot rest content with itself while the tide of freedom ebbs so far as it has during our generation.

Education in a free society and for the life of freedom is itself an experiment with consequences of great moment. What is the best educational program to teach men to be free? We do not fully know and we may only hope to find out by experimentation carefully planned, controlled, and appraised. The condition of the times will undoubtedly influence the outcome of the experiment. The best program of education for one age may not suffice for another age. Of only one thing we may be certain: No man can legitimately contend that he has an educational program that will surely work for his purpose. Indeed, there is every reason to be live that the successful program will need to have written into it a considerable degree of flexibility, to enable methods and materials to be adapted continuously to developments as they occur in the process. No standardized program has much promise.

Teacher education, in this as in so many other respects, is the larger program of education in miniature, with something added in the way of sharp focus and practical applicability. Teacher education must be an object lesson, a demonstration to those undergoing it, of the quest for the spirit and the discipline of freedom. More than that, it must provide the prospective teacher with the art and the science of the leadership and the guidance of others in this same quest. What a weight of responsibility teacher-education institutions carry for contributing to the achievement of the way of life of which we dream and to which we devoutly aspire!

There will always be those people who regard a truly experimental program of education as frustrating and defeating. Some may even call it immoral: "Have we learned nothing with certainty about education, up to now?" They will ask. "Is there no security in the ways of our fathers? Can we not take certain educational programs and practices for granted and go on from there? Is not this talk about experimentation only a display of ignorance, if not actually a way of undermining the very foundations of our social cohesion and a threat to the way of life it purports to safeguard?"

Such people miss the point entirely. They seem to assume that changes in education, if and when needed, will automatically become self-evident. Furthermore, they seem to assume that educational experimentation implies complete rejection of the past. An experiment is an effort to learn how to do something with what we have at hand. An experiment in education makes greater demands than ever upon mastery of the past and present culture of man. It seeks to sort over these treasures to see what we can make of them. It seeks to use them to achieve a greater culture for our own generation. There is nothing arrogant or disrespectful about that. Such a search for new insight has been at least modestly the purpose of the prophets of all time. It has been the creative responsibility of every past generation and the very means by which we have learned what we now know.

When experimentation is proposed as a means of discovering the nature of the needed educational program, no haphazard trial-and-error changes are implied. Significant experimentation requires careful delineation of goals, broad planning of revised methods and materials to be used, and responsible evaluation of the results. Suppose, for example, that we were to concern ourselves experimentally with the question of the relation of linguistic competency in a modern foreign tongue to interest in the people who use that tongue and understanding of their problems and their intercultural relationships in the world of today. This is but one rather specific question of importance, among many others, and even this one suggests many facets which could be studied. Each and all of these studies could be designed to yield evidence which would increase the security with which educators shape their policies and conduct their programs. Does beginning foreign language study in early childhood years, rather than later, make any difference of interest in, and understanding of, the foreign culture at, let us say, voting age? Does spoken language facility in the foreign tongue persist as long when learned as an independent technical skill as when accompanied, for learning purposes, by a cognate or parallel study of the literature, customs, political and geographical influence, and economic system of the people concerned? Does persistent spoken foreign language facility tend to develop and keep alive interest in the life of the people? These are only a few of the facets of this one question, which could be the subjects of experimentation, and which serve to illustrate the need to plan experimentation with direct reference to the purposes and values of the educational program as a whole. They also illustrate the direct dependence of teacher education upon the crucial questions of purpose and procedure in the schools where the teachers will ultimately serve.

The reader will doubtless have sensed of this book that the entire analysis of the situation in teacher education and the changes deemed desirable repeatedly implies tension between security and opportunity, between safety and adventure. This tension is found to exist among people who are concerned with guiding and controlling or actually operating teacher-education programs. It may even put in some slight appearance among the contributors to this present volume, as evidenced by positions they have taken and recommendations they have advanced. This will tend always to be so, where experimentation is proposed, for a situation worthy of experimental effort entails, conservation of some past or present values, as well as innovation. How far can innovation in education be introduced and yet be evaluated in known terms? Moreover, how far can new methods be employed, for whatever good purpose, when the experimental subjects have to go on living under relatively constant conditions in certain areas of their lives? When does the introduction of new educational ideas in practice amount morally to playing fast and loose with the fortunes and destinies of the learners? These questions will always divide teachers. Some good professional people will be extremely cautious and actually will be unable to experiment; others will only find security in trying new ways of solving the hitherto unsolved educational problem.

We shall have to live with this tension, but we must not let it reduce us to fear and inaction. The invitation to experiment in human relations and human development, even in small ways, calls for faith. We have to believe that ideas properly tested and substantiated can illuminate action in the theater of human affairs and give it significance. We have to believe that men can do better with their destiny than they have done before, if they will but try, not merely to propose, but to find the evidence of the superiority of other ways of managing themselves. We have to believe in the essential moral responsibility of those who control the enterprise of higher education. We have to believe that they will guard and protect the inviolable person of the student in any new way of teaching which they together choose to introduce for experimental purposes. Since life itself, for the self-conscious human being, is an experiment, an adventure into his unknown future days and years in the human community, it would seem that sufficient faith for significant educational experimentation is not unreasonable to ask of even our most conservative colleagues and patrons.

THEORY IS ULTIMATELY TESTED IN THE LABORATORY

Scientific experimentation implies the laboratory test of theory. Procedures for this purpose are well established in the physical sciences and technologies. The use of the laboratory in scientific investigations pertaining to the behavior of human beings, however, carries no such widely established sanction. It is sometimes argued that humans will not stand still under a microscope and hence cannot be studied scientifically. In the light of what is now known of research method in the general field of biology, this seems a very shallow objection, since "controlled" conditions are difficult to maintain throughout that field, yet significant research has been accomplished. The basic problem in securing laboratory tests of theories of human affairs seems not primarily to be one of methodology, but rather one of purpose. It seems to hurt men's pride to fancy themselves as fit subjects for scientific study and experiment. Can men learn to accept the fact that their own behavior is governed by principle and follows with some regularity patterns of cause and effect? To know this fact and to see its ramifications fully would seem likely to reveal great new horizons of freedom within which man might control his destiny; to deny it would seem a sure way to perpetuate blindness and impotence in the face of the perplexities of the future. We need to get accustomed to a search for an adequate laboratory in the sciences related to human affairs.

In the broad and general sense the community is the laboratory of education. Educational programs are verified by their consequences upon the life of the community in the same way that chemical research ultimately proves worthy as it contributes to change for the better in the standards of life for the people. This concept of the laboratory, however, while valid is too unorganized to be of much help to the chemist. He must have a much more precise situation, designed and equipped for his special purpose at a given time. Similarly, the study of educational problems requires school and community facilities designed, equipped, and perceived as means of testing particular ideas, policies, and programs. Probably the failure to risk the organization of such laboratory situations for true scientific investigation has perpetuated much unproductive educational controversy and retarded the development of educational and social techniques which often seem to have been outdistanced by material advancements in our society. If the invention of social institutions could be encouraged by laboratory experimentation as discovery and invention have been encouraged in the field of physical phenomena, there would seem to be more hope of progress in dealing with basic social and moral issues than frequently now exists.

Every school is potentially a laboratory for its teachers. The education of the teacher is never truly complete. He is constantly presented with what appears to be is, at least in some respects, a new situation in which his knowledge, insight, skill, and artistry are to be used. Each such situation has experimental possibilities, as well as possibilities for the production of already tested and predictable results. If the experimental possibilities are missed, routine results are attained and the main purpose of the educational process for the learners, namely, the experience of grappling with their own problems of education, is thwarted. Schools can be effective laboratories for the improvement of teaching, however, only if those who maintain the schools will permit, encourage, and where necessary assist in making them serve that purpose. Teacher education therefore requires far more than a systematic pre-service instructional program in college; it hinges upon a complementary community situation in which the teacher may be encouraged as a learner, as a theorist of education in the making, and as a scientific student of the educational aspect of human affairs.

It is the possible scientific significance of every act of the teacher that distinguishes him from the artisan or craftsman and that necessitates both more extended educational qualifications and more latitude in governing his own work. Industry uses thousands of workers whose performance may necessarily be more marvelously skilled than that of the teacher, but no industrial worker carries more responsibility for possibly vital consequences to follow from a particular turn of his hand than the teacher. The education of the teacher must therefore be constantly conducted with a view to laboratory proof or demonstration. The theoretical discipline of the teacher is consummated only in laboratory application. The intellectual breadth and understanding of the teacher fully manifest themselves only in the laboratory practice of his calling. The artistry of the teacher finds full expression only in the laboratory performance which is his mission. Society dare not entrust the vital influence of the teacher upon its children to any whose preparation for that work has not been shown and cannot always be shown to meet the practical test of the laboratory where children, youth, or adults are actually engaged in their own education.

Educational theory is theory of individual and social action. Every man likes to dabble in educational theory, as well he may, for his own learning depends upon his acting upon some theory, implicit or explicit. The problem of the schools is to build more tenable and more widely applicable educational theory than can be turned up by any man for himself. The individual process of learning is really an effort to discover whether productive change in a person can be brought about deliberately and thus in terms of a particular theory. The data of this inquiry are the meanings acquired by the individual, perceived by him to be significant for his own further action, and produced under the impact of an educational program embodied in a class, a school, or a teacher-guided project. The teacher sets up the conditions for such inquiries and observes and interprets their results. The continuous accumulations of such results are the data for the repeated reformulation of educational theory. In an age of large scientific development, such as our own, it has become apparent that educational theories, like theories of the behavior of the so-called inanimate world, not only deserve, but require, to be regarded as proved when experimental evidence has been adduced to support them, but not before. Theory and practice of education can only be productively developed together.

PROFESSIONAL EDUCATION FOR TEACHERS NEEDS VAST SCHOLARLY RESOURCES

Education today requires the services of the competent, confident, intelligent, and wise teacher. A person with lesser attainments and qualifications will not suffice. One who meets such a standard bears a large responsibility and deserves professional recognition comparable to that given members of the other learned professions, such as medicine and law. Education for professional qualification to teach must consequently be a most exacting regimen.

Is teaching now a profession? There can be no doubt that many teachers now in service meet the high standards of a learned profession. Many schools, colleges, and educational systems require such qualifications of persons who would join them as teachers. Neither can there be any doubt that many persons now hold teaching appointments without meeting the truly rigorous standards of qualification for a profession. Many educational institutions and systems have apparently been forced lately to engage inadequately qualified persons, either because more fully qualified ones were literally unavailable or because financial or other limitations made it impossible to compete for the services of the best personnel with industry, commerce, government service, or other fields of employment. Nothing is to be gained by arguing that the presence in teaching of a certain percentage of poorly qualified personnel disqualifies the occupation as a profession. The workers in education aspire to professional status for themselves and for their calling and they deserve it. No school can with integrity set a lesser standard when the responsibility of education is so great as it is today. Education for teaching must be conceived and built on a professional basis and the obstacles must be overcome as soon as possible.

Can the fully competent teacher be described with such clarity that his professional education may accordingly be arranged? Do the members of the profession know what they mean by good teaching? Do they have firm convictions and recommendations to offer as to how schools should be conceived and operated? Should they speak with one voice upon such matters if they are to be regarded as a profession?

Educators have presented a disunited front on many major questions of policy and procedure since the time of Socrates. Healthy and sometimes unhealthy disagreements have been publicly aired with respect to the aims of education, the nature of the curriculum, teaching methodology, and school administration. These controversies have frequently become especially heated with reference to teacher education, since the attributes and purposes of the teacher so largely determine the education of the pupils. Such free expression of differing views has sometimes led the general community to infer that the profession of education was immature, confused, and incompetent to speak with any authority, and was therefore no profession at all. Such an inference is wrong on two counts: educators do not disagree on everything important; and unanimity is not essential to a profession.

There is wide agreement among teachers, specially among teacher educators, for example, with respect to the gross discrimination of good from poor teaching. Whatever uncertainty there may be in efforts at sharp definition of teaching skills, in delineating precise methods characteristic of successful teaching, or in stating the approved "content" of the curriculum, good teaching is still recognizable in terms of the behavior of those who are taught. This concept of generally preferred practice of the teaching art is a mark of the maturity of the occupation. In addition, there are other qualifications distinguishing the teacher group from a non-professional occupation. Teachers widely recognize the foundation of their work in the scientific study of man. They are deeply committed to the great ethical and spiritual purposes characteristic of the tradition of humane culture. They are effectively organized to improve and safeguard the quality of their own collective service to the community. These and other facts attest the significance of the occupation and demonstrate the need for a type of professional education which goes far beyond mere "culture" and erudition.

At what level of professional education should teachers be permitted to enter initially upon responsible practice of their profession? Too often this question has been treated as if it were purely an economic one. "How much pre-service education will the traffic bear?" it has been asked. Obviously no profession can be content to have the qualifications of its members determined by unexamined assumptions as to how much money should be spent on them or how much they can be paid for their services. The question is rather as to what types of service the community wants its teachers to render and what minimum qualifications teachers must have to render those services. On this basis there is ample evidence to support the thesis that teachers can be safely engaged with no less than baccalaureate degree preparation which has been directed toward the professional teaching objective. Many emergency programs have provided for the employment of persons with various short course certificates. Frequently these emergency teachers have particular skills that are even superior, but the full professional responsibility can seldom be borne successfully at the outset of their service by persons whose total educational development has been foreshortened to a pre-baccalaureate level. Many people feel that the situation requires that pre-service education for teachers should extend to at least five years after high-school graduation. There is much to support this view, especially if the five years are planned to include a liberal amount of time for supervised internship or practice comparable to the clinical elements in pre-service medical education.

While the minimum length of professional education for teachers is not seriously contested within the ranks of the teaching profession, the nature and content of that education are very controversial. The authors of this present volume have no part formula for this purpose, although they have expressed their views of the matter at considerable length. They would urge widespread experimentation with teacher-education curricula, with close evaluation of processes and products. One general conclusion has been repeatedly emphasized, namely, that an adequate teacher education requires the resources of scholars from many fields. There appears to be no feasible way to draw a sharp line of demarcation between what is called general education or liberal culture and the studies more directly related to the science of education and the art of teaching. There appears to be no fully tenable distinction between the study of what to teach, whom to teach, and how to teach. Teaching requires intellectual background, social maturity, scholarly interest and skill, and practical artistry, all integrally related as they are developed and as they are applied on the job.

Thus it becomes increasingly clear that the design of a teacher-education program should be conceived and developed through the mutually respectful co-operation of members of higher education staffs drawn from all of the disciplines or fields of scholarship that are concerned with the purposes and processes of education in the community. It is only fair to recognize that many institutions of higher education are engaged in rendering types of service apart from the professional education of teachers and that many staff members of such institutions will regard their primary contributions not to be in the latter field. They should not be expected to accept responsibility for which they have no appetite or in the discharge of which they cannot make a major investment of time and energy. Those who are to be called upon to assist in planning or in giving instruction in teacher education should be ones, therefore, who not only have a lively interest but who also will commit themselves to thorough and continuous study of the problem and who will devote their professional talents unstintingly to the achievement of the goal of providing the best possible total educational experience for the prospective teacher. It has long ago become apparent that academic distinction in a special field of scholarly interest does not, in itself, make an individual an expert on teacher education. The education of teachers requires rich scholarly resources, but it also requires that those resources be applied in distinctive ways to meet the needs of the prospective teacher.

NEW ISSUES INVITE REVISION OF THE AGENDA FOR ACADEMIC DISCUSSION

Since general educational policy in a democratic community is public policy, it must be hammered out in full view of everyone and indeed with everyone entitled to participate to the fullest of his wisdom and understanding. This process is a complex and hazardous one. At times it becomes painful and even wasteful, but it is the only trustworthy way for free men to reach the decisions most basic to their freedom and opportunity. There are many pitfalls to be avoided and methodological problems to be solved if the "great debate" is to be kept on a high level of significance. What is to be done with the man of ill will, or with one who would use free discussion to destroy free discussion? How can selfishness be identified for what it is and surmounted with views representing the common welfare? What are the qualifications of the expert in such public discussions? How is the expert to be used to illuminate aspects of a question which may only be appreciated by the highly informed and the original mind? Despite uncertainties with reference to these and other questions, the distinctive quality of a free society lies in the process of participation of its members.

There is a tendency for educational discussions to become repetitive, particularly as the number of people engaged in them is rapidly expanding. This seems particularly true in relation to the perennial questions of the curriculum, which seldom can be made to appeal to people as emergency questions, precisely because they are so old. For them to be considered realistically and productively, however, they must be redefined in the light of the changed conditions of each generation and each culture.

Today it seems increasingly evident that the issues composing the problem of education are not what many people have supposed they "always were." Many of the traditional issues of education and teacher education are disappearing, under the impact of the results of scholarship and new social and cultural conditions. Some old issues remain in new frameworks of significance. Some new issues are appearing to challenge those who are to chart the course of education. It is important that attention be focused upon the issues most urgently to be considered today and that outdated controversy be put aside. Continued debate, for example, over whether educational opportunity should be extended to all, or whether particular blocks of predigested knowledge should be "required," seems hollow in the light of the general aspiration for democracy in the world. The best insights of contemporary educational specialists as to the nature of motivation and achievement in the learning process necessitate a different approach to such problems. The relation of knowledge to the determination of loyalty and ethical conduct, however, continues to baffle educational theorists and deserves to be the subject of energetic experimentation in a world whose very survival seems to depend so largely as at present upon mass support for morally sound public policy.

ADMINISTRATIVE POLICY IS EDUCATIONAL STRATEGY

The approach in the United States to the problem of educational administration differs from that of "old world" or European school systems and universities in two principal respects. The final and official determination of broad general policies in education in the United States has been made the responsibility of special lay boards of control who act for the general public, whereas in Europe such matters are determined either by faculty groups or by government through law or regulation, or by both. Furthermore, in the United States the function of educational administration has been made a matter of specialized responsibility for certain professional officers acting under the direction of the lay board of control, whereas in Europe the educational administrator tends more frequently to be fulfilling a special assignment, sometimes honorary and temporary, as a regular teacher whose major professional objectives lie in the teaching career as a whole, rather than in the special aspect of it concerned with administration. The approach in the United States has been influenced considerably by the experience of American business enterprise, although it contains many elements of the European educational tradition as to its goals.

The fixing of administrative responsibility and the use of the active participation of the lay public both seem to present unique opportunities to American educational institutions to make education a democratic public process and to safeguard its efficiency and adaptability to changing conditions. The principal problem in the use of this approach seems to be one of keeping communication open between all of the legitimately interested parties, such as faculties, students, the civic community, and the related agencies of government, and the assimilation of the contributions of all such parties to decision making in an atmosphere of freedom. The prompt and efficient making of decisions that are both enlightened and represent as fully as possible the interests of all, rather than the privilege or vested power of a few, is the major objective. This is the general problem of democratic government as located in the field of the educational system.

Certain lessons have been learned in all free countries about educational administration. Perhaps the most significant of them is that the success of a policy in actually guiding the work of a group directly depends upon the investment that each member of the group feels he has made of his own efforts and purposes in the development and adoption of that policy. A policy that may appear to be good on all objectively logical grounds, but that has been derived in a mysterious or officious way, without consultation among those who are to be directly affected by it, will tend to be perceived as either having dubious validity or, at best, properly applying only to others, not to one's self.

Another lesson is that wide participation in the development of operating educational policies need not entail equally wide participation in the management of the details of application of those policies. This distinction between policy formulation and policy execution permits teachers to take an active interest in policy matters, without the fear that doing so may involve them in time consuming and perhaps to them uninteresting analysis of particular cases in the application of the policy. One safeguard needs to be borne in mind in this connection. Frequently it happens that an administrator dealing with a succession of particular cases to be settled finds himself making or necessarily modifying a policy in the handling of those cases. That administrator, assuming him to be committed to the democratic principle of wide participation in the making of policy, will need to have his own policy-making actions reviewed and sanctioned or reoriented by the group.

A third lesson is that the adoption of a policy should liberate those to whom it applies to operate in terms of it on their own initiative and without the necessity of securing administrative approval in every instance of its application. Nothing so quickly destroys the morale of a democratic group as to find that their efforts to regularize their enterprise by securing the clear statement of policies are nullified by an administrator who shows no confidence in the ability of the members of the group to act in terms of those policies, but insists upon personally approving and directing the disposition of every situation that arises.

How do the above principles of educational administration specifically affect the work of those people in our colleges and universities whose major concern is the education of teachers? Apart from their applicability to all such persons in their capacity as members of a college or university, they seem to have a direct bearing upon the development of policies to be followed in the teacher education program. In the first place, it is evident that each institution should organize itself for the efficient fulfillment of the teacher-education function as one of perhaps many specific educational functions for which the institution may be responsible. This usually means the designation of an administrative unit within the institution, such as a faculty, a college, a school, or a department, with its appropriate administrative official in charge, to have operating responsibility for teacher-education curricula, for the guidance of students planning to enter the profession of education, and for the evaluation of student accomplishment with a view to the award of degrees, diplomas, and credentials. From time to time, it has been proposed to do without such a responsible unit, leaving the operation to be managed in some way by the institution as a whole. Unless the institution has strictly the single purpose of teacher education, this method has little promise, since "what is everybody's business may tend to be nobody's business."

In the second place, such principles imply that provision should be made for advisory participation of various kinds, throughout the institution and probably from the rank and file of the profession and the public. The teacher-education unit needs such advice as may be obtained from representatives of cognate units in the academic fields, in the operation of the general education program, and in fulfillment of various research and service functions of the institutions. Teacher education is not only a legitimate concern, but also a vital interest of many such groups. They should participate actively and continuously in formulating and revising teacher-education policies. Such participation does not and should not imply that these cognate groups must assume the responsibility or be given the authority for the decision and application of teacher-education policy in the institution. Such decision, subject to the approval of the total faculty of the institution and the legal board of control, should rest with the designated teacher-education unit, in the same way that each other unit has its sphere of special responsibility within the operating framework of the institution.

PROGRAM CHANGES IN DEMOCRATIC EDUCATION COME IN AN ATMOSPHERE OF CONFIDENCE

Doubtless there are many college faculty members and administrative officers who have long since become convinced that teacher-education programs could be improved through certain changes in curriculum or educational procedure, but who find such changes slow to come about, despite vigorous efforts on their part. In fact, it is probably the rare college faculty member who does not wish some change in the work of his institution, at least in those aspects of it which do not directly affect his own particular function. The obvious locus of the difficulty is the lack of consensus among those concerned with respect to what exactly should be done and when and by whom.

From the sociological standpoint, it is in the nature of an institution to conserve ideas and ways from the past. This is no less true of an educational institution than of any other social institution, such as a church or a family. The conservative function of a social institution is not only a fact, but it is also an obligation. One important function of the school is to serve as a conveyor of the culture without which civilized life would soon disappear.

It is also important to recognize that institutions, particularly those designated as educational, have both the function and the responsibility to produce changes in the culture, under regularized conditions but effectively, failing which they suffer the penalty of their own replacement by other devices. It is their obligation to produce change, just as truly as their obligation to prevent it, which enables educational institutions to survive and to command public recognition and support. A school therefore lives with a perpetual dilemma: What should it conserve and what should it seek to change, and when and how should it do either? A teacher-education institution is once more to be seen as at one of the controlling points in the struggle with this dilemma. What it does shows the way to others who derive their inspiration and a measure of their competency from it.

To recognize the existence of the fundamental cultural dilemma of an institution for teacher education is to perceive the great difficulty inherent in the efforts of members of those institutions to induce changes in their own goals and methods of operation. The appraisal of the extent of this difficulty goes on continuously in a faculty. How urgent is any proposed change? To what extent is a certain type of change in a race against time and catastrophe? If a change is delayed or rejected what jeopardy may attend the institution and its work? How much can an individual allow his personal comfort with conditions as they are to impede changes sponsored by others? These are questions receiving explicit or implicit answers every day. They must be asked and they must be answered, if the institution is to go on with its work and possibly even with its existence.

The important problem in this connection would seem, therefore, to be how to get the questions asked and answered with the greatest clarify, directness, significance, and intelligence. How can all of the parties concerned with such questions be enabled to contribute their greatest wisdom in the necessary consideration of these questions as to the facts of life? Here we are brought face to face with the fact that teachers are necessarily constantly learners themselves. The school for children, youth, or adults is a school for its teachers. For a teacher-education faculty to see the goal of an improved program for its students is only the beginning of the learning process, in the same way as seeing the nature of a problem to be solved in arithmetic is only the beginning of learning for a fourth-grade elementary-school class. We know a good deal about how to arrange the conditions for learning by children and there is no reason to suppose that the essential principles are any different for a group of adult faculty members.

How, then, should a teacher-education faculty approach the problem of making improvements in the program of the institution? It seems evident that they should organize themselves to provide the necessary conditions for their own learning. They will doubtless proceed less dependently than younger and less mature groups do. They need not wait upon some constituted leader to arrange the situation for them. They may find or create their own leadership. They may go after their own resource materials and find their own advisory consultants. They can follow the best practices that they have developed for many groups of their own students. The results of their learning can be put at once to the practical test. They can find out whether they have learned enough and well enough by acting on the results of their learning and locating their deficiencies for immediate correction through more learning. Such a realistic method of evaluation will soon open new horizons for them as it is increasingly doing for student groups who are receiving imaginative guidance in their laboratory experiences in preparation for teaching.

When learning is institutionalized in a school it is for the purpose of systematic provision for the necessary stimulation of the learners, for the provision of learning materials, and especially for the purpose of creating an atmosphere that sponsors learning, guards it against interference from the affairs of general community life, and rewards it with approbation for success. A teacher-education faculty needs all of these conditions for its own learning. How are they to be provided? Some of the conditions can readily be provided by the faculty for itself. Some will only be available through leadership and specific provision by administrative authorities and the by controlling board. Examples of the latter conditions are sufficient time in the scheduled work load, sufficient financial security to relieve them of otherwise obstructive worry, and recognition for the fulfillment of this learning process as a worthy achievement related to faculty status. Perhaps the most important condition of all, however, can only be provided by the sanction of the wider community. That condition is freedom from fear of public reprisal for exhibiting originality and intellectual productivity. The work of guiding the education of the teacher has been shown to be one of tremendous, even almost unbearable responsibility.

2

New Age in Teacher Education

Much has been written, both perceptive and foolish, of the influence of philosophy, politics, and business on education. Far too little, however, has been said of the influence of science. Yet science is probably the most significant fact of contemporary life, the force that best represents twentieth-century civilization. And the scientists who have concerned themselves with education have been among the most vigorous, able, and influential men of modern educational history.

Edward L. Thorndike epitomized the scientific impulse in education. In his forty years as a professor at columbia University's Teachers College he played a leading part in shaping the ideas and practices of thousands of teachers and educational psychologists. He wrote more than five hundred articles, books, and monographs which spread his views on education and the results of his psychological experiments to every public and professional library in the nation. His work, and that of his students and colleagues, was discussed in countless professional meetings, in scholarly and scientific gatherings, and in teacher-training classes. Coming to the field of educational psychology in its early, formative days, Thorndike was able to dominate its course to an extent hardly possible to one man today. Moreover, the overriding image Thorndike cast on the scientific movement in education was reinforced by his association with Teachers College. When Thorndike joined its faculty in 1899, that institution was becoming the nation's most influential center for training leaders in all aspects of education—teaching, school administration, psychology, philosophy. Through its courses, various research institutes. and the writings of its faculty, Teachers College was a potent force. Speaking of Thorndike and Teachers College, its Dean, James Earl Russell, has written—

> In developing the subject of educational psychology and making it a fit study for students in all departments, Professor Thorndike has shaped the character of the College in its youth as no one else has done and as no one will ever again have the opportunity. of doing.

There were two corollary principles to which Thorndike subscribed: (1) Psychology no longer needed to be a branch of philosophy; it could become a rigorous science, adopting the appropriate methods of the physical sciences and worthy of the credentials of objectivity and verifiability. (2) Education could and must itself become scientific, aided by all the appropriate knowledge brought to it by the physical, biological, and social sciences—especially psychology. Probably no other educational scientist, before or since, better embodied in his own work the range of scientific currents of his time.

There are, to be sure, another great names in the history of educational psychology. Among psychologists the theory of evolution has possessed no more enthusiastic exponent than G. Stanley Hall, nor has psychology ever had a more articulate spokesman or a better student of his science than William James. Abroad, Johann Friedrich Herbart urged an education based on a truly scientific psychology early in the nineteenth century. There too, the imagination of Sir Francis Galton, the experimental precision of Germany's Wilhelm Woundt, and the dedicated persistence of Alfred Binet in France are each unrivaled in the story of the relationship of the schools to the science of the mind.

Yet is was Thorndike who built a philosophy of educational science and a comprehensive system of psychology. Accepting

Hall's Zeal but rejecting his sentimentalism and anecdotal research methods. Thorndike sought to make Hall's child-study movement scientific. Inspired by James, his own teacher, he rejoiced in the experimental method of psychological research which James reported but refused to pursue. Possessed of the insights of Darwin and of the experimentalists Thorndike was able to move beyond Herbart. He escaped the trap of narrowed interests and restricted imagination which limited the scope of Wundt's own work. Taking Galton's statistical tool, he transformed and swelled Galton's own quixotic study of individual differences and Binet's intelligence test into the vast, systematic enterprise that became the"measurement movement" of twentieth century social science.

Today we take our scientific developments increasingly for granted. Yet there is far less belief among contemporary scientists and social theorists in the nineteenth century's notion of science as a panacea for all the ills of human society. Evidence has mounted that possessing knowledge, *even when it is scientific knowledge,* does not necessarily make men either good or wise. An older faith and fervor have been blunted, alike by the accomplishments and failures of science.

How different it was in Thorndike's youth! He was born in Williamsburg, Massachusetts, in 1874, just fifteen years after Darwin published *Origin of Species.* This book represents a most portentous event, not only in the history of science, but for its effect upon every line of human activity. Conservatively interpreted, the doctrine of evolution meant that man would inevitably evolve to higher levels, mentally, physically, and culturally. Thus, " to a whole generation in search of scientific assurance about the fate of man, this was a gospel of good cheer." More radically, some took Darwinism as a mandate for deliberate social action. This interpretation mean that progress was not automatic but required the intervention of men. As the physical sciences had begun to reveal and to utilize the laws guiding the operation of the natural world, there arose the belief that the social sciences could know human nature and thereby direct the course of civilization. This view made science an ally of the social and political reform movement called Progressivism. Since the progressives believed education to be a critical instrument in the building of a better world, the educational scientist who labored to discover psychological laws became a partner in the whole reform effort.

Because of Darwin animal psychology became an important avenue to knowledge about human behavior and learning. Thus, Thorndike's doctoral dissertation, a study of animal learning called *Animal Intelligence,* has become a benchmark in the development of educational psychology. In studying human mental life, Thorndike placed man squarely in the animal world. "Nowhere more truly than in his mental capacities is man a part of nature. Amongst the minds of animals that of man leads, not as a demigod from another planet, but as a king from the same race," he wrote.

Darwinism represents one main stream flowing through Thorndike's work; another is experimentalism. Older psychology had been based on rational or empirical approaches. To define the principles of mental life one practiced introspection, examining one's own ideas and processes of thought. At best the earlier psychologists observed the behavior of others, trying to deduce objectively some general laws of human mental operations. It was not until 1879 that Wilhelm Wundt founded the world's first psychological laboratory, at the University of Leipzig. Thereafter, a score of American psychologists studied with Wundt, returning to establish psychological laboratories at various American universities and dedicating themselves to experimentalism in a new, scientific psychology. When a group of educators and psychologists interested in education met in Chicago in 1893, as part of the World's Columbian Exhibition, they called their gathering the Congress of Experimental Psychology in Education. This was but one indication of the growing identification of the new psychology with the concerns of schoolmen. By making animal psychology an experimental laboratory science for the first time and by drawing educational inferences from his results, Thorndike joined the evolutionary and the experimental streams in the new, emerging educational psychology.

Early in his assault upon pedagogical views haunted by tradition and a *priori* principles, Thorndike wrote, "It is the vice or the misfortune of thinkers about education to have chosen the methods of philosophy or of popular thought instead of those of science." What did Thorndike think science had to offer educators that was superior to philosophy, tradition, or opinion? For one thing he contended that schools could be run more efficiently with the help of science. The efficiency motif was a timely argument around the turn of the century. On every side schoolmen were bombarded by shortages of money, space, and time—all of which raised questions of school efficiency. With respect to teaching methods, for example, Thorndike held that psychology could contribute to efficiency on two counts. First, methods should be made consonant with the child's nature and with the laws of learning, both of which psychology could study. In this way teaching would be facilitated, rather than obstructed, and efficiency would increase. Second, the results of learning—products like arithmetic examples, samples of handwriting, and test scores—could be used to evaluate the efficiency of a particular teaching method.

The identification of science with efficiency was widespread in those days transcending the schools. With progressive views of politics came the call for "scientific city government." In business and industry it meant "scientific management." Among the military, the gigantic, pioneering efforts that resulted in the Army tests of World War I were an attempt to create an efficient system of classifying recruits.

Science's claim to efficiency was by no means its only appeal to educators. The schools are notoriously subject to fads; and there was hope that science would give education a stability it could hardly otherwise possess, especially in a period of rapid social change. There was another, related task for science. It was widely assumed that the high prestige of science would minimize outside interference, that the indisputability of scientific "laws" would reserve educational control of educators trained in the principles and method of a scientific pedagogy. This possibility was highly valued by the leaders of the rapidly professionalizing field of education in the early year of this century.

Through the activities of scientifically minded educators and educationally minded scientists like Thorndike, the old notion of teaching as an "art" was challenged by a new and fro more rigorous definition of teaching as a "science." The effort to make education a science or, at least, to define the scientific areas which it might embrace, as international in scope. Ernst Meumann in Germany, Cyril Burt in England, Gabriel Compayrè in France and somewhat later, Jean Piaget in Switzerland were only a few of the prominent scientists participating in this enterprise. But the undoubted center of activity and enthusiasm was the United States, and Thorndike was in large part responsible.

Completely committed to the objectivity and precision of the scientific method, Thorndike was ultimately a visionary in his expectations for educational science, as the following statement testifies:

> Experiments measuring the effects of school subjects and methods seem pedantic and inhuman beside the spontaneous tact and insight of the gifted teacher. But his personal work is confined by time and space to reach only a few; their [experimental] result join the free common fund of science which increases the more, the more it is used, and lives forever.

In his earliest speeches and writings Thorndike expressed the conventional view that, once the goals and objectives of education had been set forth, psychology was to determine the best means of insuring their fulfillment. After society had decided that arithmetic and citizenship should be part of the school curriculum, the scientific researcher would investigate, adjust, and appraise the most efficient way of arranging arithmetic skills and of determining how best to form habits of good citizenship. In his first psychology textbook, Thorndike stated that the question of aims was the province of ultimate values, to be judged by ideals and not by facts. However, with his growing involvement in the scientific movement in education, and perhaps also reflecting the close alliance of educational science with the general reform movement which has come to be called progressive education. Thorndike gave science an increasingly greater part in goal-setting as well.

In the keynote article of the new *Journal of Educational Psychology* which he helped to found in 1910, Thorndike defined science's role with respect to aims as being twofold. First, psychology could make already given aims better understood by defining, clarifying, and limiting them, by encouraging the statement of educational objectives as *exact changes in behavior* that education was to bring about. In this way a goal loosely stated as: "The school will teach children to write a legible and pleasing hand" would be restated as: "At the end of Grade 2 the average child will be able to write a sentence equal in quality to step 14 on a given standardized handwriting scale; at the end of Grade 3 he shall. ..."Second, psychology could influence aims by enlarging and refining them, as in revealing facts of human nature that were previously unknown or which had been considered unimportant. By pushing into the unknown, psychology could help the schools to evolve as an ever more useful and vital social agency. In Thorndike's own work there is an excellent example of how educational psychology can enlarge the scope of education. His researches into the learning potential of adults were important in initiating and extending adult education programs through the public schools and in industry, and especially telling development in an age when Binet-type mental-age scales and the results of the Army tests supported popular opinion in the traditional view that childhood is the time for learning.

The distinction between the realms of fact and value narrowed as Thorndike's career progressed. Perhaps he fell victim to what John Stuart Mill long ago described as the inevitable temptation of the social scientist to become an adviser or even a policy maker. Thorndike came to believe that values were as much a fact of human nature as intelligence and, therefore, the province of the psychologist. Educational products and purposes must *both* be translated into quantitative statements.

Through his scientific studies of the curriculum and by means of the materials prepared for schools—text books, tests and scales of achievement—Thorndike vitally influenced professional thinking about what education *should* do. Indeed, no pedagogical philosophizing can afford to ignore the ways in which the scientific movement helped to determine modern-day conception of educational purpose.

The scientific movement was a viable phenomenon, characterized by a pletitude of activity an enthusiasm. Its strength derived from the general aura of scientism in American social thought, especially after 1859, and from the reputation and vigor of many of its early advocates. As a figure in the movement, Thorndike exerted leadership on two fronts. His system of psychology became the dominant educational psychology. This was particularly true during the first two decades of the twentieth century, before the development of strong alternative "schools" of psychology, before Freudian and Gestal theories began to influence educational thought. Furthermore, has works inspired other developments in educational science, sometimes only tangentially related to psychology. Most of these can be grouped together as aspects of the "measurement movement," the attempt to express the various dimensions of the educative enterprise in quantitative form.

Because Thorndike derived teaching procedures and the arrangement of subject matter from certain psychological "laws," a brief explication of his theories is in order. Thorndike's system of psychology is usually called Connectionism, or "stimulus-response psychology." Connectionism, is Thorndike's version of the much older "Association" psychology, best represented by British theorists in the nineteenth century and the dominant explanation for mental phenomena of its day. Both terms —Connectionism an Associationism—reflect the view that thought or learning is the result of joining things together. This might be the association of ideas or the linking of a particular perception or sensation with some action. In Thorndike's terms learning is the forming of a found between some response and a given stimulus: hence the term stimulus-response bond or, simply, S-R bond.

The major structure of Thorndike's psychological theory was laid down by the time he wrote his masterpiece, the three-volume *Educational Psychology.* Constructed from certain long-established principles of Western psychology, it also reflected that uniquely American concern with the total behavior of the individual organism which began in the nineteenth century and went by the name of "functionalism." The "functionalist" preoccupied himself with how many functions, with behavior, rather than with the description or analysis of abstract mental states. Thorndike spoke of connections between a stimulus and some motor response (though it need not be an overt action), not about connections between one idea and another. To Thorndike there is a directness in connection-making with a minimum of mediation by ideas.

Mind was described by Thorndike not as an extraphysical existence nor even as a distinct organ of the body. Rather, mind was a general term for "the sum total of connections between the situations which life offers and the responses which the man makes." Out of the doctrine of evolution had his animal studies, Thorndike constructed a theory that defined intelligence as a quantity of specific elements. Probably following the reasoning of Herbert Spencer, he claimed that animals feel things in a gross, total responses to a situation. However, man possesses the neurological capacity to select, to turn a complex impression into its many component parts. Being a highly active being, he is capable of experiencing a multitude of different details, abstracting and connecting them in ways which bring about the socalled "higher mental processes" characteristic only of human life. But "thinking" is simply having a number of particular impressions of the elements of situation. Man's superiority to other animals, said Thorndike, lies in has greater ability to select and then to form connections.

In the same way, individual men differ intellectually from one another. This is the essence of Thorndike's quantitative theory of intelligence. It places man on a continuous line of evolutionary descent and intellectual advancement. It also furnishes a rationale for the intelligence test. Since men differ in intelligence through possessing greater or lesser numbers of connections, it is possible roughly to assess any one man's total by taking a carefully selected sample. Exposing an individual to a standardized test is this sampling process.

Properly speaking, there is no one "general intelligence" in Thorndike's view. Rather, there exists a vast range of specific connections, some innate and unlearned and the rest the product of experience. Thorndike knew that the intelligence tests being constructed measured only a restricted range of types of connections, most particularly the verbal skills. He also registered an early warning against the fatalistic use of tests with children for whom they were inappropriate. In constructing his own tests, Thorndike never claimed to be measuring "Intelligence," but, instead, a statistically relevant sample of associations useful in predicting a person's ability to lean further, to form still more connections of the kinds which schools favor. Many educators were far less cautious interpreting test results, however. By and large the abuse of test scores can be laid more to schoolmen who interpret test than to the psychologists who construct them.

Throughout his career Thorndike faced the charge that his psychology was mechanistic, that it adequately explained only the most rote automatic, and habitual kinds of learning. Connectionism was frequently grouped with the conditioned response psychology of the Russian, Ivan Pavlov. Yet there were many ways in which Connectionist learning theory differed from Palvlovian conditioning. For one thing. Thorndike consistently preferred the inclusive term "situation" to the more restricted "stimulus." "The word situation....must be taken broadly," he wrote, for "the connection made is not necessarily with one particular circumstance or thing, but with the total state of affairs felt." The child kept after school does not make a connection with the isolated stimulus, sight of confining walls, but rather with the situation, sight of confining walls plus feelings of hunger plus absence of companions plus sound of companions at a distance, etc. These features of a total situation effect the response. Also, the response is neither simple nor unitary: a reaction is whatever is thought, or felt, or done as a result of the total state of affairs acting upon one. It is only for the purposes of scientific analysis, said Thorndike, that partialing-out or abstracting certain elements from a situation or a response is useful.

Since the school is concerned with learning, the connection or bond is of signal importance. Thorndike described the connection as a "tendency to respond" in a previously established way if the situation should be encountered again: thus it is the product of experience, of learning. He labeled all learned connections "habits." whether they are partially formed or strongly fixed and whether they refer to the tendency to put one's left shoe on first or to a liking for the music of Bartok. For this reason Thorndike called education the process of forming the habits desired by society. To his critics, many of whom defined habit much more narrowly, this made Thorndike the proponent of an education that would produce automations, individuals whose behavior is narrowed, nonthinking, and drill-induced.

Psychologists participating in education's scientific movement were to provide educators with a knowledge to the laws by which connections are made and broken—the laws of learning. Thorndike postulated two major laws, the laws of Exercise and Effect. Of the two, the Law of Effect is more original with Thorndike, though it had clear antecedents in the work of earlier psychologists, especially in that of Britain's C. Lloyd Morgan.

The Law of Exercise is Thorndike's restatement of the old principle of frequency or repetition to explain the forming of an association. As Thorndike phrased it, when a connection is made between a situation and a response, the strength of the connection is increased as it is used or practiced or exercised. Thus, if a child say "apple" at every sight of that fruit, the tendency to say or think "apple" at its every future appearance will be increased. the latter Connectionism came to regard Exercise as less important, denying that *mere* repetition will tend to fix connection. The Law of Effect became the central explanation of learning.

"When a modificable connection between a situation and a response is made and is accompanied or followed by a satisfying state of affairs, that connection's strength is increased; when made and accompanied or followed by an annoying state of affairs, its strength is decreased." This, formally stated, is Thorndike's Law of Effect. For education it means that the child should obtain pleasure or satisfaction or reward from his correct responses. Therefore, his lessons should enlist his interest and establish a desire for successful achievement in school. As an educational maxim this was not new; as a scientist's statement of psychological "law" this was Thorndike's bequest and represents the cornerstone of subsequent psychological interest in motivation in learning. Being scientific, derived through experimental research, the Law of Effect was a decisive force in the arsenal of progressive education. It called forth a new scrutiny of rewards, punishments, and incentives in schools. It complemented the new concern with child nature and the factors of instinct and pupil activity which were being stressed by G.l Stanley Hall and John Dewey among others.

While psychological research was carried on to determine the laws of human behavior, educational scientists also made broad-scale applications of measurement and statistics to other aspects of education. The school survey was among the most common and persisting of these efforts. To explain the schools' problems to a much interested public, to gain support for changes in curriculum and school organization, and to marshal reform interests in the schools, professional educators turned increasingly to the use of concrete facts and figures. Scores of school districts hired educational experts to survey the schools and their communities. Armed with the new language of statistics, professors of education and specialists in school administration crisscrossed the nation in the decades after 1910. Leading figures in the surveys, like George D. Strayer of Teachers College and Ellwood P. Cubberley of Stanford University, received their statistical training and their faith in the power of quantification in Thorndike's courses in educational measurement.

Related to the interest in numbers and the survey technique was the accompanying effort to construct a curriculum on scientific grounds. The first organized attempt was made by the Committee on the Economy of Time in Education appointed by the

National Education Association in 1911. Then came the less systematized but more widespread practice of the 1920s and 1930s whereby individual school districts conducted curriculum studies, often with the counsel of outside experts. Thorndike's part was strong but indirect. He had been a member of an earlier national committee on tests and standards but he did not collaborate in the work of the Committee on the Economy of Time or in subsequent activities of the curriculum survey movement. Apart from training in the principles of educational measurement and in statistics, the debt of the curriculum-science enthusiasts to Thorndike was one of inspiration. Thorndike's studies of human nature, his researches into the learning process, his psychological analysis of subject matter fields, and his oft-expressed faith in science, generated a belief that a science of curriculum making was clearly possible.

The need for concerted study of the school curriculum came from several sides. For one thing, scholarship and discovery in a number of fields, especially the sciences, raised demands for a modernized curriculum. This was a much-trod plank in the platform of educational reform. The changing character of commercial and industrial life brought pressures to teach the skills required by an ever more specialized society. The upward extension of free, public schooling to include secondary education for all meant that a kind of education originally intended for college-bound youth needed to be altered. Describing this era, one of the active participants in the scientific movement said, "We discovered that the dragnet of compulsory education was bringing into our schools hundreds of children who were unable to keep step with their companions, and because this interfered with the ordinary administration of our school systems we began to ask why these children were backwards." It was decided that part of the "backwardness" could be attributed to "nonessentials" in the curriculum. Thus, the Committee on the Economy of Time prepared its reports which outlined the minimum essentials of various school subjects. The Committee's fundamental assumption was that it is uneconomical to teach a child something he does not need to know, and that economy will result from the selection of only that knowledge which is directed serviceable.

The concern for relating the curriculum to the needs and abilities of a new kind of student cannot be separated from the desire of educational and social reformers that the school be made a more meaningful part of the lives of all children. For some this meant making the life of the society the curriculum of the schools. Equipped with standardized check lists and questionnaires, an army of investigators marched out in the scientific spirit to survey the community's ways of making a living and its habits of daily life. Responses were recorded, correlations were tabulated, and the results were translated into the lists of skills, habits, attitudes, and appreciations which were to be taught in particular schools districts. Courses of study thus prepared appeared throughout the nation. Although the major enterprise of systematically surveying community life patterns declined in popularity after the 1930s, locally appointed curriculum committees operating from the same functionalist premises continued this work for at least two more decades. Finally, vocal criticism directed at the "life-adjustment" character of this method of deciding about school subjects led to varying alternative approaches.

Thorndike stood at the very center of another phase of the scientific movement, the construction of tests and scales. Masses of achievement and intelligence tests were produced after 1910 and the output has never diminished. Today we are less familiar with the product scales which aroused so much interest in the early days of testing. Yet these measuring instruments, developed especially for handwriting, drawing, and composition, illustrate perfectly Thorndike's philosophy of scientific measurement. Consider has own handwriting scale as an example of the techniques he used. A large number of handwriting samples were arranged in a series of graded steps. Each step represented an improvement in some aspect of the quality of handwriting. The ranking-system—based on the pooled opinion of handwriting experts who had agreed on the arrangement—allowed a pupils's own writing to be compared to and matched with the samples of the scale. This meant the pupil's writing *quality* could be assigned a *Quantitative* value; that is, quality could be expressed in quantitative terms. Such scales represented the essence of Thorndike's belief that questions of quality are restable in terms of quantity. Thus men do not differ by virtue of being heavy or lean, tall or short, wise or foolish, good or bad. These categories imply a qualitative distinction which Thorndike rejected. Rather, men differ in the *amount* of weight, height, intelligence, and virtue they exhibit. Therefore, where statements in *amount* are lacking, it is not because numbers furnish an inadequate language. Instead, said Thorndike, it is because our science is still very young.

There is general recognition of Thorndike as a figure in the scientific movement in education. His place in the history of psychology is even better known. However, it is noteworthy that Thorndike is not usually placed among the Figures of the school reform movement of his century called progressive education, despite the many ways in which he furthered its goals. It is no less interesting that latter-day critics of education do not list him among the culprits responsible for modern school practices although today's schools bear the clear imprint of educational science. Rather his more noisome detractors have identified themselves with the progressive education movement. Some of the ways in which Thorndike belongs to and stands apart from the course of progressivism in American education are worthy of consideration.

Today, it is hardly possible to read an educational policy statement that does not mention individual differences. Whether the topic be the education of the gifted, the need for a "solid" curriculum, the expansion of higher education, or the improvement of mathematics teaching, there is implicit or explicit commitment to the proposition that the school must take account of individual differences. True in more than tow thousand years of recorded educational history there have been frequent, if sporadic, expressions, of concern for individual differences. But it is only with the advent of modern psychology that the *facts* of human variation have been available, contributing to a radically altered conception of the school. Earlier psychology concerned itself with the mind in general, not with specific minds. Not until the work of Francis Galton and James M. Cattell was there sustained interest in individual minds. However, when psychology began to investigate the nature and extent of human variation in intellect and personality it did so with a vengeance and, again, the United States was the center of such study.

According to Thorndike. Psychology must extend its restricted study of individual responses in reaction time and its perceptual acuity experiments to controlled investigation of the ways in which individual children and adults differ in native capacity and patterns of learning Science must transform the sentimental and haphazard concern for the child, shown by the child-study societies, into systematic analyses of the school population. The long-standing American enthusiasm for rugged individualism must be sustained by a precise and accurate knowledge of the nation's human resources. Thorndike enlisted educational science on behalf of both an efficient treatment of the child as an individual and for general educational planning. His work on individual characteristics was climaxed by the third volume of *Educational Psychology* in 1914, the most complete and comprehensive treatise on the subject of its day.

Thorndike proposed several school measures that were compatible with progressive theory. First, he recommended that special provisions be secured for children at either extreme of the range of abilities. Second, he declared that attempts to bring all children "upto grade" were fallacious and impossible of realization; instead Thorndike showed that equal practice opportunities actually increased differences in achievement between children. Third, he gave scientific sanction to the modern pedagogical dictum that the teacher must discover where each child stands and lead him from there, that education must begin with and take its lead from human nature as individually expressed.

Determining the characteristics of human nature and how they are expressed in various children was not the stopping point in Thorndike's view, however. Aided by science, education must *change behavior.* The school was to *use* its knowledge of human nature to mold children in accord with social mandates. Thus did Thorndike differ from the Naturalists who preceded him While Rousseau contended that education must be compatible with nature, the dictates were from nature and not from society or from reason. Hall, too, believed that the best education interferes least with nature. Thorndike would have no such neutral conceptions of the school. Like Dewey, but unlike some of the later progressives enamored of an image of a "child-centered" school, Thorndike denied that nature is inherently good; rather it is whatever man can make of it. "That the natural is the good is a superstition which psychology cannot tolerate. Still less, however, can psychology tolerate the superstition that there can be any foundation for educational achievement other than the best that human nature itself affords," he said. And, again, "Original nature has achieved what goodness the world knows as a state achieves order, by killing, confining, or reforming some of its elements."

Thorndike did not permit the facts of a gigantic and hitherto unrealized spectrum of human differences to lead him to lower his expectations of the schools. "I avoid nothing because it is difficult," he once said. The existence of a science is predicated on the belief in that regularity of action called "law," which science seeks to discover and explain. Thorndike was convinced that "It is folly to give up the attempt to get rational principles for teaching because the teacher's task varieties with the individuals taught."

Beyond describing individual differences, educational science sought to explain their cause. Thorndike early concluded that heredities is the major reason for human variation in intellect and character, that no other factor is more significant than innate and inherited inequalities in the capacity to learn. He denied John Lock's doctrine that at birth each child's mind is a white tablet to be written upon by experience alone. Instead, he argued that every child possesses a legacy of possibilities and experience realizes these possibilities. Thorndike's formulation was opposed by most of the theorists of the progressive education movement who believed that education is the *source* of intelligence, that the schools could build intelligence in the society by making enriched and functional learnings available to all. Thorndike seemed a determinist, since his theory meant that nay individual's nature and future possibilities are predetermined by heredity and that he would modify and limit schooling on the basis of revealed differences. But Thorndike denied the accusation of determinism, holding that once educators clearly know the respective roles of heredity and environment, the responsibilities of the school—its limits and its options—could be set reasonably. We serve education better by understanding it than by praising it, he said in 1914.

Despite the energy and effort which Thorndike exerted to bring about improvements in the schools, his science was not satisfactory to those reformers who claimed that education's powers were well high limitless. His explanation of the sources of differences between men was unacceptable to those who believed that education can create a democracy of equal. For his part Thorndike rejected this progressive thesis as a sentimentalism and an obscurantism which permits laxity in school and society alike. In his St. Louis address to the American Association for the Advancement of Science in 1935 he said:

> Ethics, politics and philanthropy have been guilty of neglecting individual differences, partly because doing so simplifies all problems, and partly because of the retention of theological and sentimental prejudices in favor of the similarity and equality of man.

Although there was basic agreement between Thorndike and the educators of the progressive movement about the need to consider individual differences in school planning, their interpretation of these differences had to vary. They held fundamentally opposed philosophical views of the nature of man and society.

On other fronts, too, this incompatibility intruded. There was substantial initial agreement between Thorndike and the educational progressives about the subject matter of the curriculum; but differences concerning the nature of the mind and the learning process led to an eventual and irreconcilable quarrel. When a psychologist. of Thorndike's stature said there is no such thing as general intelligence, he gave support to those waning a broadened curriculum. He undermined the existing argument that the established sequence of studies was universally suitable when he described the mind as myriad of specific connections and not as a muscle which must be exercised on a classical core of subjects.

Thorndike's attack upon the ancient doctrine of formal discipline aroused considerable agitation in educational and psychological circles. Beginning with the Thorndike-Woodworth experiment in 1901, there arose continual discussion of the question: How much of what is learned in one situation is transferred to another? The predominant view had been that certain subjects—particularly the more abstract studies such as mathematics—disciplined the mind, training its various faculties of memory, perception, and reasoning so that the individual would be equipped in any future situation. This dogma of formal discipline said that transfer results from the strengthening of powers or faculties rather than from the usability of some particular content or method of study. Considerable skepticism existed among psychologists of the late nineteenth century, largely as a result of the theories of Herbart and the famous memory experiment of William James. There was also doubt among educators, but at the turn of the century, faculty psychology and formal discipline were still accepted guides to curriculum selection and teaching practice.

Thorndike entered the fray early. "Now surely the sensible way to reason is not to set up an abstract notion of a proper discipline and argue about whether different studies fulfill its qualifications," he wrote in 1899, "but to see empirically what the different studies give to their followers." His first study found that practice in one kind of task, such as learning to estimate the area of a rectangle, did not result in improvement in estimating areas of differing shapes. His own later experiments corroborated these first results, showing little transfer to ease subsequent learning. What transfer did occur was attributed to the presence of common or identical elements in the two situations. Although

Thorndike later objected when others said that *no* transfer existed, he maintained that there was less harm in assuming too little transfer than in inferring that significant amounts occur.

The issue of transfer was not settled by Thorndike and the many other researchers who went to work on the question; and it is with us still. But the effect of the doubt cast by the transfer studies was critically important to the curriculum reform government. A review of the 1903 edition of Thorndike's *Educational Psychology* described the book as providing a "powerful argument to those who would adapt school programs to the needs of life as directly as possible." The contention that the curriculum should be made up of subjects useful in life already existed, as an alternative to the dominant belief in the mental disciplinary value of certain other subjects. The function of psychology was to give the criterion of usefulness scientific support, and it did so beautifully, If transfer does not occur or if its effects are minimal, then subjects must be chosen for their direct utility in life, the argument ran. Since learning is specific the schools must provide direct experience with the skills and knowledges required by life. Proposals to teach by "problem" or "project" methods received support as well. Thorndike make numerous statements favoring a lifelike, concrete, and directly useful education. Progressive theorists like William Heard Kilpatrick used the language of Connectionist psychology, at least in the early days before rival psychologies emerged which were philosophical more compatible.

Among psychologists, Thorndike's formulation of the Law of Effect is considered one of this signal contributions to learning theory. It is especially paradoxical that educators have virtually ignored this contribution which has coincided so well with their own concern for pupil interests and with making learning satisfying and pleasurable. Rather they chose to attack him on the basis of the Law of Exercise. He was labeled a reactionary in education, a proponent of rote-learning and teaching by drill methods. This charge was made despite the fact that, from the beginning of this career, Thorndike make Exercise and Effect companion laws. Long before the renounced Exercise as a major law of learning in 1929, he stated that mere practice does not strengthen a connection and does not insure learning.

It is not because Thorndike's complete psychology was unavailable that it was misrepresented by many of the most influential educational leader of his day. The reason may well be laid to Thorndike's consistent criticism of those who were entrapped by a teaching methodology which assumed that learning could be simply achieved that schools operated in the reform principles of progressive education would make learning easy—indeed, almost automatic!There is no royal road to learning or teaching, Thorndike said. Schools with happy, unrestrained children studying vital problems and lifelike "units" would still require exacting teaching if real learning were to occur. Some of the educators who welcomed Thorndike's research on transfer of training were as guilty of a belief in automatic learning as the older proponents of formal discipline had been. They sometimes assumed that pleasant surrounding, a sympathetic teacher, movable furniture, and a serviceable curriculum would insure the rich learning in which the founders of progressive education had believed. Thorndike's scientific training did not permit him to share this naivetè. in 1914 he told a group of educators:

> A child's mind is never a witch's pot to be set in action by educational incantations. Its defects are not curable by faith. To discipline it means to improve the specific habits. To develop it means to add bonds productive of desirable response and to weaken the opposite.

For his unflinching and unabated use of terms like "habit," "repression," and"systematic practice" Thorndike was criticized. His views on heredity's limitations upon learning ability seemd too harsh to a nation proudly extending universal education upward and to a profession wanting to believe in no inherent limit on the school's power to build a better society. As the successful years of leadership early in the century passed, one by one, into the 1920s and 1940s, Thorndike's pedagogy slid more and more from fashion. Yet in these same years the other achievements of the scientific movement were securely established in the schools. Still, it might be remembered that fashions in education, as elsewhere, often follow cyclical patterns. And, hopefully, it might once again be said of Thorndike's work, as The himself once said of science, that its ideals of accuracy and honesty are destigned to live on, in honor.

3

Psychology as Science

The motive for a man's life resides within himself and in the spirit of his times. Something of the personality of Thorndike can be gleaned from his professional writings and speeches and from the commentaries of his students and colleagues. The only published autobiographical material is the regrettably brief piece Thorndike prepared for A History of Psychology in Autobiography, edited by Carl Murchison. It is included here in its entirely.

AUTOBIOGRAPHY: EDWARD LEE THORNDIKE

I have no memory of having heard or seen the word psychology until in my junior year at Wesleyan University (1893–1894), when I took a required course in it. The textbook, Sully's *Psychology,* aroused no notable interest, nor did the excellent lectures of Professor A. C. Armstrong, though I appreciated and enjoyed the dignity and clarity of his presentation and admired his skill in discrimination and argument. These discriminations and arguments stimulated me very little, however, and this was later true also of the writings of James, Ward, and Stout. There is evidently some lack in my equipment which makes me intolerant of critical studies unless fortified by new facts or decorated by a captivating style.

The candidates in a prize examination were required to read also certain chapters from James's *Principles.* These were stimulating, more so than any book that I had read before, and possibly more so than any read since. The evidence is threefold. I bought the two volumes (the only book outside the field of literature that I voluntarily bought during the four years of college) and read all save parts of the most technical chapters. Though not, I hope, more impertinent than the average collegian, I reproached Professor Armstrong for not having given us James in place of Sully as our text. When a year later, circumstances permitted me to study at Harvard, I eagerly registered for the course available under James.

During the first semester at Harvard (1896–1897) my program was half English, one-fourth psychology, and one-fourth philosophy, the last at the suggestion or requirement of Professor Royce. The subtlety and dexterity of Royce's mind aroused admiration tinged with irritation and amusement. Most of the students saw him as a prophet, but to me then he seemed too much a performer. Under no circumstances, probably, could I have been able or willing to make philosophy my business. Its stars shone brightly at Harvard in those years (1895–1897); Royce and Santayana were at or near their full glory, and Palmer was, as ever, the perfect expositor, but what I heard from them or about them did not attract me. Later I read the *Life of Reason* with extraordinary interest and profit, and learned to value the integrity and sincerity and impartiality of Dewey's writings on philosophy as well as on psychology and education; but in general my acquaintance with philosophy has been superficial and casual. Work in English was dropped in favor of psychology in the course of the first graduate year, and, by the fall of 1897, I thought of myself as a student of psychology and a candidate for the Ph. D degree.

Münsterberg was in Germany from the fall of 1895 to the fall of 1897. During the second half of 1895–1896, Mr. Hackett and I had made experiments in a course under the direction of Professor Delabarre, who had charge of the laboratory. During 1896-1897 I first attempted to measure the responsiveness of young children (3–6) to facial expressions or movements made unconsciously as in mind-reading experiments. I would think of one if a set of numbers, letters, or objects (I cannot now recall which or how many). The child, facing me across a small table, would look at me and guess which. If he guessed right, he received a small bit of candy. The children enjoyed the experiments, but the authorities in control of the institution would not permit me to continue them. I then suggested experiments with the instinctive and intelligent behaviour of chickens as a topic, and this was accepted. I kept these animals and conducted the experiments in my room until the landlady's protests were imperative. James tried to get the few square feet required for me in the laboratory, and then in the Agassiz Museum. He was refused, and with his habitual kindness and devotion to underdogs and eccentric aspects of science, harbored my chickens in the cellar of his own home for the rest of the year. The nuisance to Mrs. James was, I hope, somewhat mitigated by the entertainment to the two youngest children.

During the two years of study at Harvard, I had supported myself by acting as tutor to a boy. We roomed together, and the incessant companionship and responsibility was burdensome, though he was cheerful, cooperative, and fonder of me that I deserved, and though I learned much practical psychology and pedagogy from the experience. A year free from such labor seemed desirable, so I applied for a fellowship at Columbia. I received the appointment, and upon inquiry was informed by Professor Cattell that an extension of my work on the mental life of animals would be suitable for a doctor's thesis. So I continued these experiments with chickens at my parent's home during the summer. I tried white rats also, but I was stupid in handling them and the family objected to the smell, so I let them go.

I came to New York, bringing in a basket my two most educated chickens, from whom I then expected in due time to breed, and so test the influence of acquired mental traits upon inherited capacity, a foolish project in view of the slow breeding rate of fowls. I also expected to test the permanence of their learning over a long interval, but never did, the first of a regrettable list of enterprises left incomplete.

Cattell was not only kind, but highly efficient, providing a room in the attic which was ample for my purpose, and giving, as always, sound advice. The freedom from work and worry for money was a great boon. The present policy of universities is to reduce grants for scholarships and fellowships relatively to the number of students, replacing them by loan funds, and this may be wise. But, so far as I can judge, scholarships at Harvard and a fellowship at Columbia increased my productive work in science by at least two years and probably improved its quality.

The motive for my first investigations of animal intelligence was chiefly to satisfy requirements for courses and degrees. Any other topic would probably have served me as well. I certainly had no special interest in animals and had never taken a course in biology until my last year of graduate work, when I worked hard at it and completed a minor for the doctor's degree. The work with monkeys, done in 1899–1901, was done from the mixture of duty, interest, and desire for good repute which motivates most scientific work. The extension of the fruitful experimental method to representative primates was obviously important. I would have gladly continued the work with the higher apes, but could not afford to buy or maintain them.

In the spring of 1898, I was offered two positions, one as a teacher of psychology in a normal school, the other at a much lower salary as a teacher of education in the College for Women of Western Reserve University. I chose the latter, partly because my brother expected to go there and partly because of the route of Western Reserve. I spent the summer in reading the facts and important theories about education and teaching. This could then be done if the history of educational practices was omitted. After a year at Cleveland, I was given a trial at teaching psychology and child study at Teachers College, and there I have spent the past thirty-one years.

I have recorded my beginning as a psychologist in detail because it illustrates what is perhaps the most general fact about my entire career as a psychologist later, namely, its responsiveness to outer pressure or opportunity rather than to inner needs. Within certain limits set by capacity and interest I did in those early years and have done since what the occasion seemed to demand. Thus for various courses taught at Teachers College I wrote the *Elements of Psychology, Notes on Child Study, Educational Psychology (in three editions, from 1908 to 1914), An Introduction to the Theory of Mental and Social Measurements, and The Psychology of Arithmetic.* It has always seemed to me better for an instructor to present his contributions in black and white than to require the labor and risk the errors of note-taking. Thus I have made somewhat laborious researches on mental inheritance, individual and sex differences, memory, work, fatigue, interest, the interrelations of abilities, the organization of intellect, and other topics in educational psychology, because in each case the matter seemed important for theory or practice or both. Thus I planned and directed the psychological work of the New York State Commission on Ventilation, prepared tests for the selection of clerical employees, and served on the Committee on Classification of Personnel in the Army and in various other enterprises because I was told by persons in whom I had confidence that it was in the line of duty. Thus I have written textbooks for children to show that psychology does apply in detail to the work of the classroom Thus, in 1919, at the request of the faculty of Columbia College, I undertook the responsibility of preparing annually an intelligence examination suitable for use in the selection and placement of freshmen; and in 1922, at the request of Justice Stone, then Dean of the Columbia Law School, I conducted a three-year investigation which resulted in the Capacity Test adopted in 1928 as a part of the system of selection of entrants to the Columbia Law School.

Obviously I have not "carried out my career," as the biographers say. Rather it has been a conglomerate, amassed under the pressure of varied opportunities and demands. Probably it would have been wiser to plan a more consistent and unified life-work in accord with interest and capacity, but I am not sure. Even in the case of great men there is considerable evidence that the man's own interests and plans may not cause a better output than his responses to demands from outside. So James wrote the *Principles* with wailing and gnashing of teeth to fulfill a contract with a publishing firm. *Pragmatism* and *The Will to Believe* were done when he was free to choose. An ordinary map of science has probably less reason to put his own plans above those which the world makes for him. So I do not complain of the restrictions imposed by the necessity of earning a living by various drudgeries to which I have been assigned. And I reproach myself only moderately for not having looked and thought longer before leaping to this, that, and the other job.

In the last dozen years I have been enabled by grants from the Carnegie Corporation to carry on two investigations, which I did choose and plan, one on the fundamentals of measurement of intellect and capacity, the results of which appeared as *The measurement of Intelligence,* the other on the fundamentals of learning, the results of which have appeared in *The Fundamentals of Learning* and in *The Psychology of Wants, Interests, and Attitudes.* These do seem to me by far the best work that I have done and I cannot help wondering what would have happened if similar support had been available in 1905 or 1915.

The impetuosity to which I have referred has influenced my work in detail. I often have to do corrective and supplementary experiments and discard work because in its course a better way is found.

Another weakness has been an extreme ineptitude and distaste for using machinery and physical instruments. Presumably my work have been better, and certainly it would have seemed better, if I had been at home with apparatus for exposing, timing, registering, and the like.

The training which I have most keenly missed has been a systematic course in the use of standard physiological and psychological apparatus and extended training in mathematics. Perhaps the first would not have profited much in view of my extreme incapacity. I did not lack capacity for mathematics and tried to remedy the second deficiency by private study, but something else always seemed more important. I managed to learn the essentials of statistical method somehow, and have handled some fairly intricate quantitative problems without, I think, making more than one mistake (which I was able to correct promptly at the suggestion of Dr. T. L. Kelley). But I feel incompetent and insecure in the abstract algebraic treatment of a quantitative problem and am helpless when the calculus is necessary.

Young psychologists who share one or more of my disabilities may take comfort in the fact that, after all, I have done useful experiments without mechanical ability or training and have investigated quantitative relations with very meager knowledge of mathematics.

As personal features on the other side of the ledger I may put intelligence, good health, strong eyes, the interest in work and achievement which Veblen has called the instinct of workmanship, impartiality, and industry. As environmental features I may note home life with parents of superior intelligence and idealism, many profitable courses in Wesleyan, Harvard, and Columbia, especially those in abnormal psychology with James, statistical methods with Boas, and neurology with Strong, university colleagues eminent in psychology and other fields, and the great body of published work in science.

The last is of course the most important. Though an investigator rather than a scholar, I have probably spent well over 20,000 hours in reading and studying scientific books and journals.

I have tried to make two lists, one of authors all or nearly all of whose writings I have read, and another of authors not included in the above to whom I owe valuable facts or suggestions. But the first list of thirty or so names grades off into the names of many more, much of whose writing I have read, and the second list, which is very long, cannot be accurate because of faults of memory. So I may note only that the writings of James and Galton have influenced me most, and that factual material seems to benefit me more than what is commonly called discussion and criticism. Although, as has been stated, my tendency is to say "yes" to persons, my tendency seems to have been to say "No" to ideas. So I have been stimulated to study problems, to which Romances, Wesley Mills, Stanley Hall, Alexander Bain, Kraepelin, Spearman, and others seemed to me to give wrong answers, more often than to verify and extend work which seemed sound. Of late years this negative or critical tendency seems to have weakened and given place to an interest in questions to which the answers are conflicting or inadequate, and in questions which have not even been faced.

Up till the war I was able to keep fairly well informed of the findings of psychologists in respect to animal psychology, individual psychology, and educational, psychology, but since 1917 I have been able only to follow specially important work and that which I had to know about in connection with my own researches. In spite of the saving of time due to the *Psychological Abstracts*, my reading is now less and less adequate each year.

I have a suspicion that our scientific code, which demands that an investigator should acquaint himself with everything, good, bad, and indifferent, that has been done on the problem which he is investigating should be somewhat relaxed. Personally I seem to have profited more from reading important books outside of the topics I had to investigate, and even outside of psychology, than from some of the monographs and articles on animal learning, intelligence tests, and the like, which our code required me to read.

We are especially urged in these psychological auto-biographies to describe our methods of work, but I seem to have little or nothing useful to say in this regard. In the actual work of advancing knowledge of human nature we may use three methods. We may observe and think about the facts that come our way; we may deliberately gather by observation or experiment facts which we see can be got and which seem likely to be instructive; we may put a question that we know is important and then do our best to get facts to answer it. I have done all three; most often the last. The most fruitful methods often come to mind late in the course of/an investigation. When one does everything that he can think of, the doing often makes him think of something else. So the idea of the delayed-reaction experiment (which has proved the most valuable of my methods of studying animal mentality) came to me after two years of work with animals. So the idea that the difficulty of a task for intellect (or any other ability) can be measured only in the case of a task composed of enough elements to involve all of intellect (or of the ability, whatever it may be), and nothing but it, came only after 30 years of study of intellect, and over a year of special investigation of means of measuring difficulty for intellect.

Concerning conditions favorable and unfavorable to scholarly and productive work in science. I have little or nothing instructive to report. Peaceful successful work without worry has rarely tired me, though if I drop below a certain minimum amount of sleep, a headache results. Noise does not disturb me unless it is evidence of distress, as of a person or animal in pain. Surety of freedom from interruption is of course beneficial. Social intercourse except with intimate friends is fatiguing, and all forms of personal conflict, as in bargaining, persuading, or rebuking, are trebly so. Physical exercise is enjoyable, but not, so far as I know, beneficial. A general background of freedom from regret and worry is almost imperative, and I early decided to spend so little and earn so much as to keep free from financial worries. In order to reduce one cause for worry, it has been my custom to fulfill my contractual obligations as a professor before doing anything else. The good opinion of others, especially those whom I esteem, has been a very great stimulus, though I have come in later years to require also the approval of my own judgment.

Since my own history is so barren of interest and instruction I may add a few notes of general observation. Excellent work in psychology can surely be done by men widely different in nature or training or both. James and Hall were essentially literary men, one with an extraordinary sense of fact, the other with extraordinary imagination and prophetic zeal. On the other hand, some of our present leaders were first trained in physics or engineering.

Excellent work can surely be done by men with widely different notions of what psychology is and should be, the best work of all perhaps being done by men such as Galton, who gave little or no thought to what it is or should be.

Excellent results have come from the successive widenings of the field of observation to include the insane, infants, and animals, and from the correlation of mental events with physiological changes. Should we not extend our observations to include, for example, history, anthropology, economics, linguistics, and the fine arts, and connect them with biochemistry and biophysics

After Darwin's publication of Origin of Species in 1859, whole new lines of investigation opened up in the social sciences as well as in biology and zoology. Concepts like "survival of the fittest," "natural selection," and "adaptation" were applied to man's culture and institutions, to human activities of all kinds including education. The imprint of the evolutionary thesis is manifest in every line to Thorndike's endeavors. Part of one acknowledgement of psychology's debt to Darwin, from a lecture delivered at the University of California in 1909, is reprinted here.

DARWIN'S CONTRIBUTION TO PSYCHOLOGY

Psychology, as you all know, means the science of mental, as opposed to physical, facts—the study of thoughts and feelings, as opposed to physical objects. But the science of mental facts may mean to different individuals and at different times very different things; and to understand Darwin's contribution to it we must for a moment consider some of them.

To most of the writers on psychology of the first half of Darwin's century, it meant naming, describing, and classifying our states of mind and our so-called mental powers...

But psychology, at least to-day,...means the study of intellects and characters in all their relations to the bodies which possess them. Human psychology shares with physiology, anthropology and sociology the study of all human nature and activity. Psychology in general shares with zoology the study of all animal nature and activity. Now in the activities and the behavior of man , as of any other animal, Darwin was interested. He was preeminently a naturalist. Only when the mind played a part in the general economy of life—only when it could be studied from the outside by careful and impartial observation of its effects, did he feel special interest or show special capacity in studying it. It was to psychology as the science of human and animal behavior that he contributed...

First of all, of course, Darwin gave psychology the evolutionary point of view. Psychology had studied the human mind itself alone and had taught that our minds were all made after one pattern mind, which worked as it did for no intelligible reason, but just because it did. Darwin showed psychologists that the mind not only is, but has grown that it has a history as well as a character, that this history is one of hundreds of thousands of years, and that the mind's present can be fully understood only in the light of its total past.

Psychology has by no means fully mastered this lesson. Human learning is still too often described with total neglect of animal learning. But each decade since the *Origin of Species* appeared has shown a well marked increase in comparative and genetic psychology. Of our own countrymen, for instance, William James, Stanley Hall, and John Dewey have consistently worked at psychology on a genetic basis. Psychology has also been careless in *applying* this lesson. The ostensible followers of Darwin have sometimes shown far too little of his industry in mastering facts and of his caution in making inferences from them. The kind of thinking that considers the pleasure humans take in swimming fully explained as a relic from the minds of our ancestors who were fish, or that accounts for human coöperation in industry by reference to ants, bees and wasps, may take the name, but has not the spirit, nor, in reality, the method of Darwin. But, side by side with such extravagant speculations and unnatural history, careful observations and experiments have been made with reference to animal learning, to the mental powers of primitive man, and to the mental evolution of the human species.

Only those of expert acquaintance with the recent history of psychology would appreciate a list of the psychologists who have thus been Darwin's followers, or a review of the investigations which they have made; but you will all perhaps be interested to know the present status of the doctrine of mental evolution—the present belief concerning the genealogy of human intellect and character.

I must warn you that we shall be dealing with the battle of investigation at its very outposts, hearing the latest returns, but not knowing how far they will be finally confirmed; and that very many of my statements may be amended by later and better work. But I can only report what, with present knowledge, seems to me the course of development of the human intellect. Of the development of human character, I cannot, for lack of time, speak at all. And for the same reason, I must begin our mental history, not at the very beginning, but half way in its course, with the fishes.

You know that starting from this point our bodily decent is roughly as follows: fishes begat amphibia; amphibia begat reptiles; reptiles begat mammals; some early mammals begat the primates; some early primates begat man.

The existing fishes have intellects of a sort, in the sense that they can learn—can so change their natures as not to do the same thing in the same circumstances. The unfit object they first tried to eat, they later reject; the unfit place they first went to, they later avoid. The nature of their learning will be clear from a simple but typical instance.

If the common Fundulus of the New England coast is confined by a wire screen at one end of an aquarium upon which direct sunlight shines, it reacts to the situation by swimming toward the shaded end of the aquarium. When it pokes its head against the screen it changes direction, swims alongside the screen, and them again to ward the shaded end. It will thus in the course of time swim at nearly every square inch of the screen. If now a small hole has been left in the screen, say in the upper right-hand corner, the fish will, in the course of such instinctive swimmings toward the shade and changes of direction, swim through the holds and reach the shaded end, where it will remain in physiological peace. If the experiment is repeated again and again, say at intervals of twenty minutes, the fish will make, sooner and sooner, fewer and fewer of the useless darts at the screen, will make the appropriate movements of swimming to the right, rising up, and swimming through the hole. Whereas at the first trial it spent five or ten minutes in getting out, it will now spend less and less time. Eventually, after many trials, it will have eliminated all the futile movements,—will, when confined by the screen, swim to and through the hole directly in five or ten seconds.

The fish has learned to respond to the particular situation in an adaptive way. It has modified its behavior to suit the situation. Its learning consists in the stamping in or strengthening of the connection between that situation and the particular response of swimming to and through the hole, and the weakening and final elimination of the connections between that situation and the movements which resulted only in the perpetuation of the unsuitable situation. Sensitiveness to a situation, a variety of responses, the selection of the fit one and its association with the situation, are the four essentials of its learning. No "ideas" of "thinking" of the human sort are necessary to account for it.

Such learning by directly connecting certain responses with a situation and disconnecting certain others from it, was undoubtedly characteristic of the fishes of long ago who were our forefathers. They learned, but they learned without thinking about the situation or thinking beyond the situation. They learned very few things.

The amphibians and reptiles, which come next in the line of descent, show the same sort of intellect, the only know difference being that in general they can be sensitive to more kinds of situations, can make more kinds of responses, and can connect the later with the former in more ways.

In the case of the mammals, other than the primates, special studies have been made of dogs, cats, rats, mice, raccoons, and guinea pigs, which agree in finding this same learning by the direct selection of one response for association with a situation as the main component of the animal's intelligence. With it there are, possibly, obscure traces of the life of ideas, of thoughts of things past and to came, of things bound to the actual present situation only by connections made in the animal itself. But the early mammals, who are in the direct line of descent to man, probably progressed beyond the reptiles only by being able to learn more and different habits, not by learning them in a more human way.

In the monkeys, which have been studied somewhat elaborately by four psychologists, the same learning without thought, the same responding to the situation of the moment without recalling the past or foreseeing the future, the same trial and success method, is the rule. The monkey in general does not call up ideas, select the ideas that seems fit, and act upon it. He acts impulsively, not intellectually, doing not what he thinks of doing, but what he feels like doing. But he feels like doing an enormous number of things; and at times, when one of those things is notably successful, he drops his previous behavior and adopts the successful act so suddenly that he *seems* to have formed not a habit, but a notion.

It is safest to doubt that having ideas, thinking about things instead of poking, pulling, biting, clawing and chattering at them, plays a large role either in existing primates or in the early primates who came between the mammals in general and those mammals whom we would accept as brother-men. But there can be no doubt that in the number of kinds of situations to which they respond, in the number of responses they makes, in the number of connections they can make between situation and response, and in the love of mental activity for its own sake, the primate group—the present monkeys, chimpanzees, gorillas and the ancestors of them and of us—are far in advance of other mammals and in a line that leads straight to the human mind.

For the demonstrable intellectual difference between the year-old baby and the monkeys is not that he has many ideas while they have few or none. He, too, has few or none. It is that he responds to more things and in more ways. He differs from the monkey as the monkey differs from the dog and as the dog differs from the fish.

The arousal of the human yearling by all sorts of sights and sounds, and his varied, incessant manipulations of all sorts of objects, seem a random, futile play. They do not seem to preserve him or the species. But it is this behavior, which we significantly call "monkeying with" things, that produces ideas. By responding to one thing in so many contexts and with so many acts, the little child comes to respond to it by no act at all, but by thinking it, having an idea of it. By extending the animal learning far enough, it of itself produces ideas, and ideas produce all the rest.

When once the mind begins to function by having free ideas, all the phenomena of reasoning soon appear. The adult seems to differ enormously in intellect from the year-old baby. And in practical efficiency he does. But the psychological factors of an adult intellect are all observable in the average child of three. Roughly speaking, between his first and third birthdays a child becomes intellectually a full human being.

How slowly or how abruptly the change came from early ancestors not intellectually above the present primates to our nearer ancestors possessing, like two-year-old children, free ideas of at least the common objects around them and their own common bodily acts, no one has attempted to estimate. It was a radical change in its consequences; but psychologically it would require only an extension of instincts and capacities already present in the primates. It could well have come, according to pure Darwinian principles, from small variations repeatedly selected. Thus in mind, as in body, man is a part of nature. His intellect is no new creation, but a simple, though extended variation from the general animal type as found in our nearest physical relatives, the primates. Among the minds of animals that of man is chief, but also kinsman ruler, but also brother.

The second great influence of Darwinism upon psychology was its stimulus to the study of the concrete particulars of intellect and character in individual men. You will remember that the voyage on the *Beagle* aroused in Darwin a permanent interest in the variations within species and in the gradations of species one into another. You will also remember that during most of his life thereafter he studied the variations of animals and plants from the type of the species, especially under the varying conditions supplied by domestication. His work turned the emphasis from the type to the variations from it. Biologists could no longer think of the animal and plant kingdom as a collection of replicas, occasionally imperfect or defaced, of originals made in some supernatural mint. Just as there is continuity, gradation, change little by little, as we pass backward to more and more remote ancestors, so within each species and between many species there is continuity, gradation, change little by little, as we pass sideways to more and more distant cousins. Psychology adopted somewhat reluctantly the new point of view. It used to speak in terms of the mind—a pattern mind, possessed by all men. But now it studies "minds" rather than "the mind," and makes the differences which distinguish human individuals as significant as the likenesses which mark us as members of one species, and does not doubt that our common humanity goes with a very wide range of variation. Moreover, these intellectual and moral variations among men show as a rule continuity, gradation, change little by little.

Language encouraged us to think of men as grouped into clean-cut classes, good and bad, intelligent and stupid, quick and slow, and the like, and the pre Darwinian psychology, in cases where it did get away from the doctrine of a single pattern mind, usually jumped to the equally false popular view of two or three or more patterns still distinct, with gaps between. What psychology would not do was to think of intellectual and moral traits along continuous scales, as physical science thinks of length, temperature, weight, or density. But this just what it must do to get insight into or control over the facts. And this it is now doing as a result partly of the general emphasis on quantitative methods in all sciences and partly of the special emphasis on variability and continuity in living things due to the work of Darwin.

The last line of influence from Darwin's work that I shall try to describe is the least definite, but perhaps the most important of all—his influence in making psychology a natural science—in depriving teleological or supernatural causes from their last remnant of power in the minds of scientific men.

Primitive thinking explains events of every sort by supposing that someone wishes the event to take place. The wind blows because Poseidon wishes a storm. It thunders because Zeus wishes to show his wrath. The crop is good because Demeter so decides. Primitive thinking tries to control events by wheedling or bribing someone, just as a little child teases his mother to make a snowstorm or to stop the rain. Men soon learn, in certain very easy cases, that this explanation by someone's wish, by personal design, does not work. The successions of day and night, for instance, are easily seen to be regular, and to neither need nor heed the wishes of men or gods. The sun does not stand still at any one's caprice. Only a fool will hope to delay its setting by sacrifices or to hasten its rising by prayer. You may still beseech some person to speed to its mark the stone that you throw, but you would not expect him to hold suspended in air the stone you drop.

The progress of common knowledge first, and of the refined knowledge which we call science, later, gradually repudiated the caprices of persons—of gods, goddesses, fairies, and elves—as explanations of one physical event after another. The movements of the stars, the behavior of all bodies in motion, the action of heat and light, the affinities of the chemical substances—as fast as men learned enough, personal wants were forced to abdicate rule over each of these. Magic and begging were abandoned as means to control them. But every case was a struggle, and even the most thoughful, the most scientific men were not converted to natural causation with all their hearts and minds. As a rule, even they kept all the superstitions they could. At a time when they would not have sung an incantation to make water boil quicker, they would have change formulas to make base metals change into gold. After they had ceased to pray someone that fire might leave wood unharmed, they would still pray that the wind might change.

By Darwin's time men of science had, of course, given up the cruder forms of belief in the regulation of nature by personal caprices; but they kept a refined form of it in the case of living matter. For they did not see any natural way by which the varieties of animal and plant life could have come into existence with all their adaptations to the world in which they existed. They had gradually become thorough naturalists in theory astronomy, physics, chemistry, and, last of all, in their geology; but they did not see how to rely on nature alone in biology. They still reasoned, like primitive men or babies, that animals and plants were as they were because someone had chosen that they should be so. They could not find within nature any cause for the specific forms which living matter wore. Men of science before Darwin, his grandfather among them, had proposed causes inherent in the natures and surroundings of animals and plants themselves. But the forces they invoked were not adequate. So for species and adaptation science still accepted a cause outside of nature in the time-dishonored form of someone's personal wish.

Darwin showed a natural way. He found within nature forces able to have produced species and their adaptations. The wish for birds with the feathers of which men may keep themselves warm or dry was shown to be as unnecessary to explain the birds' existence as the wish for water is to explain the combination of oxygen and hydrogen, or the wish of the gods to play marbles is to explain the spheroidal form of the earth and moon.

And Darwin's work did not suffer the caprice of persons to be considered a cause of mental events, of human psychology, of the history of men and nations. These also are to be understood, not by divining the intentions which they might possibly serve, but by examining them and the natural world of which they are a part. These, also, are to be controlled, not by devices to change someone's intentions, but by straightforward work with nature itself. Science and true religion now teach man to be throughout, in psychology as in physics, honest with nature and with himself. No excuse is left for hoping and fearing instead of thinking—for teasing and bribing instead of working. Our intellects and characters are no more subjects for magic, crude or refined, than the ebb and flow of the tides or the sequence of day and night.

Thus, at last, man may become ruler of himself as well as of the rest of nature. For, strange as it may sound, man is free only in a world whose every event he can understand and foresee. Only so can he guide it. We are captains of our own souls only in so far as they act in prefect law so that we can understand and foresee every response which we will make to every situation. Only so can we control our own selves. It is only because our intellects and moral—the mind and the spirit of man—are part of nature, that we can be in any significant sense responsible for them, proud of their progress, or trustful of their future...

To all human thinking and conduct Darwin taught two great principles. The first is the principle of evolution, or continuity—that each succeeding segment of the stream of life, each successive act in the world drama is the outcome of all that have gone before and the cause of all that are to come. The second is the principle of naturalism—that in life and in mind the same cause will always produce the same effect, that the bodies and minds of men are a part of nature, that their history is as natural as the history of the stars, their behavior as natural as the behavior of an atom of hydrogen. If there were time I could show how this same contribution has acted to transform our views of all human institutions, of the state, the church, education, and every future of civilization, and or treatment of every practical concern of life.

Gladstone and Lincoln lived in the thick of human business, and devoted their exceptional talents to the affairs of state. Each led a great nation, one through a generation of steady development, the other through the nation's greatest crisis. Darwin, making experiments in his quiet garden at Down, seems utterly remote from such leadership of men. Yet so far as such subtle problems can be calculated, we must conclude that Darwin will in the end have had the greatest influence upon social institutions, even upon government itself. For, in the long run, the only cure for national ills and the only foundation for progress is science, sure and verifiable knowledge, directing a good will toward men. And this good-will itself can be aroused and increased only by use of the facts and laws of science. Even now, in the treatment of subject races, in legislation for criminals and dependents, in the care for public health, and in the new view of the family, we may see the influence of Darwinism beginning to spread to statesmanship and social control.

I venture to prophesy that when, a hundred years from now, men again celebrate the work of Darwin, there will be no more doubt of his transformation of the world's activities than of his transformation of its thinking. If the chief art of reason is life, so also the chief duty of life is science, the search for truth. The best citizen is the one who advances most the common good. The surest, perhaps the only sure, means of advance is increase in truth. To the search for the truth Darwin gave an intellect of wonderful fairness and care, and a life of perfect devotion.

4

Education as Science

The Influence of Improvement in One Mental Function on The Efficiency of Other Functions

Our chief method was to test the efficiency of some function or functions, then to give training in some other function or functions until a certain amount of improvement was reached, and then to test the first function or set of functions. Provided no other factors were allowed to affect the tests, the difference between the test before and the test after training measures the influence of the improvement in the trained functions on the functions tested.

It is possible to test the general question in a much neater and more convenient way by using, instead of measures of a function before and after training with another, measures of the correlation between the two functions. If improvement in one function increases the efficiency of another and there has been improvement in one, the other should be correlated with it; the individuals who have high rank in the one should have a higher rank in the other than the general average. Such a result might also be brought about by a correlation of the inborn capacities for those functions. Finding correlation between two functions thus need not mean that improvement in one has brought increased efficiency in the other. But the absence of correlation does mean the opposite. In an unpublished paper Clark Wissler, of Columbia University, demonstrates the absence of any considerable correlation between the functions measured by the tests given to students there. Naomi Norsworthy, of Teachers College, has shown (the data were presented in part at the Baltimore meeting; the research is not yet in print) that there is no correlation between accuracy in noticing misspelled words and accuracy in multiplication, nor between the speeds; that there is little or no correlation between accuracy and speed in marking on a printed page misspelled words, words containing r and e the word boy, and in marking semicircles on a page of different geometrical figures.

Perhaps the most striking method of showing the influence or lack of influence of one function on another is that of testing the same function-group, using cases where there are very slightly different data. If, for instance, we test a person's ability to estimate a series of magnitudes differing each from the nest very slightly, and find that he estimates one very much more accurately than its neighbors on either side, we can be sure that what he has acquired from his previous experience or from the experience of the test is not improvement in the function-group of estimating magnitudes but a lot of particular improvements in estimating particular magnitudes, improvements which may be to a large extent independent of each other.

The experiments, finally, were all on the influence of the training on efficiency, on ability as measured by a single test, not on the ability to *improve*. It might be that improvement in one function might fail to give in another improved ability, but succeed in giving ability to improve faster than would have occurred had the training been lacking.

The evidence given by our experiments makes the following conclusions seem probable:

It is misleading to speak of sense discrimination, attention, memory, observation, accuracy, quickness, etc., as multitudinous separate individual functions are referred to by any one of these words. These functions may have little in common. There is no reason to suppose that any general change occurs corresponding to the words "improvement of the attention, or of the power of observation, or of accuracy."

It is even misleading to speak of these functions as exercised within narrow fields as units. For example, "attention to words" or "accurate discrimination of lengths" or "observation of animals" or "quickness of visual perception" are mythological, not real entities. The words do not mean any existing fact with anything like the necessary precision for either theoretical or practical purposes, for, to take a sample case, attention to the meaning of words does not imply equal attention to their spelling, nor attention to their spelling equal attention to their length, nor attention to certain letters in them equal attention to other letters.

The mind is, on the contrary, on its dynamic side a machine for making particular reactions to particular situations. It works in great detail, adapting itself to the special data of which it has had experience. The word *attention*, for example, can properly mean only the sum total of a lot of particular tendencies to attend to particular sorts of data, and ability to attend can properly mean only the sum total of all the particular abilities and inabilities, each of which may have an efficiency largely irrespective of the efficiencies of the rest.

Improvement in any single mental function need not improve the ability in functions commonly called by the same name. It may injure it.

Improvement in any single mental function rarely brings about equal improvement in any other function, no matter how similar, for the working of every mental function-group is conditioned by the nature of the data in each particular case.

The very slight amount of variation in the nature of the data necessary to affect the efficiency of a function-group makes it fair to infer that no change in the data, however slight, is without effect on the function. The loss in the efficiently of a function trained with certain data, as we pass to data more and more unlike the first, makes it fair to infer that there is always a point where the loss is complete, a point beyond which the influence of the training has not extended. The rapidity of this loss, that is, its amount in the case of data very similar to the data on which the function was trained, makes it fair to infer that this point is nearer than has been supposed.

The general consideration of the cases of retention or of loss of practice effect seems to make it likely that spread of practice occurs only where identical elements are concerned in the influencing and influenced function.

The particular samples of the influence of training in one function on the efficiency of other functions chosen for investigation were as follows:

1. The influence of certain special training in the estimation of magnitudes on the ability to estimate magnitudes of the same general sort, i.e., lengths or areas or weight, differing in amount, in accessory qualities (such as shape, color, form) or in both. The general method here was to test the subject's accuracy of estimating certain magnitudes, e.g., lengths of lines. He would, that is, guess the length of each. Then he would practice estimating lengths within certain limits until he attained a high degree of proficiency. Then he would once more estimate the lengths of the preliminary test series. Similarly with weights, areas, etc. This is apparently the sort of thing that happens in the case of a tea-taster, tobacco-buyer, wheat-taster or carpenter, who attains high proficiency in judging magnitudes or, as we ambiguously say, in delicacy of discriminating certain sense data. It is thus like common cases of sense training in actual life.

2. The influence of training in observing words containing certain combinations of letters (e.g., s and e) or some other characteristic on the general ability to observe words. The general method here was to test the subject's speed and accuracy in picking out and marking certain letters, words containing certain letters, words of a certain length, geometric figures, misspelled words, etc. He then practiced picking out and marking words of some one especial sort until he attained a high degree of proficiency. He was then re-tested. The training here corresponds to a fair degree with the training one has in learning to spell, to notice

forms and endings in studying foreign languages, or in fact in learning to attend to any small details.

3. The influence of special training in memorizing on the general ability to memorize. careful tests of one individual and a group test of students confirmed Professor James' result. These tests will not be described in detail.

These samples were chosen because of their character as representative mental functions, because of their adaptability to quantitative interpretations and partly because of their convenience. Such work can be done at odd times without any bulky or delicate apparatus. This rendered it possible to secure subjects. In all the experiments to be described we tested the influence of improvement in a function on *other functions closely allied to it.* We did not in sense-training measure the influence of training one sense on others, nor in the case of training of the attention the influence of training in noticing words on, say, the ability to do mental arithmetic or to listen to a metaphysical discourse...

When one undergoes training in estimating certain magnitudes he may improve in estimating others from various causes. Such training as was described in our previous paper gives one more accurate mental standards and more delicacy in judging different magnitudes by them. In the case of estimations of magnitudes in terms, of unfamiliar standards such as grams or centimeters, the acquisition of the mere idea of what a gram or centimeter is, makes a tremendous difference in all judgments. This will be seen in the case of N' s estimation of area. She was told that an inch was 2.54 centimeters, and with that as practically the sum of her knowledge of the size of a centimeter made judgments of a certain inaccuracy. The mere examination for two minutes of areas 1, 10, 50 and 100 sq cm. in size reduced this inaccuracy to 37 percent. of what it had been. The acquisition of definite ideas is thus an important part of the influence of improvement in one function on the efficiency of other functions. Even this, however, may not be operative. With some subjects in some cases the new ideas or the refinement of old ideas produced by the training seem impotent to influence judgments with slightly different data.

It is hard to prove whether or not or to what extent the delicacy in judging by means of such ideas in the case of one set of data is operative with the different data used in the test series. Surely it sometimes is not.

The training might also give ideas of how to estimate most successfully habits of making the judgments in better ways, of making allowance for constant errors, of avoiding certain prejudices. These habits might often concern features in which the function trained and the functions tested were identical. For instance, the subjects who judged area of various shapes made their judgments before training by looking at the 10, 25 and 100 sq. cm. areas given them as guides; after training they never looked at these but used the mental standards acquired. This habit is a favorable one, for a person can look at a 25 sq. cm. area in the shape of a square and still think various-shaped areas from 30 to 50 sq. cm. are under 30. The mental standard works better.

The training might give some mysterious discipline to mental powers which we could not analyze but could only speak of vaguely as training of discrimination or attention. If present, such an effect should be widely and rather evenly present, since the training in every case followed the same plan. It was not.

For functions so similar and for cases so favorable for getting better standards and better habits of judging the amount of improvement gotten by training in an allied function is small. Studies of the influence of the training of similar functions in school and in the ordinary course of life, so far as we have made such, show a similar failure to bring large increases of efficiency in allied functions.

In the three articles of which this is the last we have endeavored to present as succinctly as possible the results of our experiments. It has not seemed worth while to subject them to a minute analysis, for the reliability of any individual determination is not sufficient to warrant special conclusions from it. The general attitude which comes from the examination of all the facts we have demonstrated, not a set of precisely formulated judgments, is what we have aimed to produce.

The nest steps in the study of the interdependence of mental functions would seem to be the exact analysis of the influence of one on the other where such is present and the discovery of its amount and nature in cases of practical importance, for instance, in the case of the training given in school subjects, in occupations, in games, etc. Under the first head we should hope to see experiments carefully devised, as these rough ones of ours were not, to detect the exact elements of any function that were changed by training, to measure such changes and to find which of such changes brought about increased efficiency in other functions and how. Under the second head we should put determinations of the exact improvement in the efficiency of various functions by commonly practiced educational disciplines and measures of the influence of the training of certain mental functions by school subjects on the efficiency of other functions.

THE PRINCIPLES OF TEACHING

The aims, materials and methods of education: The word *education* is used with many meanings, but in all its usages it refers to *changes.* No one is educated who stays just as he was. We do not educate anybody if we do nothing that makes any difference or change in anybody. The need of education arises from the fact that *what is* not what *ought to be.* Because we wish ourselves and others to become different from what we and they now are, we try to educate ourselves and them. In studying education, then, one studies always the existence, nature, causation or value of changes of some sort.

The teacher confronts two questions: What changes to make? and "How to make them?" The first question is commonly answered for the teacher by the higher school authorities for whom he or she works. The opinions of the educational leaders in the community decide what the schools shall try to do for their pupils. The program of studies is planned and the work which is to be done grade by grade is carefully outlined. The grammar-school teacher may think that changes in knowledge represented by the ability to read a modern language ought to be made in boys and girls before the high school, but the decision is rarely his; the primary teacher may be obliged to teach arithmetic although her own judgment would postpone giving the knowledge of numbers until the fifth or sixth grade.

What changes should be made in human nature by primary grammar and high schools and why these and not other changes should be the aim of the schools, are questions usually answered under the heading "Principles of Education." How most efficiently to make such changes as educational aims recommend, is a question usually answered under the heading "Principles of Teaching", or "Methods of Teaching", or "Theory and Practice of Teaching", or "Educational Psychology." This book will try to answer this later question—to give a scientific basis for the art of actual teaching rather than for the selection of aims for the schools as a whole or of the subjects to be taught or of the general result to be gained from any subject. Not the *What* or the *Why* but the How is its topic.

It is not wise however to study the *How of teaching* without any reference to the *What* or the *Why.* If a teacher does not appreciate, at least crudely, the general aims of education, he will not fully appreciate the general aims of school education; if he does not appreciate the general aims of school education, he will not fully appreciate the aims of his special grade or of any one special subject; if he does not have fairly clear ideas of what the year's work as a whole or of what each subject as a whole ought to accomplish for the scholars, he will not know exactly what he is about in any particular day's work. The teacher must be something more than the carpenter who follows without reflection the architect's plan, or the nurse who merely administers the physician's prescriptions. His relation to the administration of the school system and the program of studies is more like that of the builder who is told to make the best house he can at a cost of ten thousand dollars, using three laborers, a derrick and such and such tools and providing especially for light, ventilation and protection against fire. Superior authorities say, 'Make the best boys and girls you can, using arithmetic, geography, school regulations and so on, proving especially for knowledge, good habits of thought, worthy interest, bodily health, noble feelings and honest, unselfish conduct.' The builder must often study how to dig a foundation, how to erect a frame, how to lay a floor and the like with reference to what is to be built; the teacher should often study how to utilize inborn tendencies, how to form habits, how to develop interests and the like with reference to what changes in intellect and character are to be made. The teacher should know about educational aims and values as well as about such principles of teaching as directly concern his own activities in the class-room...

The aims of education: Education as a whole should make human beings wish each other well should increase the sum of human energy and happiness and decrease the sum of discomfort of the human beings that are or will be, and should foster the higher, impersonal pleasures. These aims of education in general—good-will to men, useful and happy lives, and noble enjoyment—are the ultimate aims of school education in particular. Its proximate aims are to give boys and girls health in body and mind, information about the world of nature and men, worthy interests in knowledge and action, a multitude of habits of thought, feeling and behavior and ideals of efficiency, honor, duty, love and service. The special proximate aims of the first six years of school life are commonly taken to be to give physical training and protection against disease; knowledge of the simple facts of nature and human life; the ability to gain knowledge and pleasure through reading and to express ideas and feelings through apoken and written language, music and other arts; interests in the concrete life of the world; habits of intelligent curiosity, purposive thinking, modesty, obedience, honesty, helpfulness, affection, courage and justice; and the ideals proper to childhood.

The special proximate aims of school life from twelve to eighteen are commonly taken to be physical health and skill; knowledge of the simpler general laws of nature and human life and of the opinions of the wisest and best; more effective use of the expressive arts; interests in the arts and sciences, and in human life both as directly experienced and as portrayed in literature; powers of self-control, accuracy, steadiness and logical thought, technical and executive abilities, cooperation and leadership; habits of self-restraint, honor, courage, justice, sympathy and reverence; and the ideals proper to youth.

With respect to the amount of emphasis upon different features of these general ideals, the best judgment of the present rates practical ability somewhat higher and culture of the semi-selfish sort somewhat lower than has been the case in the past. No sensible thinker about education now regards the ability to support oneself as a mean thing. Every one must gain power at school as well as at home to pull his own weight in the boast, to repay in useful labor what the world gives him in food and shelter. The cultured idler is as one-sided as the ignorant and clownish worker and may be even more of a danger to the world. The schools must prepare for efficiency in the serious business of life as well as for the refined enjoyment of its leisure.

The best judgment of the present gives much more weight than has been the case previously to health, to bodily skill and to the technical and industrial arts. The ideal of the scholar has given way to the ideal of the capable man—capable in scholarship still, but also capable in physique and in the power to manipulate things.

Very recently thinkers about education have dwelt more and more upon the importance of aiming not only to prepare children for adult life and work but also to adapt them to the life of childhood itself. Aim more to make children succeed with the problems and duties of childhood and less to fit them for the problems and duties of twenty years after; let education adapt the child to his own environment as well as to some supposed work of his later years—such are the recommendations of present-day theories of education.

In actual practice aims often conflict. A gain in knowledge may mean a loss in health; to arouse ideals may mean less time for drill in correct habits; in zeal for the development of love of the beautiful the interest in the dry, cold facts of science may have to be neglected. The energy of any teacher, and of scholars as well, is limited. All that can be expected is that none of the aims of school education shall be willfully violated and that energy should be distributed among them all in some reasonable way.

The degrees of emphasis on the different proximate aims vary (1) with the nature of the individual to be educated and (2) with the nature of the educational forces besides the school which are at work. Thus (1) the emphasis in a school for the feeble-minded is not the same as in an ordinary school; the emphasis in a high school representing a selection of the more ambitious, intellectual and energetic is not the same as in a school where the selection is simply on the basis of the ability of the parents to pay tuition. (2) The emphasis in a primary school attended by the children of recent immigrants will differ from that in a school in a suburb inhabited by American professional and business families. A high school in a farming community in the Southwest should not pattern its ideals after those proper to a school in New York City.

The special problem of the teacher: It is the problem of the higher authorities of the schools to decide what the schools shall try to achieve and to arrange plans for school work which will attain the desired ends. Having decided what changes are to be made they entrust to the teachers the work of making them. The special problem of the teacher is to make these changes as economically and as surely as is possible under the conditions of school life. His is the task of giving certain information, forming certain habits, increasing certain powers, arousing certain interests and inspiring certain ideals.

The study of the best methods of doing so may be carried to almost any degree of detail. The principles of teaching may mean the general principles applicable to the formation of all habits or the highly specialized rules of procedure for forming the habits of correct use of *shall* and *will*; they include the laws valid for the acquisition of any knowledge and the discussion of the particular difficulties in teaching the spelling of *to, two* and *too*. But the problem is always fundamentally the same: Given these children to be changed and this change to be made, how shall I proceed? Given this material for education and this aim of education, what means and methods shall I use?

The scientific basis of teaching: The work of teaching is to produce and to prevent changes in human beings; to preserve and increase the desirable qualities of body, intellect and character and to get rid of the undesirable. To thus control human nature, the teacher needs to know it. To change what is into what ought to be, we need to know the laws by which the changes occur. Just as to make a plant grow well the gardener must act in accordance with the laws of botany which concern the growth of plants, or as to make a bridge, well the architect must act in accordance with the facts of mechanics concerning stresses and strains, or as to change disease into health the physician must act in accordance with the laws of physiology and pathology, so to make human beings intelligent and useful and noble the teacher must act in accordance with the laws of the sciences of human nature.

The science of biology, especially human physiology and hygiene, give the laws of changes in bodily nature. The science of psychology gives the laws of changes in intellect and character. The teacher studies and learns to apply psychology to teaching for the same reason that the progressive farmer studies and learns to apply botany; the architect, mechanics, or the physician, physiology and pathology.

Stimulus and response: Using psychological terms, the art of teaching may be defined as the art of giving and withholding stimuli with the result of producing or preventing certain responses. In this definition the term stimulus is used widely for any event, which influences a person—for a word spoken to him, a look, a sentence which he reads, the air he breathes, etc., etc. The term response is used for any reaction made by him—a new thought, a felling of interest, a bodily act, any mental or bodily condition resulting from the stimulus. The aim of the teacher is to produce desirable and prevent undesirable changes in human beings by producing and preventing certain response. The means at the disposal of the teacher are the stimuli which can be brought to bear upon the pupil—the teacher's words, gestures and appearance, the condition and appliances of the school room, the books to be used and objects to be seen, and so on through a long list of the things and events which the teacher can control. The responses of the pupil are all the infinite variety of thoughts and feelings and bodily movements occurring in all their possible connections.

The stimuli given by the teacher to arouse and guide the pupil's responses may be classified as:

A. Stimuli under direct control
   - The teacher's movements—speech, gestures, facial expression, etc.

B. Stimuli under indirect control
   - The physical conditions of the school—air, light, heat, etc.
   - The material equipment of the school—books, apparatus, specimens, etc.
   - The social conditions of the school—the acts (including spoken words) of the pupils and the spirit which these acts represent.
   - The general environment—acts of parents, laws, libraries, etc.

These responses may be classified as:

A. Physiological responses, such as deeper breathing, sounder sleep, vigorous exercise and the like.

B. Responses of knowledge, such as connecting a sense stimulus with an appropriate precept, abstracting on element from a complex fact or making associations of ideas.

C. Responses of attitude, such as the connection of attention, interest, preference and belief with certain situations.

D. Responses of feeling, such as connecting sympathy, love, hate, etc., with certain situations.

E. Responses of action or of conduct and skill, connecting certain acts or movements with certain mental states.

The value of psychology: If there existed a perfect and complete knowledge of human nature—a complete science of psychology—it would tell the effect of every possible stimulus and the cause of every possible response in every possible human being. A teacher could then know just what the result of any act of his would be, could prophesy just what the effect of such a page read or punishment given or dress worn would be—just how to get any particular response, of attention to this object, memory of this fact or comprehension of that principle.

Of course present knowledge of psychology is nearer to zero than to complete perfection and its applications to teaching must therefore be often incomplete, indefinite and insecure. The application of psychology to teaching is more like that of botany and chemistry to farming than like that of physiology and pathology to medicine. Anyone of good sense can farm fairly well without science, and anyone of good sense can teach fairly well without knowing and applying psychology. Still, as the farmer with the knowledge of the applications of botany and chemistry to farming is, other things being equal, more successful than the farmer without it, so the teacher will, other things being equal, be the more successful who can apply psychology, the science of human nature, to the problems of the school.

The Scientific Study of Teaching

The efficiency of any profession depends in large measure upon the degree to which it becomes scientific. The profession of teaching will improve (1) in proportion as its members direct their daily work by the scientific spirit and methods, that is by honest, open-minded consideration of facts, by freedom from superstitions, fancies or unverified guesses, and (2) in proportion as the leaders in education direct their choices of methods by the results of scientific investigation rather than by general opinion.

Throughout this book the student has been given training in thinking scientifically about teaching, and has been prepared to base his professional work upon facts and to examine every act of teaching in the light of known laws of human nature. One thing more is essential to the proper intellectual attitude of a teacher toward classroom problems—the verification of results.

Testing the Results of Teaching

The importance of tests: No matter how carefully one tries to follow the right principles of teaching, no matter how ingeniously one selects and how adroitly one arranges stimuli, it is advisable to test the result of one's effort—to make sure that the knowledge or power or tendency expected has really been acquired. Just as the scientist, though he has made his facts as accurate and his argument as logical as he can, still remains unsatisfied until he verifies his conclusion by testing it with new facts. So the teacher, after planning and executing a piece of work as well as he can, must 'verify' his teaching by direct tests of its results and must consider uncertain any result that he cannot thus verify.

Their difficulty: It is true that some of the most important results of teaching cannot be verified at all by the teacher himself. The permanence of interests, the effect of moral inspiration in childhood on adult behavior and the fortification of the pupil's heart against degrading forces that will assault it years after school is done, are of necessity not subject to full or accurate verification. The results of a teacher's work upon the life of the pupils out of school are also to a large extent inaccessible to adequate observation. Finally, certain changes in human intellect and character, such as nobler ideals, new ambitions and stronger powers, are hard to test even within the sphere of school and classroom life. The deeper ideals and ambitions are often cherished in secret and revealed only by some sudden access of intimacy or by unusual events. The strength of mental powers is not hard to test but the result is almost always the result to delayed capacity—of mere inner growth—as well as of the teacher's efforts; hence, the facts are hard to interpret.

In many cases, however, a teacher may not only hope and believe that a desired result has been obtained; he may know. In many cases he can do more than simply try the best plan he can devise; he can try, test the results, find the failures in them, and, with this new knowledge, devise a remedy. Such actual verification of the success of one's work is possible in the case of changes in knowledge, skill and all definite habits. One should be able to tell absolutely whether Johnny Smith gets ideas or only words when he read, whether Mary Jones can sew well enough to be worth five dollars a week to a dressmaker, whether Fred Brown does or does not treat his classmates with more justice than he did three months ago.

Their value to the teacher: Testing the results of one's teaching is useful not only because it gives a basis for improvements in one's methods, but also because it is one chief means of gaining knowledge of the mental content and special capacities of individuals. In applying the principle of apperception a teacher is constantly led to test the results of knowledge previously given as a preliminary to giving more. For the main thing in fitting stimuli to the mental make-up of pupils is not a host of ready-made devices to secure the cooperation of previous experience; it is rather constant readiness in testing for the presence of the essentials, in diagnosing the exact result of previous lessons.

Their value to the class: Testing the results of teaching is useful to the class as well as to the teacher, and to the class directly as well as indirectly through the betterment of future steps in teaching. Any scholar needs to know that he knows as well as to merely know; to be ignorant and know that you are so is far more promising than to be ignorant and not know it. By expression and use new ideas and habits get a double value; boys and girls in school need to know what progress their efforts have achieved and to guide their efforts by objective facts as well as by their own sense of progress.

It is common opinion that examining a pupil, finding out 'whether he knows his lesson' is the least part of teaching, is something that anyone can do. And it is fashionable amongst many teachers to spend the greater part of their time and still more of their energy in giving children opportunities to learn a great deal rather than in making sure that they learn something. The type of testing that uses the entire recitation simply to make sure that the pupil has studied certain pages of a book and remembered what he has learned is a small part of teaching and can be done by even a poor teacher. But the real verification of the work of teaching, that makes sure of just what the pupil knows and feels, that tests his comprehension and attitude as well as his memory, that prevents waste and prepares the way for better teaching of that pupil in the next topic and better teaching of that topic with the next class, is a most essential part of teaching and is one of the hardest things to do well...

Testing the results of teaching and study is for the teacher what verification of theories is to the scientist—the *sine qua non* of sure progress. It is a chief means to fitting teaching to the previous experience and individual capacities of pupils, and to arousing in them the instinct for achievement and the capacity for self-criticism. The test for knowledge, skill, appreciation and morality is in each case appropriate action. A valid test is one in which the response in question (knowledge or skill or ideal or whatever it may be) and only that response will produce a certain observable result.

Testing the General Results of School Work

The importance of tests of methods. What the teacher should do with respect to each act of teaching each pupil, the leaders in education should do with respect to the general methods of teaching a subject recommended to all teachers. Expectations of results, even if based on right principles, must be corroborated by actual verification.

As a rule the best present judgment about the efficiency of a method of teaching will rest upon its harmony with the principles derived from the facts of human nature and upon its success or failure as measured by the opinion of those who try it. The best present judgment will not be mistaken very often or very much, but there could be safer tests of the worth of methods. For when a principle derived from the facts of human nature is applied under the peculiar conditions of school life it may need modification; and the opinions of even the best teachers concerning the value of a method may be shortsighted and partial. What is needed is the comparatively sure decision of that superior variety of opinion which is called science.

The characteristics of scientific judgments of methods: The judgments of science are distinguished from the judgments of opinion by being more impartial, more objective, more precise, more subject to verification by any competent observer, and by being made by those who by their nature and training should be better judges.

Science knows or should know no favorites and cares for nothing in its conclusions but their truth. Opinion is often misled by the 'unconscious logic of its hopes and fears', by prepossessions for or against this or that book or method or result. Science pays no heed to anything but the facts which it has already made sure of; it puts nothing in the scales but objective evidence. Opinion trusts its personal impressions, bows to authority and follows the crowd. Anyone's opinion constantly favors the methods he is used to and is suspicious of new ideas except his own; it accepts without verification and rejects without a fair trial. Science seeks precise quantitative measures of facts by which changes and correspondences may be properly weighed; opinion is content to guess at amounts of difference and likeness, to talk in the vague terms of more or less, much and little, to rate a method as better or worse without taking the pains to find out just how much better or worse it is. Science reveals the sources of its evidence and the course of its arguments, so that any properly equipped thinker and verify for himself the facts asserted to be true. Opinion offers itself to be accepted or rejected, but not to be verified or intelligently criticized. Science is the work of minds specialized to search after truth and selected as fit for the work by their equals and superiors in it. Opinion is the occasional thought of those who, though important and capable people, are yet only amateurs in the work of getting truth.

Science would decide between two methods, say of teaching reading, by giving each an adequate trial, by measuring exactly the changes in bodily welfare, knowledge, interests, habits, powers and ideals caused by the two, and by comparing impartially the results in the two cases. It would, for instance, arrange that method A should be tried in ten or twenty classes and method B in ten or twenty other classes of equal ability and advantages taught by equally competent teachers. It would make sure that the two groups of teachers tried equally hard and that the two groups of classes were alike with respect to school-room equipment, the amount of time given to reading and the like. It would measure with precision the accomplishment of each pupil in reading itself, in spelling and writing, in knowledge of facts gained, in appreciation of good literature, in interest in reading, in such habits as might be influenced by the special training of reading, in power to learn new things and so on through the list of all the changes which instruction in reading may produce.

The prospects of scientific investigations of teaching: Obviously such a scientific basis for the professional work of teaching is in every way desirable. But for may reasons only a beginning has been made. The main reasons are perhaps, first, that strictly scientific methods have only lately begun to be used in the case of facts of human activities and, second, that the complexity of the problems of teaching is so great as to make scientific treatment of them very intricate and laborious. There are a score of competent scientists engaged in the study of physical science for every one that is at work on the problems of social institutions. The task of knowing completely the facts and explanation of the mental and moral development of any one child is comparable to the study of the geology of an entire continent or the chemistry of all metals.

The infrequency of the effort to investigate questions of teaching in the spirit and by the methods of science and the difficulty of the task itself are, however, no excuse for their neglect. The scientific study of teaching is at least as important as the scientific study of medicine and, though difficult, is in no way impossible. Even the subtle changes in powers, interest and aspirations can be measured; for sooner or later they must be manifested in actual facts. Even the remote influences of teaching on life after school can be known if the investigator has unlimited time and energy. The immediate influences of various sorts of teaching upon the knowledge and habits directly concerned, may be studied scientifically with much less difficulty and with promise of quick returns in knowledge. There should be no need to guess at the value of methods of teaching spelling or beginning reading or Latin grammar.

Such investigations lie beyond the scope of the activities of most teachers. The time, the training, the scientific frame of mind and the zeal which they require can only rarely be at the disposal of the teacher, who has so many other things to learn and to do. To advance scientific knowledge of education is a most worthy occupation for anyone who is able to succeed in it but it is not the duty of all or of many teachers. The burden of making exact measurements of children's attainments, of inquiring deeply into the what and why of the facts of school life and of feeling responsible for the verification or disproof of hypotheses about methods may be assumed voluntarily by the investigator, but it should not be imposed upon an already too busy teacher. Teachers should respect and encourage the labors of science but they should not feel bound to share them. The leaders in thought about education, on the other hand, *should* feel bound to study scientifically the field in which they claim to rank as experts. Since their opinions will be accepted by the profession as a whole, it is their duty to verify each opinion by a test of the results to which it leads.

THE MEANING OF EDUCATION

Man changes the world in which he is. He changes the earth's form, whether he only scrapes out a hole in which to hide, or removes mountains to join oceans. He changes its living beings when he kills one bird or when he plants or destroys a forest. His fellow men and his own nature are no less truly changed by what he is and does.

The art of human life is to change the world for the better—to make things, animals, plants, men and oneself more serviceable for life's ends. Trees grow regardless of man's intent, but he prunes or trains them the better satisfy his own wants, or plants others for the common good. Children, too, grow in part by inner impulses apart from man's direction, but man tries to change their original natures into forms which serve his needs. Each man singly tries, by producing certain changes and preventing others, to make the world of things and men better for himself; a group of men living together, so far as they possess wisdom, try to make things and men better for the group as a whole.

If human arts and industries are classified according to *what* is changed, education is grouped with government, hygiene, medicine, business administration, and the like, as one of the arts busied with the production and prevention of changes *in human beings.* There are no hard and fast barriers separating one of these divisions of human activity from another. The meanings of the terms—moral education and government, physical education and hygiene, industrial education and the direction of labor—overlap in the case of each pair. Education is not a word confined rigidly to specified occupations of man, but refers vaguely to more or less of human activity in the production and prevention of changes in other human beings. In the broadest sense, man is an educator in every act that changes any other man.

Education is the production and prevention of changes. Its facts are a selection from the changes that go on in the world. Science, or knowledge, in reporting the ways of the world, groups all these changes oftenest according to the objects which change. Thus in astronomy it reports the nature and changes of the stars; in chemistry, those of the atoms; and in biology, those of plants and animals. The objects whose changes we study under education are living animals, usually those of the human species.

The changes going on in any one object are of many sorts. Thus a man is a mass of matter subject to laws of gravitation, electrical conduction, and the like, so that some of the changes in him are for physics to study; he is also a concretion of atoms of nitrogen, oxygen, hydrogen, carbon and the like, so that some of the changes in him are for chemistry to study; other changes in men belong under anatomy; still others, under physiology; still others are referred to the many specialized sciences of intellect and character.

Which of the changes that go on in an animal shall be studied under the heading *Education*, is for science a matter of useful selection rather than of absolute necessary appropriateness. Thought can be logical, systematic and fruitful, no matter where it draws the line between educational and noneducational. It is customary to include under education the changes in intellect, character and skill, and to exclude the changes in the body's gross physical and chemical propertied, such as the rate at which it falls, or the depth at which it floats. But the exact selection from the facts of a man's life which shall be called his education, may be decided by convenience. A thinker about human education may choose his subject matter freely from whatever sciences concern man. Physiology, the science of digestion, excretion, circulation and the like: psychology, the science of intellect and character; sociology, the science of man's behavior with other men in a community: pathology, the science of disturbances of efficient life; even parts of physics and chemistry—all may contribute to the science of education. No clear boundary separates man's education from the rest of his life. In the broadest sense his education is his life.

THE NEED OF EDUCATION

Such education as man gives himself to-day prevents each new generation from stagnating in brutish ignorance, folly and pain. But far better education is needed to reduce the still appalling sum of error, injustice, misery and stupidity ...

Man improves education as he improves any other human activity—by open-minded thought about it, by learning the results of existing forms of it, by experimenting with other forms, and by clearing up and making reasonable our notions of what changes we should make in human beings and of how we should make them.

Such impartial scientific study of man's efforts to change himself for the better has been receiving more and more attention within the past twenty years.

In the case of school education, for instance, the actual changes wrought in boys and girls by this or that form of education are being measured, old and new methods are being tested by experiment in the same spirit of zeal and care for the truth that animates the man of science, and the educational customs which have been accepted unthinkingly by "use and want" are being required to justify themselves to reason.

Such scientific study faces five problems or groups of problems, namely, those of:

1. *The aims of education:* What changes should be made in human beings by schools and other educating forces?

2. *The material or subjects of education:* What is the original nature of the human beings whom we have to change? What are the principles or laws of human nature and behavior that we need to know in order to change men for the better?

3. *The means and agents of education:* What forces are at our command in the task of producing and preventing changes in human beings?

4. *The methods of education:* How should these means and agents be brought to bear upon the subjects of education so as best to realize its aims?

5. *The results of education:* What have been the actual effects of different methods, means, and agents acting upon different kinds of human beings?

INTELLECT AND CHARACTER ARE DUE TO INTELLIGIBLE CAUSES

No response of any human being occurs without some possibly discoverable cause; and no situation exists whose effect could not with sufficient knowledge be predicted. Things do not happen by mere chance in human life any more than in the fall of an apple or in an eclipse of the moon. The same situation acting on the same individual will produce, always and inevitably, the same response. If on different occasions it *seems* to produce different responses, it is because the individual has changed in the meantime and is not the same creature that he was. At the bottom of the endless variety of human nature and circumstance there are laws which act invariably and make possible the control of human education and progress by reason. So the general rule of reason applies to education: *To produce a desired effect, find its cause and put that in action.*

This rule, too, may seem obvious and commonplace. In truth, however, a very great amount of educational effort has been and is haphazard, the result of whatever impulses the educator by nature and habit has in each particular emergency rather than the result of a rational plan to produce a certain change by the most probably available causes. Thus, if a child repeatedly fails to understand a statement or enact an order, the parent will often repeat the identical statement or order but in a very loud voice, even though the use of reason would have shown that the child heard the words perfectly. And when this addition of more intensity fails, the parent often adds still more, confusion and terror being the response in the child. By nature and previous habit the parent *feels* like yelling the words that have been misunderstood, as a man feels like shaking his fist at the rain that is spoiling his crops.

The commonest erroı of the gifted scholar, inexperienced in teaching, is to expect pupils to know what they have been told. But telling is not teaching. The expression of the facts that are in one's mind is a natural impulse when one wishes others to know these facts, just as to cuddle and put a sick child is a natural impulse. But telling a fact to a child may not cure his ignorance of it any more than patting him will cure his scarlet fever.

Human nature in general is so complex and so little known, and human individuals are so various in their natures and change so much and so subtly, from day to day, that one is tempted to give up the effort to understand them and adopt aimlessly whatever treatment he happens to feel like using. Even superior teachers would have to confess that again and again they say this or ask that or order the other, not because they know any good reason why the statement, question or command should produce the desired response, but just because they do not know what to do and because that particular statement or question happens to come to mind. To thus act with no reason may, under certain circumstances, be excusable, but such teaching by the push of instinct or pull of chance is essentially irrational and inferior. There is always a reason for every fact in human behavior. There is, for every emergency, something which is better to do than something else; and there should be always a better guide than one's haphazard impulses.

The practical consequence of the fact that human nature and behavior are knowable, the same effect being always due to the same cause, should then be to encourage insight, experiment, and reason in man's dealings with himself. Scientific spirit and method will be rewarded in education as in the physical sciences.

THE MATERIAL FOR EDUCATION: THE ORIGINAL NATURE OF MAN

The different original natures of men represent variations around one central tendency or 'type'—the ordinary or average original nature of man as a species. Thus, though men vary notably in inborn ability to reason, their variations are around a central tendency, the average capacity of mankind to reason, which is clearly distinct from the average capacity of earthworms or caterpillars. Though to the situation 'being alone in the dark', different responses would be made by different infants, even though all had been treated alike, yet their responses would center about an average distressed behavior, whereas deep-sea fish would respond to being alone in the dark with stolid equanimity.

The original equipment of the central or average or typical human being consists, over and above his strictly physical, chemical and physiological nature, in tendencies to respond to certain situations by certain sensations, feelings and acts. These tendencies may be called the original mental make-up of man as a species.

When the situation is simple, the response uniform and the connection between the two close and hard to modify, the tendency is usually called a reflex. Thus, since the original make-up of man leads him to respond to bright light entering the eye by contracting the pupil, doing so promptly and surely and rather unalterably, the tendency is called the papillary reflex.

When the situation is more complex, the response more variable and the connection between the two more easily modified, the tendency is called an instinct.

Thus the tendency of man to respond to the situation—*unfamiliar large animals approaching him rapidly with open jaws*—by trembling, running and hiding, is called one of the instincts of fear.

When the situation is very complex, the response very variable and the bond between them very modifiable, the words 'capacity', 'predisposition' and the like are often used instead of instinct.

Thus the fact that man as a species by original nature has tendencies which, when the proper situations are provided, grow into thought, speech and music, would be expressed by such terms as 'the capacity for reasoning' 'the predisposition toward articulation, imitation and the other factors in speech', and 'musical capacity.

THE USE OF UNLEARNED TENDENCIES BY EDUCATION

Such is the original stuff of human nature, out of which the circumstances of life and training have fashioned each of us. As the potter must know his clay, the musician his instrument or the general the raw recruits out of whom he hopes to make a disciplined force, so education has to reckon with these unlearned tendencies. To change men's wants for the better, we must heed what conditions originally satisfy and annoy them, since the only way to create an interest is by grafting it on to one of the original satisfiers. To enable men to satisfy their wants more fully, the crude curiosity, manipulation, experimentation and irrational interplay of fear, anger, rivalry, mastery, submission, cruelty and kindliness must be modified into useful, verified thought and equitable acts.

The task of education is to make the best use of this original fund of tendencies, eradicating its vicious elements, wasting the least possible of value that nature gives, and supplying at the most useful time the additions that are needed to improve and satisfy human wants. This task is complicated by the fact that original tendencies are often 'delayed'—that is, appear only when a certain stage of mental growth is reached—so that education has to wait perhaps longer than it wishes before it can count upon them. It is further complicated by their transitoriness. Many tendencies appear for a time, but wane if not given exercise and reward; so that education has to strike while the iron is hot. If the response is sought too early, effort is wasted: if this is sought too late, the effort may fail altogether. It is further complicated by the discords between the behavior to which original nature prompts and the behavior which the welfare of man in his present civilized state requires. Man's original equipment dates far back and adapts him, directly, only for such a life as might be led by a family group of wild men among the brute forces of land, water, storm and sun, fruits and berries, animals and other family groups of wild men. But man has created a new world, in which his original nature is often at a loss and against which it often rebels.

Some original tendencies should be cherished almost as they are. Some must be rooted out of children—by withholding the situations that would call them forth so that they die a natural death from lack of exercise; or by making their exercise result in pain and discomfort; or by substituting desirable habits in place of them. The great majority of original tendencies, however, should neither be preserved in their exact original form, nor be altogether annihilated, but should be so modified and redirected as to further the improvement and satisfaction of men's wants under the conditions of humane and rational living.

Thus the indiscriminate manipulation of objects is modified into instructive play with sandpiles, blocks or ball; and later into the intelligent use of tools, pencil, pen, typewriter, engine, printing-press and the like. Thus the satisfyingness which originally accompanies notice and approval by anybody is redirected to form special attachments to the approval of parents, teachers, one's own higher nature, and heroes, living and dead, who are chosen as ideal judges. Thus the original incitement of 'another trying to get the food or victory or admiration which we crave' is replaced gradually by rivalry with others in all work and play, then by rivalry with our own past records or with ideal standards. Thus out of 'collecting and hoarding at random whatever is handy and attractive to the crude interests in color, glitter and novelty', habits of intelligent scientific collecting and arranging may be formed, and the interest in collecting may be made a stimulus to getting knowledge about the objects collected. Thus the original interests the tendencies to be satisfied by and annoyed by, to like and dislike, are turned into acquired interests in efficient workmanship, kindly fellowship, the welfare of one's family, friends, community and nation, and finally into the love of truth, justice and the happiness of mankind as a whole.

It has been a common error in education to try to make such changes all at once—to demand rationality and morality offhand—to stick ideal considerations and motives into children in a few large doses—to expect them to work, study, be just and be wise because we tell them to. Nothing but harm comes from expecting such miracles. Little more is gained by telling a man to think, or to be accurate, or to have good taste, or to honor truth and justice, than by telling a tree to bear fruit, or a duck to keep out of the water. The eventual nature which is desired for man has to be built up from his original nature.

he strengthening, weakening and redirecting of original nature begin soon after birth, so that by the time a child enters school he is already in many respects a product of our complex environment of clothes, furniture, toys, tools, language, customs and ideas. School education starts from acquired as well as original tendencies. But the original roots of intellect, character and behavior are still potent. Education which works with rather than against them—which conserves their energy while modifying them into more desirable forms—will have a tremendous advantage. Merely to let children act out what they are to read and make what they are to understand—that is, to enlist their original tendencies to bodily activity and manipulation in the service of knowledge-getting—enormously facilitates school work. Recognition of the original strength, in boys, of the interest in things and their mechanisms, and of the original strength, in girls, of the interest in the thoughts and feelings of persons, will similarly increase the effectiveness of high school management. The first necessity in education everywhere is to know what man will be and do apart from education.

THE MATERIAL FOR EDUCATION: THE LEARNING PROCESS

The Laws of Habit Formation

All the changes that are produced in human intellect character and skill happen in accord with, and as the result of, certain fundamental laws of change. The first is the Law of Exercise, that, other things being equal, *the often or more emphatically a given response is connected with a certain situation, the more likely it is to be made to that situation in the future.* Thus, by repeatedly inducing a child to respond to the question 'How many are four and two?' by saying, 'Six', a bond is formed between that situation and that response. This law may be more briefly stated as: 'Other things being equal, *exercise strengthens the bond between situation and response.*

This law needs no comment. It is the most commonly recognized law of human behavior. The need is rather of emphasis upon the other things which may be unequal. Chief among them are the *consequences of the response,* whose power in learning is recognized by the Law of Effect.

The Law of Effect is that, other things being equal, *the greater the satisfyingness of the state of affairs which accompanies or follows a given response to a certain situation, the more likely that response is to be made to that situation in the future.* Conversely, the greater the discomfort or annoyingness of the state of affairs which comes with or after a response to a situation, the more likely that response is *not* to be made to that situation in the future. Suppose, for example, that when a child responds to the situation, *being asked, 'How many are four and two*? by saying 'Six', he is always given kind looks, candy and the approval of his fellows. Suppose, on the contrary, that he always received rebukes, blows and jeers. This law may be stated more briefly as: *Satisfying results strengthen, and discomfort weakness, the bond between situation and response.*

Old connections between situation and response are weakened, and new connections are created, only by force. Human nature does not do something for nothing. The satisfyingness and annoyingness of the states of affairs which follow the making of the connection are the chief forces which remodel man's nature. Education makes changes chiefly by rewarding them. The prime law in all human control is to get the man to make the desired response and to be satisfied thereby.

The Law of Effect is the fundamental law of learning and teaching. By it a crab learns to respond to the situation, *two paths,* by taking the one, choice of which has in the past brought food. By it a dog will learn to respond to the situation, *a white box and a black box*, by neglecting the latter if opening it in the past has been promptly followed by an electric shock. By it animals are taught their tricks; by it babies learn to smile at the sight of the bottle or the kind attendant, and to manipulate spoon and fork; by it the player at billiards or golf improves his game; by it the man of science preserves those ideas that satisfy him by their promise, and discards futile fancies. It is the great weapon of all who wish—in industry, trade, government, religion or education—to changes men's responses, either by reinforcing old and adding new ones, or by getting rid of those that are undesirable.

Selective Activities

Human nature is selective throughout. Of any total state of affairs or situation, some one part may be, and commonly is, predominant in arousing response. Thus, of the turmoil of outside events, certain particular vibrations of the air and of the ether are effective in stirring man's receptors to feel and act, while the higher soundwaves and the infra-red and ultra-violet ethereal vibrations are not. Out of a baby's total surroundings, the familiar face of its mother or the moving brightness of a toy, provokes attention to the neglect of the rest. The interested reader's thoughts are determined by the meanings of the words of the book—the size of the type, the length of the lines, the noises in the room, and other features of the total gross situation being comparatively without influence. Suppose the total situation to be *a school class in geometry engaged in the consideration of the problem, 'If two parallel lines are cut by a transversal, the alternate interior angles are equal.* Not only may the figure and the problem be the only part of the total situation that is active in determining a boy's thoughts, but the one tiny element of the parallelness of the two lines may have special predominance. Suppose that the situation—*thinking of a bicycle*—aroused the thought 'Greek.' Evidently, one small feature of the situation determined the response.

We have then, as a general law of human learning, the fact that *one part or element of a situation may be prepotent.* The response made will then be that which is connected, by original nature or by the laws of exercise and effect, with that part or element or feature. This may be called the Law of Partial Activity. It may be stated more briefly as:—*Connections may be with elements of a situation as well as with the situation as whole.*

The second law of selective thinking, which we may call the Law of Analysis, states the conditions under which even a very subtle element comes to have responses bound to it. It is that: *When any response has been connected with many different situations, alike in the presence of one element and different in other respects, the response is thereby bound to that element; so that when that element appears, even in a very different total situation, it will tend to evoke that response.* Thus, having been led to respond by saying and thinking, 'Four', to the situations: *Four apples, how many? Four dots, how many? Four boys, how many? Four feet, how many? Four ounces, how many? Four handfuls, how many?* etc., the child tends to respond to *Four peas, how many? Four girls, how many? or Four chairs, how many?* by saying or thinking 'Four'. The element of 'fourness' tends to evoke a response of its own wherever it occurs.

By virtue of this law of analysis we are able to acquire habits of response to elements which are never experienced by themselves alone, which are always melted into amalgams with other elements. Man can thus respond to yellow, blue and green, regardless of what the colored object is; to long, short, big and little, regardless of what the measured object is; to heat, mass, square root, gas, liquid, solid, animal, vegetable, mineral, good, bad, greater, equal, before, caused by, and all qualities, conditions and relations, regardless of any particular things that may be before his eyes.

Such habits of response to threeness, fourness, fiveness, dogness, catness, molecules and atoms, vertebrateness and invertebrateness, multiplication and division, but, and, if, equality, cause and effect, and the innumerable other abstract elements with which human thought and conduct are concerned, give man his power over nature and himself. They are the most important habits to be formed by education—the essence of human learning.

The process of forming connections in thought, feeling and conduct is thus enormously intricate. Man's learning is not made up merely of connecting a million or so total responses—such as putting on his hat, thinking of sixteen, or saying *elephant*—each with some one of a million total situations, such as 'walking out of his own front door with his hat in his hand on a sunny day', 'being asked what the square of four is', or 'seeing *elephant* on a printed page and being asked to pronounce the first word in line three.'

Human learning involves, on the contrary, a complex arrangement of tendencies within tendencies and a hierarchy of habits. The printed letters, elephant, for example, may connect as a whole with the sound of the word made aloud or in inner speech: each group of them, such as ele or pha or nt, tends also to evokes whatever sounds it has gone with in the person's experience: the ph has not only bonds leading to the sound that has been made in response to it, but also bonds, that must now be held in check, between the p and its customary sound-value and between the h and each of its sound-values. Each letter has indeed also some slight tendency to still finer bonds. The element of shape in the t, for example, has an appreciable tendency to arouse the response of thinking of a telegraph pole; each may arouse its letter name instead of its various customary sound-values, and so on.

As a further result of the laws of Analysis and Partial Activity, any one total situation may be responded to in many ways, its various aspects and elements producing, one after another, their special responses. This process of trying this, that and the other promising response of thought or action is the first step in reasoning. The second step is the selection of the most promising among them to serve as the situation to provoke further ideas on the subject.

THE PSYCHOLOGY OF ARITHMETIC

When the analysis of the mental functions involved in arithmetical learning is made thorough it turns into the question, 'What are the elementary bonds or connections that constitute these functions?' and when the problem of teaching arithmetic is regarded, as it should be in the light of present psychology, as a problem in the development of a hierarchy of intellectual habits, it becomes in large measure a problem of the choice of the bonds to be formed and of the discovery of the best.

Our theories about schooling, recreation, and the higher life are all somewhat blinded by an unscientific expectation that somebody will grow wheat and bake bread and make shoes and build railroads and manage factories by some such necessary order of nature as makes the sun shine and the rain fall. This blindness is often accompanied by a certain condescension, or even scorn, toward productive labor, which is perhaps a relic of the long centuries of idealization of the leisure class. There is a very real danger that schooling may unfit a community to produce by itself its own necessities, and lead it to depend on industrial mercenaries imported to do all the dirty work.

As a psychologist, considering the intricate hierarchies of customs and traditions and checks and balances by which the instinctive tendencies of man are directed into the operations of modern industry and trade, the writer wonders that the whole apparatus does not crack with the strains to which it is subjected or explode from the passions which it harbors in its vitals. He feels most devout thanks for his daily bread. So he looks with favor on a mixture of schooling and productive labor, and is unwilling to assume that the latter is a curse to be postponed as long as possible. He sees hope in adult schooling as a means of social health, and is ready to exchange early schooling for it nearly at par.

The present quantitative distribution of schooling in our best communities is almost entirely a matter of public indiscriminate compulsion for certain early years and of entirely private volition thereafter. This seems improvable. Public welfare depends as truly on who goes to school after fifteen as on how many go to school till fifteen. The continued schooling of some individuals is so useful to nation that it should be assured. Adult schooling is a promising means for gaining flexibility in caring for such individuals. The facts of adult ability to learn should caution us against attaching too much weight to youth in the laws and customs which decide who shall be forced or encouraged to go to school.

5

Intellect & Learning and Progress

THE NATURE OF INTELLECT

We have learned to think of intellect as the ability to succeed with intellectual tasks, and to measure it by making an inventory of a fair sampling from these tasks, arranging these in levels of intellectual difficulty, and observing how many the intellect in question succeeds with at each level (and, if we wish, how long a time each success takes). From this grades inventory, we may compute measures of altitude or level, of width or range or extent at each level, and of total area...

Such a definition in terms of tasks accomplishable, and such a measurement in terms of the contents of a graded inventory is sound and useful, but is not entirely satisfying. One cherishes the hope that some similar, more unitary fact exists as the cause of intellect and that variations in the magnitude of this fact may provide a single fundamental scale which will account for levels and range and surface. Moreover, one realizes the desirability of search for the physiological cause of intellect, regardless of whether that cause be single and simple or manifold and complex....

The fact of human life of whose nature we seek a more exact description is the ability to deal with things or persons or ideas by the use of ideas. We contrast intellectual power over things, as by ideas about length or weight or heat, with nonintellectual power over things, as by strength or skill or acuity of vision. We contrast intellectual power over people, as by consideration of facts about them, with nonintellectual power over them, as by good temper or courage or physical charm. We contrast intellectual power over ideas, as by using other ideas to gain success with them, with nonintellectual power over them, as by industry or patience.

The facts and arguments which as shall present do not, however, depend for relevance or value upon the acceptance of this particular identification and demarcation of intellect. They will apply nearly or quite as well to any preliminary description which any competent psychologist would devise for those features of life wherein the Aristotles differ most widely from the inmates of asylums for idiots, and wherein the life of a man thinking effectively about mathematics or medicine or manufacturing differs from the life the same man eating, drinking, swimming or playing tennis without, as we say, an idea in his head.

If a score of competent psychologists should list on the one hand all the products whose production depends primarily upon intellect—all the tasks for success with which intellect is the *sine qua non;* and on the other all the products or tasks which they regarded as nonintellectual—success thereat being independent of intellect—they would show very substantial agreement. Where they appeared to differ, the differences would be unimportant for our purpose. Very seldom would the same task appear on opposite sides of the ledger. When it did, the difference would resolve itself into a difference in favor of a narrower restriction of intellect (for example, to ability to deal with abstract ideas or to ability to deal with relations), or in favor of a wider extension of it (for example, to certain tasks where ideas are not at work, at least not obviously). The facts and arguments which we shall present will apply regardless of such shrinkage or swelling in the area regarded as intellectual....

Beginning, then, with this loosely determined group of products which intellect produces, tasks at which intellect brings success, we may inquire concerning its observable or surface nature as a fact in human behavior or its deeper nature as a fact of fundamental processes in the mind or brain. We may investigate the thinking and action of men who have much intellect to discover more precisely and fully the features in which they differ from men who have little; or we may try to discover more ultimate causes of these differences. We may compare a man's obvious life, when he is using his intellect little or not at all, with his life when he makes large use of it, other factors remaining the same, to see just what the differences are; or we may try to discover hidden forces which produce these differences. We may study the nature of intellectual tasks, the production of intellectual products, or the nature of the ultimate power or powers whereby a man can succeed such tasks. There may be, of course, much to be revealed concerning facts intermediate between the description of intellectual tasks and the discovery of their ultimate cause.

The standard orthodox view of the surface nature of intellect has been that it is divided rather sharply into a lower half, mere connection-forming or the association of ideas, which acquires information and specialized habits of thinking; and a higher half characterized by abstraction, generalization, the perception and use of relations and the selection and control of habits in inference or reasoning, and ability to manage novel or original tasks. The orthodox view of its deeper nature, so far as this has received attention, has been that the mere connection or association of ideas depends upon the physiological mechanism whereby a nerve stimulus is conducted to and excites action in neurons A, B, C, rather than any others, but that the higher processes depend upon something quite different. There would be little agreement as to what this something was, indeed little effort to think or imagine what it could be, but there would be much confidence that it was not the mechanism of habit formation.

THE HYPOTHESIS THAT QUALITY OF INTELLECT DEPENDS ON QUANTITY OF CONNECTIONS

The hypothesis which we present and shall defend admits the distinction in respect of surface behavior, but asserts that in their deeper nature the higher forms of intellectual operation are identical with mere association or connection forming, depending upon the same sort of physiological connections but requiring *many more of them.* By the same argument the person whose intellect is greater or higher or better than that of another person differs from him in the last analysis in having, not a new sort of physiological process, but simply a larger number of connections of the ordinary sort.

More exactly our hypothesis is as follows: Let c represent whatever anatomical and physiological fact corresponds to the possibility of forming one connection or association or bond between an idea or any part or aspect or feature thereof and a sequent idea or movement or any part or aspect or feature thereof. Then if individuals I_1, I_2, I_3, I_4, etc., differing in the number of c's which they possess but alike in other respects, are subjected to identical environments, the amount or degree of intellects which any one of them manifests, and the extent to which he manifests "higher" intellectual processes than the other individuals, will be closely proportional to the number of c's which he possesses. If we rank them by intellegence-examination scores, the order will be that of the number of c's. If we rank intellectual processes in a scale from lower, such as mere information, to higher, such as reasoning, the individuals who manifest the highest processes will have the largest number of c's.

The view of common sense, of educational science, and of those who have constructed tests for measuring intellect, has been that intellect is a power to respond *correctly,* that the *quality* of the responses is a primary criterion of the degree of intellect. The teacher and the test-maker would insist that correct judgments and valid inferences required more intellect than the wrong judgments and faulty inferences.

The hypothesis which we present accepts this view, but makes a sharp distinction in this regard between the original intellectual capacity which a man has and the actual intellectual products which he produces. It credits the quality of the ideas that a man acquires, and the truth or falsity of the judgments which he makes, and, to some extent, even the validity of the inferences which he draws from any given data, largely to his training. The average man today has better ideas about lightning than Aristotles had, can make more correct judgments about eclipses than Moses could, and, if trained in science, may well draw more valid inferences from observing the action of acids on metals than either Aristotles or Moses did. With approximate equality of training, the quality of intellectual responses is an essential index of intellectual capacity, but it may be decaptive if the inequalities are great.

Our hypothesis limits itself to the original capacity. If by original nature, apart from all training, a man possesses tendencies to be right rather than wrong in his judgments, to hold true rather than false ideas, to make justifiable rather than unjustifiable inferences, more or less than other men, in so far forth those tendencies are due to his having more or fewer c's [possibilities of forming connections] than other men.

The essential element of our hypothesis is that it offers a purely quantitative fact, the number of c's, as the cause of qualitative differences either in the kind of operation (e.g., association *versus* reasoning) or in the quality of the result obtained (e.g., truth *versus* error, wisdom *versus* folly), so far as these qualitative differences are caused by original nature....

What is essential to the hypothesis is that by original nature, men differ in respect of the number of connections or associations with ideas which they can form, so that despite identical outside environments, some of them would have many more than others. "The number of c's a man has" means simply the original constitutional basis of the number of ideational connections which he has....

Negatively, the hypothesis asserts that no special qualitative differences are required to account for differences in degree of intellect; the higher processes or powers have no other basis in original nature than that which accounts for differences in the number of bonds of the associative type.

The reader who is impatient with these subtleties may forget them all with no great loss. The gist of our doctrine is that, by original nature, the intellect capable of the highest reasoning and adaptability differs from the intellect of an imbecile only in the capacity for having more connections of the sort described.

The bearing of the hypothesis upon the problem of measurement lies in the fact that we may be able for many purposes to *replace our measurement via a sample inventory of tasks, by a more or less direct measurement of* C [one's possibility of forming more connections]. If we can get access to C so as to measure it (and if the hypothesis is valid) we can measure intellectual capacity, and can measure it perhaps at a very early age. If also one C does vary from another simply by consisting of a larger number of c's we have a single variable in the most convenient of all units.

HUMAN LEARNING

It is a general law of mental action that the response to any external situation will depend upon the condition of the person as well as upon the nature of the situation. If the situation is itself an inner one, that is, a part of the person's mind, the response will depend not only on it but also on the rest of him. What a person learns as a consequence of any situation is a consequence of his nature as well.

The condition of the person is conveniently considered as consisting partly of rather permanent and fixed mental sets such as are commonly returned to by the words *instinct, temperament, purpose, and ideal*, and partly of more temporary and shifting sets such as are named fatigue, sleepiness, the disposition to add rather than subtract, and the intention to be as unfriendly as is consistent with good manners.

The general fact that the status of the person at the time influences his response is sufficiently obvious, being illustrated by almost every moment of any person's life. More careful and systematic evidence of the choice and direction of connections and the determination of responses by the set or attitude of the person, as influenced by the instructions given him or by the general nature of the task, has been reported by the psychologists who have studied the thought processes.

Equally obvious are the influences of those more permanent attitudes or sets of mind in a person which belong to him as Frenchman or German, Christian or Jew, teacher or physician, father or son, optimist or pessimist, realist or romanticist, extrovert or introvert, hard-boiled or sensitive, energetic or inert.

The attitude or set or adjustment of a man is a chief determiner not only of what he thinks and does but also of what he will welcome or reject—of what will satisfy or annoy him. If you are set to speak French, you are discomforted by the thought of an apt English phrase which would have rejoiced you under ordinary conditions. If you are a beginner at golf, you are content with a drive which in later expertness may be intolerable to you.

Every connection is made by a particular person or mind or brain in a particular status. Every after-effect of every connection is an effect upon a particular person or mind or brain in a particular status. Expectations, intentions, purposes, interests, and desires refer to dynamic factors as real as the situation-response connections between hearing *four times five* and thinking *twenty,* or seeing c a t and saying "cat."

Some of you have perhaps thought or felt that the view of learning as connecting which I have presented in the previous lectures is too mechanical and fatalistic, leaving no room for the control from within by purposes of the man's own making. Some of my fellow-students of psychology and education certainly think so.

What I have just said concerning the ubiquitous and potent influence of mental sets or dispositions, including the total make-up of the person so far as it may be active in any given case, seems to meet these criticisms.

The influences which cooperate with the situation to determine the response are as complicated, variable, purposive, and spiritual as the learners themselves are. The chief role in the drama of learning is not played by the external situations, but by the learner. The reason why I have said much about frequency of connections, satisfyingness of connections, identifiability of situations, availability of responses and the like, and little about the purposes or mental sets or total minds which direct and organize them is not that I belittle the latter. It is rather that the general importance of the latter is obvious, and that the variations of individual idiosyncrasy do not seem specially fruitful for study. So far, then, there should be no quarrel between an honest connectionism or associationist and an honest purposivist. Both equally believe that individual attitudes, adjustments, dispositions, sets, interests, and purposes work with the situations of each moment to determine what connections these shall make.

The quarrel, if any, will be over the connectionist's account of the constitution and development of these attitudes, sets, purposes, or selves.

What is any given set or attitude or disposition of mind made out of? More broadly, what are a person's interests and purposes made out of? Still more broadly, what is his *total mind or self or entire system of tendencies* that may cooperate with the external situations? The answer which I must in honesty give, though aware of the difficulty which I should have in defending it, is that all these are in the last analysis made out of connections and readinesses, original or acquired, including those multitudinous connections whereby satisfyingness and annoyingness are attached to certain events in the mind.

If I observe any special set or purpose, such as the tendency to divide rather than multiply or the desire to give opposites rather than meanings, or the lust for fame, or patriotism, or general benevolence, and list what I find in it, the list contains ideas, connections with totals and with elements, readinesses to connect, interests, and the like-all produced by original tendencies or past connectings and rewardings. If I attempt to analyze a man's entire mind, I find connections of varying strength between (a) situations, elements of situations, and compounds of situations and (b) responses, readinesses to respond, facilitations, inhibitions, and directions of responses. If all of these could be completely inventoried, tellings what the man would think and do and what would satisfy and annoy him, in every conceivable situation, it seems to me that nothing would be left.

I read the facts which psychologists report about adjustments, configurations, drives, integrations, purposes, tensions, and the like, and all of these facts seem to me to be reducible, so far as concerns their powers to influence the course of thought or feeling or action, to connections and readinesses. Learning is connecting. The mind is man's connection-system. Purposes are as mechanical in their nature and action as anything else is.

I shall not defend this doctrine. It will be more interesting and broadening to use the time at our disposal to present a doctrine which is, or at least is supposed to be, in sharp contrast with the connectionism which these lectures have presented.

What I shall say about Gestalt-theory and learning will probably be unsatisfactory to its advocates, partly because of necessary brevity and incompleteness, and partly perhaps because of inability on my part to understand it. I hope at least to be neither unfair nor misleading.

Gestalt-theory is a protest against three extreme forms of psychological atomism, and a constructive doctrine of the organization of mental life.

1. It denies that a state of mind consists simply and solely of a sum or mosaic of elements, an enumeration of which would state all that one needs to know or can know about that state of mind. It declares that the whole mental state is more than an additive combination of these parts, having a pattern or configuration or form not reported by their

enumeration, and that the parts when in such a state of mind are not as they would be when out of it, or in some other state of mind, each being modified by the community.

2. It denies that a given part or element of condition or action in the Brain, say, conduction through neurone A and across the synapse to neurone B, will always produce the same result, asserting that this will depend upon what the condition of other neurones is, and upon what other neurones are acting at or near the time and how they are acting. The total result of a complex brain activity is not then predictable by knowledge of what each part of it would produce if active alone. It declares that there are physiological patterns or configurations, having a potency beyond that of the sum of the potencies of their parts. Koffka, for example, writes that "association may be explained in terms of the physical configurations of the nervous system," and that "these configurations...will now prove of special value in clarifying the achievements of intelligence."
3. It denies that a longitudinal segment of behaviour, say, writing cat when asked to do so, or putting on one's coat when one feels cold, or reciting the alphabet, or responding to "What is the product of nineteen times seventy-eight?" by the necessary computations, consists simply and solely of certain elements of thought, feeling, and action in a certain sequence. It declares that such a segment or strand or flow of behaviour often has, or rather is, also a configuration or pattern, or several such. It is not beads connected by various clasps, but a necklace. It is not a series of tones, but a melody. It is not men walking in a column, but a procession.

The first of these three pairs of denials and assertions has relevance to the psychology of learning in two ways. First, it emphasizes the general difficulties of any too simple theory of learning by the addition of elements. This will be brought out even better by the third denial and assertion, and will be considered later. Second, it directly exposes the special difficulties of explaining the learned or acquired element in perception by certain exaggerated and perverted forms of the traditional British associationism, according to which, for example, the mind first got yellowness, circularity, solidity, four-inch-diameterness, orangy taste, and orangy odor, and then put them together to perceiver an orange. This seems as unnecessary and fantastic to an associationist or connectionist of to-day as it does to Wertheimer, Köhler, Koffka, or Ogden....

The denial that a given small fraction of status or action in the brain always produces the same result and the assertion that there are physical patterns or configurations in the brain with powers over and above the powers of the conductions and connections and other elementary facts in the neurones which are in the pattern are important. We want a psychology of learning which is in harmony with the facts which are known or are likely to be learned about the action of the neurones. The connectionist frankly admits that his belief in the influences of sequence in time, belongingness, and satisfying consequences in making one state of affairs more likely to evoke another rests not only on observations of behavior, but also on the probability that learning in general is caused by modifiability in the paths which conduction follows in the neurones. He frankly admits that his explanations of abstraction and generalization, though chosen because of observations of behavior, are made more attractive to him because they require from the neurones nothing beyond growth, excitability, conductivity, and modifiability.

I regret that I cannot give evidence for or against the alleged physiological configurations or discuss them usefully. For I cannot imagine at all clearly what they are supposed to be. I cannot tell wherein the configurative brain-process which makes a person find the opposite of a given world differs from that which makes him find the product of two given numbers, except that one is the *x* which produces the ones result and the other is the *y* which produces the other result. I cannot even tell whether they are composed of conductions in neurones, or of something else, or of conductions plus something else.

The connectionist welcomes the factual criticisms of an over-simplified conduction system made, for example, by Köhler, and hopes that the study of the organization of thought and conduct by gifted psychologists may lead to advances in knowledge of the organization of brain action. The connectionist, indeed, realizes the difficulties of explaining human nature as a system of connections between neurones perhaps even more clearly and acutely than the Gestaltist does. But on the whole, he finds reason to think that it is being and will be so explained. Stresses and strains, equilibria, and other qualitative features sometimes attributed to the physiological configurations, do not seem hopeful to him. He is also somewhat suspicious of them because for a time they were offered as a substitute for psycho-vitalism. Vitalism in the case of learning (or anything else) is likely in practice to be an abandonment of science, a cowardly retreat to causes whose action is unpredictable and uncontrollable by man. We do not want it or anything like it.

The connectionist welcomes the labors of a Franz or a Lashley which cast doubt on certain theories of the localization of cerebral functions. He is glad to support any competent worker who explores the possibilities of theories of selective resonance or the like as substitutes for the doctrine of spatial proximity of axones to dendrites or of permeable synapses. He will suffer gladly criticism on the factual level. But when he is told by speculative vitalists "Thus far shall neurone action go and no further; the remainder of learning is due to vital forces, above and beyond any mechanisms," he pays no attention. He is too busy, for instance in studying neurology or biophysics.

The third denial and assertion are, of course, the most important for our purpose. The denial that a piece of behavior is fully described by stating what thoughts and feelings and acts are in it and what order they have should encourage or force all students of behavior and of the modifications in it which we ascribe to learning to more careful observations and more thorough analysis. The assertion that the unit of behavior is, often or always, a configuration or pattern subject to the principle of closure, and tending to become as clear and definite as possible, is a challenge to show a better theory of organization within the situation-response sequence.

The denial seems correct and wise. Human behavior is not an undifferentiated series of events. Much of it falls into units longitudinally, each with a beginning and an end. Suppose, for example, that a child is playing with his blocks, that you approach and offer him a bit of cooky, that he reaches for this, grasps it, puts it in his mouth, and continues to play. The fraction of the behavior beginning with his awareness of your offering and ending with his deposit of it in his buccal cavity has a genuine unity. It is a pattern or configuration, if you please, set off against a ground, akin in a real sense to other units in form, though the offerer, the thing offered, the position of the child, the exact nature of the reaching movements, the grasping, and the insertion may not duplicate exactly any previous sequence. If we call the states outside the child from the first instant of his awareness of the offering to the end, the situation, and call what he does from that first instant until he returns to his play again, his response, it is true, as Ogden writes, that "situation and response operate together as one unit, the general pattern of which as it unfolds itself is constantly conditioned by subtle variations both in the situation and in the organic readiness for response." The behavior sequence *playing with blocks* ——→ *awareness of mother with cooky* is genuinely different from the sequence just described. It leads on to something new rather than back to the *status quo ante*. It ends in something reasonably called suspense, a problem, or a tension, rather than in something reasonably called a result or a resting phase. It does not so obviously begin and end.

Much of the stream of life is made up of such little unitary dramas as the child's awareness of the person with food and his response thereto, set off, by breaks in belongingness, from the *status quo ante* and the *status quo post* and set up in relief above the minor contemporaneous events. But not, I think, all. There are spells of shorter and less coherent sequences and also very long series of sequences related not as the parts of a configuration to its total, but as incidents in a general plan, or as steps in a useful routine, or even as connections cooperating by little more than addition.

If the units with beginning and end into which the behavior of a man often divides itself are all to be called configurations, that term must be made so elastic as to be well-nigh useless. Consider three of the commonest behaviors of our lives—conversing, driving automobiles, and, more rarely, walking. A friend says, "Whom are you going to vote for on Tuesday?" and you reply, "I think that probably I shall vote for Hoover, but I am not sure." Responding to the sound of whom uttered after a pause and with a certain inflection by a sense of impending inquiry in re some person is a unit of a sort. Responding to "are you going" by certain ideas and readinesses is a unit of a sort. Responding to "Whom are you going to vote for?" by understanding it is a unit of a different sort, with more finality to its end. Responding to "on Tuesday" by understanding it is a unit of a still different sort, with more finality to its end than the behavior to "Whom" or "are you going," and with much less internal complexity and interdependence of parts than the behavior to "Whom are you going to vote for?" Responding to the entire question by the entire answer is a unit of a still different sort. Responding to the total status up to the moment of saying "probably" by saying it is a unit of a still different sort. Some of these units conform fairly well to the specifications of a *Gestalt* or *configuration;* some do not, for example, the *understanding "whom"* unit, or the *understanding* "on *Tuesday*" unit, or the *saying "probably"* unit.

A man is driving his automobile. During much of the time there are no obvious divisions into longitudinal units. He is set or adjusted or disposed toward driving the car, and he maintains certain rather steady responses of posture, grip, and pressure on the gas, varying these slightly so is to maintain the satisfyingness of going at the desired speed on the right side of the road. It seems pedantic to cut up a minute of such driving into a dozen separate units. The state of affairs is rather a smooth flow. It is only when he sees a hill, or tries to pass a car ahead, or slows up for a turn that we have states of affairs usefully thought of as having beginnings and ends.

A man is walking home from work, with his mind set to get home. Some units are obvious, as when, arriving at corner A, he turns to the left, or as when, arriving at a cross street, he stops and looks up and down for traffic. Some are important, though not so obvious, as when the situation-changes of each footfall release the motor action of the next step forward, right and left alternating with probably not one mistake in 10,000. When the effects of the mile of walking produce an increase in fatigue or thirst or a reduction in nervousness, we have a very important situation-response connection which may being and grow and wane and vanish by infinitesimals.

Turning a corner and seeing whether a street is safe to cross can be treated as configurations, but such situation-response units as ordinary walking displays seem too mechanical and such situation-response units as the reduction of nervousness seems too lacking in form.

In general, few of the units into which behavior may be divided are configurations in the strict sense of things "the unitariness of which defies analysis," which "are transposable like melodies," and which "when they appear or disappear do so altogether." A heard or a seen word calling up its meaning and a person or object calling up its name are two of the commonest units or cases of "belonging" with clear beginning and end, but each of these is analyzable and is *not* transposable. It seems therefore extreme to assert as Koffka does that "all learning requires the arousal of configural patterns," or that "repetitions without the achievement of a configuration remain ineffective whenever they are not positively harmful," or that, "In the broadest sense, practice means the formation of a figure rather than the strengthening of bonds of connection." The configurationist is in a stronger position when he accept the formation of connections as the explanation of much learning, reserving configuration to be a principle of organization.

Learning the symbols of shorthand, the vocabulary of a foreign language, to smile under this, that, and the other discomfiture, to add more rapidly, to typewrite, to judge lengths or to draw lengths more accurately—these are samples of thousands of sorts of learning where the unity is the simple belonging of situation and response, not an unanalyzable *Gestalt.*

Dynamically, configurations and closure are invoked to do certain things in hebavior supposed to be too hard for a certain sort of connection-system, namely, one made up by the mere addition or subtraction of sequences, and perhaps to be too hard for any system of connections. The configurations are supposed to change the man by establishing and perfecting themselves, tending by some inner power to become as good and as sharply defined as possible.

I hope that the sort of connection-system which I have described in these lectures is more acceptable than the kind against which configurationists like Köhler and Koffka and Ogden direct their criticisms—criticisms from which I have profited, and with which I often agree. We have seen that the influence of belonging is as genuine as that of frequency or repetition. We have seen that one very common type of connection is that between a situation and an order to attain a certain result, the subsidiary connections by which that result is attained being left undetermined. We have seen that a process of varied reaction with selection and weighting of tendencies very often is intermingled with the routines of habit. Few or no habits are absolutely "fixed." Even reaching for the spoon that is always at the right of one's plate at breakfast contains a quantum of exploration with guidance by sight or touch or both.

We have seen that even a rather simple segment of behavior may display a subtle, piecemeal activity of situations and an elaborate coöperation of connections.

We have seen that connections are treated differently according to their acceptability and their consequences. Connections which thwart the man's purpose are rejected and replaced by others. Satisfyingness is not a deity invoked occasionally to select a few exciting and crucial connections. It is constantly at work, getting food safely into our mouths, keeping our handwriting up to a certain standard of legibility, and guiding almost every sentence that we speak.

The connectionist theory of life and learning, a summary account of which I have given, is doubtless neither adequate nor accurate. Its explanations of purposive behavior, abstraction, general notions, and reasoning are only a first and provisional attack on these problems. It has many gaps and defects. But I cannot see that such a connection-system requires aid from closure or Prägnanz. The facts which they explain seem explainable nearly or quite as well by varied reaction guided by the satisfyingness of the results attained, and this seems far simpler and more in accord with what the neurones are and can do.

6

The Nature of Individual Differences

The life of a man is a double series—a series of effects produced in him by the rest of the world, and a series of effects produced in that world by him. A man's make-up or nature equals his tendencies to be influenced in certain ways by the world and to react in certain ways to it. To describe even one man's intellect and character fully, at even any one time, it would be necessary to list all the world's happenings that he might possibly encounter, and to state in each case how he would feel and think and act in response to that happening.

If we could thus adequately describe each of a million human beings—if, for each one, we could prophesy just what the response would be to every possible situation of life—the million men would be found to differ widely. Probably no two out of the million would be so alike in mental nature as to be indistinguishable by one who knew their entire natures. Each has an individuality which marks him off from other men. Each has not only a mind, the mind of the human species, but also his own, specialized, particular, readily distinguishable mind. Even in bodily nature, indeed, men differ so much that it would be hard to find, amongst a million, two whose features are just alike, who are equally susceptible to every disease, who have identical bodily habits. The differences in intellect and character are far greater.

We may study a human being in respect to his common humanity, or in respect to his individuality. In other words, we may study the features of intellect and character which are common to all men, to man as a species; or we may study the differences in intellect and character which distinguish individual men.

The study of the facts and laws applicable to all men by virtue of their common humanity gives education its fundamental rules for the control of changes in intellect and character. The study of the facts and laws of individual differences enables us to apply these principles economically in the case of each individual whom we seek to educate.

In studying individual differences, it is customary to reduce the infinitude of tendencies to think and feel and act in certain ways in response to the varied situations which life offers, to the more general, and so fewer, tendencies which the psychologist calls abilities, interests, habits, qualities of mind, or mental traits. Thus the hundreds of connections between the situations represented by all the possible problems in addition and the responses represented by all their solutions, are reduced to the one trait, "ability to add." Thus the many inborn connections between, on the one hand, seeing and touching blocks, sand, strings, wire stones, water, and other material objects, and on the other hand examining, packing, pulling, putting together, taking apart, forming and re-forming those objects, are comprised in the one trait, "The instinct of constructiveness" or "the interest in manipulation." Thus by such a term as "memory for figures" we refer to the permanence of many connections—the thought of a battle with its date, the thought of a person with his address or telephone number, the thought of a city with its number of inhabitants.

Individuals are commonly considered as differing in respect to such traits either quantitatively or qualitatively, either in degree or in kind. A qualitative difference exists when the individuals have different amounts of the same trait. Thus, "John is more attentive to his teachers than James is," "Mary loves dolls less than Lucy does," "A had greater devotion to his country than B had," are reports of quantitative differences, of differences in the amount of what is assumed to be the same kind of thing. A qualitative difference exists when some quality or trait possessed by one individual is lacking in the other. Thus, "Tom knows German, Dick does not," "A is artistic, B is scientific," "C is a man of thought, D is a man of action," are reports of the facts that Tom has some positive amount or degree of the trait "Knowledge of German" while Dick has none of it, that A has some positive amount of ability and interest in part while B has zero, whereas B has a positive amount of ability and interest in science, of which A has none, and so on.

A qualitative difference in intellect or character is thus really a quantitative difference wherein one term is zero, or a compound of two or more quantitative differences. All intelligible differences are ultimately quantitative. The difference between any two individuals, if describable at all, is described by comparing the amounts which A possesses of various traits with the amounts which B possesses of the same traits. In intellect and character, differences of kind between one individual and another turn out to be definable, if defined at all, as compound differences of degree.

If we could list all the traits, each representing some one characteristic of human nature, and measure the amount of each of them possessed by a man, we could represent his nature—read his character—in a great equation. John Smith would equal so many units of this, plus so many units of that, and so on. Such a mental inventory would express his individuality conceivably in its entirety and with great exactitude.

No such list has been made for any man, much less have the exact amounts of each trait possessed by him been measured. But in certain of the traits, many individuals have been measured; and certain individuals have been measured, each in a large number of traits. I shall state first some of the more important results of the measurements of individual differences in the case of single traits, differences in the amount of the same kind of quality or thing.

Individual Differences in Single Traits

It is useless to recount the traits in which men have been found to differ. For there is no trait in which they do not differ. Of course if the scale by which individuals are measured is very coarsely divided, their differences may be hidden. If, for example, ability to learn is measured on a scale with only two divisions: (1) "ability to learn less than the average kitten can" and (2) "ability to learn more than the average kitten can," all men may be put in class two, just as if their heights were measured on a scale of one yard, two yards, or three yards, nearly all men would alike be called two yard high. But whenever the scale of measurement is made fine enough, differences at once appear.

Their existence is indubitable to any impartial observer. The early psychologists neglected or failed to see them precisely because the early psychology was partial. It believed in a typical or pattern mind, after the fashion of which al minds were created, and from which they differed only by rare accidents. It studied "the mind," and neglected individual minds. It studied "the will" of "man," neglecting the interests, impulses, and habits of actual men.

The differences exist at birth and commonly increase with progress toward maturity. Individuality is already clearly manifest in children of school age. The same situation evokes widely differing responses; the same task is done at differing speeds and with different degrees of success; the same treatment produces differing results.

There can be little doubt that of a thousand ten-year-olds taken at random, some will be four times as energetic, industrious, quick, courageous, or honest as others, or will possess four times as much refinement, knowledge of arithmetic, power of self-control, sympathy, or the like. It has been found that amongst children of the same age and, in essential respects, of the same home training and school advantages, some do in the same time six times as much, or do the same amount with only one tenth as many errors.

The Influence of Education

The intellect and character given to an individual by sex, race, and near ancestry furnish the starting point for the general education which he gets from the fortunes of life and the special education which society prescribes for his and its own good. Sometimes these environmental forces bring him into conformity with others, rounding off the corners of his individuality to make it more like the type: in other cases the environment increases initial differences and adds to the total variety of human nature. To what extent the differences that come to exist amongst individuals are to be attributed to differences in their nurture, is known uncertainly, if at all. I shall attempt only to show the attitude a thinker must take toward the general question.

There is no doubt that differences in home, school, books, friends, political status, and the like, may cause differences in the intellect and character which a man comes to possess—in his eventual nature. Two identical original natures, if brought up in 1900 BC. and AD. 1900 or in Berlin and Peking, would result in very different eventual natures. The Japanese of today are probably almost or quite identical, in original nature, with their great-grandfathers. All or nearly all of the differences between the two groups are attributable to differences in environment. Any man's individuality is determined in large measure by his language, occupation, religion, customs, and ideas. These against are determined in large measure by his nurture.

But the influence of the environment is subject to two important limitations. Any environmental force has far less effect if it is *avoidable.* If a boy born in China can, if his nature sufficiently impels, go to a modern school, the influence of the old-fashioned Chinese schools, even though they outnumber the modern schools a hundred to one, is far less than if they are the unavoidable form of education.

If the custom of slavery is universal, men who are by original nature just and humane will inhumanely deprive the babies born in slavery of common human rights. But if the custom is called in question at all, so that the force of society's approval of it is avoidable—if a man can flee in fact or in thought to the company of those who distrust slavery—then the effective force of that custom is enormously weakened. A man may, in respect to it, determine his eventual nature by his original nature.

Similarly, before any alcoholic beverages were known, no man, however intemperate his original nature, could be a dipsomaniac. But, once total abstinence is avoidable, the determination of a man's behaviour toward liquor may be made largely by his original nature. He may shut his ears to all tales of the misery caused by drink, may not attend to any of the facts which would facilitate abstinence, may respond to all restraining forces by neglect, and seek out, as a result of the inner impulsion of his inborn make-up, the rare opportunities for alcoholic intoxication.

The second limitation to any environmental force is that it acts differentially, the result being determined by the original nature acted upon as well as by the force itself. Even in those who do not avoid it, it has all degrees of welcome. Being slaves does not make all men slavish, much less equally slavish. Evil communications may ennoble the manners of some men. "The environmental stimulus adequate to arouse a certain power or ideal or habit in one man may be hopelessly inadequate to do so in another. Washing bottles in a drugshop was, if a common story is true, adequate to decide Faraday's career; and the voyage on the Beagle is reputed to have made Darwin a naturalist for life. But if all the youth of the land were put to work in drugshops and later sent on scientific expeditions, the result would not be a million Faradays and Darwins, or even a million chemists and naturalists. All that one man may need to be free is a vote; but even a long education in self-direction may be inadequate for another. Being told a few words suffices to secure the habit of reading in one child, while the child beside him remains illiterate after two years of careful tuition. The amount of stimulus required in some cases is so infinitesimal that the power seems to spring absolutely from the man himself. In other men no agency is found potent enough to arouse a trace of the desired result."

As a result of these limitations, it is hard to find differences between one and another man of the same era and general social condition that are clearly due to differences in training. The great scholar is not made by attendance at a university; rather his own nature made him seek that influence scorned by so many others. Many a drunkard remains so in spite of fewer temptations. Saloons being inaccessible, he drinks at home; whiskey being debarred, he takes to "bitters" or patent medicines; one suspects that if alcohol did not exist, he would soon discover cocaine. Each nature in some measure selects its own environment, and each nature may get from an environment a different influence, so that the relative achievements of, say, the boys who this year being school in America, will probably be more closely parallel to their relative original talents and interests than to their relative advantages in home and school environment.

The Significance of Individual Differences

We have seen that individuals differ in whatever trait of intellect or character is examined. The variations from the ordinary, common, or typical man range continuously to such extreme conditions as appear in the idiot and the genius, or Nero and Lincoln. But the great majority cluster somewhat closely around the "average man." Clear and useful divisions into separate classes are impossible with respect to either the amount of some single trait or the total constitution of the mind.

The differences that characterize men of the same time, country, and social status are largely original, determined directly by the germs from which the individual develops, and so indirectly by the ancestry from which he springs. Each original nature has so great power of selecting and avoiding the forces of social and educational environment that the fundamental powers, interests, and ideals of such men are largely determined before they are born. Over the particular connections with ideas which we call knowledge, and the particular connections with acts which we call skill, training has greater power; and, of course, unavoidable differences in training, such as go with differences between 1700 and 1900, England and China, slave and free, are far more potent.

All the sciences and arts of controlling human nature must accept the original variety of human nature as a condition for thought and action. The economist must not consider men as all seeking with steadfast rationality to buy as cheap and sell as dear as they can. The religious worker should not hope to arouse uniformly the same sense of guilt and longing for justification to which he and his intimates testify. The scholar may as well expect all men to be passionately eager to use the left rather than the right hand, as expect them to prefer linguistic or mathematical erudition to ignorance. The teacher who has not learned by ordinary experience that each child is to some extent a separate problem, demanding for his best interest an educational theory and practice to fit him, should learn it once for all from psychological theory.

Specialization of schools is needed not only to fit pupils for special professions, arts, trades, and the like, but also to fit the schools to original differences in the pupils. Specialization of instruction for different pupils within one class is needed as well as specialization of the curriculum for different classes. Since human nature does not fall into sharply defined groups, we can literally never be sure of having a dozen pupils who need to be treated exactly alike.

All thought and action will be more reasonable and humane if we look for variety in men and examine each nature in a scientific spirit to learn what it really is, instead of idly judging it by some customary superstition. For example, the most pitiful waste and unreason in human affairs is behavior whereby one makes himself suffer to secure for another a good which is to the other a nuisance or a pain. A parent who sacrifices his own joys to protect his children against the healthy, beloved, and noble struggles of life; a philanthropist who lessens his own welfare to teach factory-workers refinements, knowledge of which can only embitter their inability to secure them; a religion that spends life in stimulating the fears and worries of men whom fear and worry will never lead to right living, but only to more worry and fear—in such gratuitous miseries, false diagnosis of human hearts is prolific.

The most necessary elements in the life or reason and justice are, first, an awareness of what individual human natures really are and really want; and then an appreciation of the relative worth of the myriads of wants thus revealed. This valuation of human wants, in turn, is improved chiefly by knowing what they are and how each competes or cooperates with all the others. Only in proportion as such a science of the nature and behavior of individual men exists can man know what his duty is or know how to do it.

THE DISTRIBUTION OF EDUCATION

The general spirit of our country for the past hundred years has been to make great efforts to increase the amount of education but to pay relatively little attention to its distribution. The plea of reformers has been for more education, regardless of who received it. There has been an indiscriminate urge toward more schools, longer school years, and later compulsory-attendance ages. Education of any sort for any person has been recommended as a national investment without much consideration of the differences in safety and income which may attach to the investment in certain boys and girls rather than in others. The mere volume of education has been taken as a measure of idealism, somewhat as the mere volume of gifts to beggars of all sorts used to be taken as a measure of philanthropy and charity.

In so far as any attention has been paid to the question of who were receiving much and who were receiving little education, the general tendency has been to try to equalize the distribution, by aiding backward communicates, increasing the number of days schools were in session, delaying the permissible age for leaving school, enforcing attendance laws, and other lines of effort designed to raise the amount for those who were receiving less than others. The doctrine that equalization of education is beneficent, partly by remedying certain definite accidents and injustices and partly by a mysterious power to advance democracy and social justice, has been very popular. Its influence has been potent, not only in the distribution of education so as to give most to those who have least, but also in the efforts of teachers to bring backward pupils up to grade and in the establishment of special classes for the deficient and dull.

It may be doubted whether either the policy of striving for indiscriminate increase in the volume of education or the policy of favoring especially those who would otherwise have very little schooling was ever the best for the general welfare. A very strong argument could have been made at any time in the last half-century for exercising careful discrimination in the distribution of education, the most being given to those who would use it best for the common good. A fairly strong argument could also have been made that those who would use more education best for the common good would be those who already had a great deal of it—for example, promising young students of science, who, with more education, might make discoveries of great benefit to the world, or promising young physicians, clergymen, engineers, and the like, who, with more education, might serve their communities much better. However, so long as there were many children who had only a few years of schooling, each of less than a hundred days, the benevolent doctrine of changing distribution in such a way as to favor the least educated was rarely questioned. The prevention of illiteracy and the extension of education so that every child would have at least a thousand days of schooling seemed a wise as well as a humane policy, even if not in the end the wisest.

When the school year was lengthened, the age of compulsory attendance raised to fourteen or sixteen, and provision made for special classes for the very dull, some thinkers began to consider the interests of the intellectually able pupils and the public's interest in making the most out of its human resources. These thinkers asked, "Who are receiving the most education? Are they the ones who will use it best for the common good?" But they asked these questions usually in such forms as: "Who are going to college?" "Who should go?" "Who are proceeding on to high school?" "Who should?"

When the questions are asked in these forms, the answer to the first is that the high schools do get a selection that is superior in intellect, and the colleges and professional schools a selection that is still more so. The fact concerning the relation of intelligence to grade reached among the American soldiers of the World War, the facts revealed by surveys of high-school population, and the facts shown by the tests of intellect or "scholastic aptitude" which have been more and more widely adopted by colleges since 1920, were, in spite of numerous individual misfits and dubious educational investments, accepted as comforting. Those who were found at the higher levels of schooling were much abler than those who had been eliminated by the way.

The question "Who are receiving the most education?" is not, however, answered adequately by answering the questions: "Who go to college" "Who go to high school?" "Who attend medical schools?" or any other questions that ask who receive certain higher levels of education. "Most education" may mean two things: most education in actual amount of educational effort spent on a person or most education in amount of change made in the person. The former is roughly measured by the money spent on the pupil or by the days or years of schooling the receives. The latter is roughly measured by the amount he learns, or the grade he reaches, or the abilities which promotions, degrees, and diplomas are intended to represent. Both meanings are important, but they must not be confused. The facts just mentioned about the superior quality of students in higher institutions do not prove that the ablest children are receiving the most education in yeas. They may conceivably prove that the ablest children to learn the most and advance the farthest, though having little more, or no more, education in the first meaning than the average or the dull.

The problem of providing schooling in some reasonable relation to the intellectual ability of the recipients is only one part of the general problem of the quantitative distribution of education. It would be a very inadequate treatment of the matter to use intellectual superiority alone as the measure of fitness for more education. Moreover, the problems of the qualitative distribution of education are at least as important as those of quantity. We have to ask not only, "How much schooling shall each sort of individual receive?" but also, "What kind of schooling shall it be?"

There is no time to do more than mention these questions and recommend them as worthy subjects for thought and research. I must use the time that remains to reinforce your memories of the message I have tried to deliver.

Zeal to produce more schooling, that is, to increase the amount of schooling given in our country, has been one of America's fine idealisms. Such zeal should be maintained, but with it there should be equal zeal to distribute this education so that those will have most who can use it best. What evidence we now have indicates that the ablest receive very little more than the least able. For every boy in the top forty of our 785 who stayed in school beyond the age of eighteen, there were nearly ten boys below average ability who did so. The passion for equalization which had a certain nobility when a large percentage of children barely learned to read and write becomes unwise, almost ridiculous, when the question is of spending our resources to keep in school boys of sixteen, or seventeen, or eighteen who would be happier and more useful at work or at play. Our increased resources should be used to aid young men and women whom nature and nurture have chosen to profit from schooling.

Doubtless, great ability will often manage to get education outside of schools or to get along without it, but those who can do so much for the world with so little are the very ones who should be given more. In the wars we are incessantly waging against disease, misery, depravity, injustice, and ugliness, we should not provide our best marksmen with the poorest weapons nor ask our bravest to fight with their naked hands.

EDUCATION AS CAUSE AND AS SYMPTOM

If communities could be controlled like chemicals in test tubes or animals in cages, we should be led by the facts...to vary the quantity and quality of education in certain communities for a time and observe the consequences year by year thereafter and also to introduce thousands of families of known abilities and interests into certain communities and observe the consequences.

It is unfortunate that we can very rarely proceed by such experiments as by taking a dozen cities which were identical in all relevant matters with another dozen and increasing the quantity of education by a known amount for n years in one dozen but not in the other. When suitable experiments are impracticable, the more fundamental analysis may be made more or less well by the techniques of partial correlation and multiple correlation or of Sewall Wright's path coefficients. In the social sciences suitable experiments usually are impracticable as they certainly are in our problem of how far the quantity or quality of education determines the goodness of life for good people in states and in cities.

On the whole, the facts which I have reported probably attach less causal efficacy to schooling, home life, and special forms of training than the general opinion of educators has attached to them. They certainly do not support the promises of educational evangelists that, it all the children for a generation or two had enough education of the right sort, they would be healthy, wealthy, and wise, living in peace and amity, free from vulgarity and meanness, busy with noble thoughts and deeds.

If one has been nourished by the hope of reforming the world in short order by extending schooling to all to age 21 (or 61, for that matter), he will be disappointed to find that the quantity and quality of a state's schooling in 1900 caused less than 20 percent of its welfare status in comparison with other states in 1930. If one has imagined that giving the intellectually underprivileged the advantages of a home where the parents have able minds and encourage intellect in their offspring would cause the genes of a moron to develop into a mind equal to that of the average present-day European, or cause the genes of a "dull normal" to develop into a mind able to graduate from a reputable law school, he will be disappoint to learn that differences in home life and training probably cause less than a fifth of the variation among individuals in I.Q.

But are not such facts healthy and profitable? Suppose that the quantity and quality of education in a community caused 50 or 60 percent of its status in the goodness of life for good people a generation later. Then the great extension of education in the United States during the three generations from Horece Mann's day to our own, and in England, France, and Germany during the same time, should have brought a near millennium. Since it obviously has not done so, some mysterious force of evil must have counteracted its force and we must live in terror of an overpowering diabolism.

Suppose that family environment caused 75 percent of the variation in I.Q., so that genes whose I.Q.s, if reared in the average family would be 100, would, if reared in a family ranking in the 98th percentile for favorableness to intellect, become boys and girls with I.Q.s of about 130. This is as if the variation in plants was caused 75 percent by the soil and cultivation and only 25 percent by the seed. In the case of plants no-body would regard this as a matter for congratulation. It would mean that generation after generation the quality of the soil must be maintained to avoid a disastrous regression in the quality of the crops. Thistles would grow from wheat if conditions were not kept right.

Why should it be regarded as desirable for man? Only because we have been accustomed and attentive to the possibility of improving the conditions of human life and unaware of the possibilities and advantages of improving the human genes. A moderate amount of consideration of heredity and human affairs will show how enormously more advantageous it will be to have a 75 percent determination by heredity and induce the able and good to have children than to have a 75 percent determination by environment and induce the able and good to take boarders.

Mankind has its genes, its tools and apparatus, its customs and institutions. We should make the most and best out of all of these. The way to do so is to learn the truth about them and act accordingly. School education is one of the most important of human institutions, and free schooling for those who can use it for human welfare is one of the finest and most beneficent. But we honor education more by understanding it than by praising it, and we should not ask too much from it. There is a certain attractiveness in thinking that education has limitless possibilities and appealing to it, whatever our difficulty or distress may be. But the attractiveness of such an attitude is like the attractiveness of an infant's appeal to his mother in confidence that she can gratify his every wish. After childhood such appeals seem, and are, weak and stupid. So should the appeals of this, that, and the other public or private interest to education to save this, that, and the other valuable, or at least valued, feature of life. Least of all should educators expect too much of education. Like men of science they should measure and know, and like good engineers they should when advisable allow a factor of safety. What is more contemptible than an ignorant educational reformer (or conservative) selling his wares to a trustful public, taking a profit from spreading guesses and lies!

EDUCATION: THE OPPORTUNITY OF THE HIGH SCHOOLS

The problem before the high school is to give to the boys and girls from fourteen on who most deserve education beyond a common school course such a training as will make them contribute most to the true happiness of the world. The high school should consider the natures of these boys and girls, what they are, what they can do, and what their share of the world's work is to be; it should consider the demands which the world will make upon them, the particular needs which the high school pupil is to supply; and in the light of the human nature it has to work with and the human wants it has to supply should choose its course of study, devise its methods and plan its scheme of administration. No high school is successful which does not use an intelligent sympathy with, and a sympathetic insight into, the life of boys and girls. The high school was made for them, not they for the high school. No high school is successful which does not have in mind definitely the work in life it students will have to perform, and try to fit them for it.

The present situation with respect to high school education may be briefly described as follows: The high schools offer to pupils from about fifteen to about nineteen, who have made satisfactory progress in school up to then, the opportunity to study Latin and one or more other languages, algebra and geometry, the English language and literature, English composition, the history of America and of Europe, and the elementary parts of the several sciences. Many of them offer also courses in bookkeeping, business arithmetic, and the like, in so-called commercial courses. A few of them offer courses in manual training and the technical arts, including domestic art and science for the girls and scientific agriculture. But these business and technical courses are usually considered not so respectable as the course comprising languages and mathematics, and are often used as a refuge for pupils who do not seem able to do the latter. The high school accepts also the task of preparing students for the tests required for entrance to college.

We so take it for granted that the customary and respectable thing is thoroughly good, in fact nearly the best possible, that our natural attitude toward the high school, unless it becomes aggressively annoying, which it rarely does, is one of peaceful, careless satisfaction. It is, we say, the "People's College," where all can go and receive the education proper to their ages and needs. But if we re-read the programme outlined above, thinking meanwhile of the boys or girls in the late teens that we know intimately, thinking also of the three-fourths of high school pupils who drop out before they finish its course, we shall be ready to consider the possibility that in many and important ways the high school has not mastered its problems or even fully appreciated it. It can, and should be, better fitted to boys and girls; it can and should fit them better for what they have to do.

It makes little difference what features of youth are taken; nearly all will furnish illustrations of the chance for progress.

For instance, we can do more to fit the high schools to the poor. If a gifted boy lives in a town where there is no high school, that town should pay the expense he incurs in going to the nearest. If a gifted boy must earn money to help the family, the best thing a school system can do is to get him a job out of school hours. It is a far more important work for schools to keep the best boys and girls in school than to weed out the dull. An employment bureau is more needed than promotion-examinations. If the boy can't be helped to earn enough outside of school hours, the school hours should be shortened in his case. It is far more important to have him in school two hours a day or two days a week than to save some one a little trouble in assigning lessons.

By the present arrangements of high schools, there is no choice between all school and no school. The boy or girl in whose case a high school education will be an investment, bringing a return to the State of a hundred percent. Or more, may be debarred from it by the brute fact that his father is dead or that there are eight children in the family to be supported.

In the second place, we can do more to fit the high school to that class of boys and girls, the majority, by the way, who are not primarily interested in or efficient at dealing with ideas, but whose talent is for the manipulation of things, for using tools and machines rather than books, for cooking for a party rather than writing compositions about it, for performing experiments and making collections rather than learning rules.

Of the boys and girls who ought to enter the high schools of the county next fall, three times as many are fit to study agriculture or household sanitation as are fit to study Latin and algebra.

It is a foolish arrangement by which systematic school training from fourteen to eighteen is restricted so largely to the class who can and will do well as scholars, who are idea—rather than thing-thinkers. Systematic education is as necessary and as profitable for the future dentist, engineer, architect, builder, plumber, electrician, or housekeeper, as for the future teacher, lawyer or writer. The time has passed when the rule of thumb was enough for the building trades; when science was a luxury to the farmer, when old wives' lore passed on from mother to daughter was the best available education for housewifery and motherhood. The time is in fact at hand when the technical and the industrial occupations and the work of the housekeeper will be actually more dependent for success upon expert knowledge than the work of the clergyman or literary man. The progress of science in the nineteenth century, continuing at an increasing rate, has put the "hewer of wood" in possession of a solid course of study in forestry, equal in dignity to that of priest or lawyer and made it possible for the "drawer of water" (*alias* the engineer in hydraulics and irrigation) who really knows his work to study a lifetime.

The present arrangement is the result not of a rational adaptation of the high school to the interests of society, but of a more or less fortuitous historical development. Modern high school education is a growth from the training of priests and of "gentlemen" in the sense of a hundred years ago. The linguistic training and superficial knowledge of the "humanities" in which it abounds was quite appropriate in the case of the generation of future ministers and "general" who needed to talk agreeably about things in general and not appear at a loss in the company of others trained in the same manner. But the training that was efficient in enabling one to make a good impression among the educated class of a hundred years ago is about the last thing one would rationally choose for the 600,000 children in our high schools to-day. Heaven forbid that we should try to turn out a quarter of a million agreeable talkers as the product of the high school. Let the most ardent advocate of the traditional curriculum choose at random fifty names from the entering class of his local high school; let him find out what each of them has done, what they like to do and can do well, what their older brothers and sisters are doing; and if he has the germs of open-mindedness he will admit that not one in three of them should give, as nearly all now do, a fifth of their time to the study of the traditional algebra and geometry, and that not one in five should study Latin. If, instead of taking the fifty who do enter, he could with omniscience choose the fifty or five hundred who ought to be the ones to continue with systematic education,—the future leaders in trades, business, industries and professions,—he would find a still larger majority of those whose own development and social usefulness demand a training in connection with the real world of nature and the constructive arts.

At this point some reader who has been brought up to a superstitious reverence for that potent word "culture" and to an association of "utilitarianism" with idiocy, the devil and the plague, will need enlightenment. If culture means knowledge of and participation in the best that has been taught and felt and done, studying chemistry, physics and physiology, or practicing forestry, sanitation and nursing, are as truly cultural as reading poems or learning the events of history, and much more so than reading forty lines daily of Caesar's *Gallic War* or contemplating the mysteries of mood and tense. If culture means a knowledge of the sort of thing they say Matthew Arnold knew to perfection, its pursuit is itself a trade, the trade of literary man and moralist, a trade that, like any other, may be pursued nobly or ignobly, from true zeal for excellence or from sordid selfishness, a trade which has an èclat and gives its adept a fame which science, invention and the industrial arts lack, but which intrinsically is no more honourable than its less showy rivals.

The use of the world utilitarian as a term of reproach and despite is due to a pardonable but none the less unfortunate lack of knowledge. Since the nobler souls have been willing to seek truth and beauty and honour, regardless of whether or not there happened to result any increase to their own individual happiness thereby, it is argued that we ought diligently to search for and use in schools those particular subjects of instruction and means of training which would give little or no increase to the happiness of the world at large. As if one could make anybody unselfish by making him useless, or a disinterested lover of truth and beauty by teaching him things of no practical interest to anybody! As if being good for nothing was the most exalted variety of goodness! The most pitiable feature of this fallacy is the frequency with which opponents of utilitarianism make their own greedy profit out of preaching against it....

I may only ask attention to a few specially relevant facts. First, there is knowledge enough which ends only organisation and adaptation to the high school pupil. Second, we cannot leave the matter to natural instincts; our neglect of it in formal education means that we entrust it to verbal traditions of the ignorant, to the charter of servants, and the woman's column of the newspapers. Third, the experience of medical education, the professional training of nurses, and the teaching of biology in high schools and colleges shows that teaching the facts of science concerning embryos goes on in much the same way as teaching the facts about bacteria or the liver, and warrants the expectation that the small fraction of such a course devoted to a matter-of-fact scientific acquaintance with the development of the human embryo would reduce rather than stimulate undesirable curiosity. Fourth, it is true that girls from sixteen to nineteen are more interested in romance, coquetry, and other activities preliminary to family life than they are in family life itself, and no one should expect such a course to have great popularity; but the course will be supported by those general intellectual interests which support a course in chemistry, biology or hand work. Finally, parents do not know enough to give the training and the churches or other philanthropic agencies would spoil it by inefficient teaching and futile moralising.

It is high time to turn back from these illustrations to the text itself, fitting the school to boys and girls and fitting them for life.

It may be claimed that the traditional training in the languages and mathematics, and the teaching in other subjects patterned on that training, does precisely fit for life by affording a general discipline for the intellectual powers, and that the work of lesson getting in the traditional curricula is the most economical preoperative for future efficient work and unselfish recreation of whatever sort. But it is very hard to find any basis in *facts* for this claim, and it is easy to find abundant evidence against it. The claim itself appears in educational theory usually as an excuse, as a defensive argument. Only when Latin lost its high place as a utility in commerce and the professions, and began to lose its eminence as the key to the world's knowledge and supposedly best literature, was its disciplinary value discovered. Only when problems about four men working fourteen days at a fourth of a stone wall ceased to apply to every-day practices on the farm did they begin to give universal accuracy and logic. Wherever education is put to a competitive test to produce efficiency in life, for instance in professional schools, it is forced to rely on special training in the special things that are to be done efficiently. We do not give our lawyers more Latin or our physicians more mathematics to make them logical and accurate. But apart from these suspicious facts, definite experiments have shown the high degree of specialization of the intellect and the inability of training in one study to mysteriously transform the whole intellectual outfit. Moreover, the time has utterly passed when the languages and mathematics could boast any superiority in respect to the power, small for any school study, to improve the mind as a whole. Right methods of thinking can be inculcated as well in forestry, electrical engineering, nursing or the sciences concerned with agriculture, and the chances of transfer of these methods to the general activities of life is greatest where the subject is most like, not most abstracted from, the general activities of life. The high school should give mental discipline and give as much of it as possible, and just for that reason it should, to discipline best for life, discipline in those problems which are most like those of life.

7

The Values of Studies

Among the many means used in school education the 'studies—that is, the portions of the arts and sciences which are learned—are the most notable. The problem of deciding what each of these is good for as an educational instrument, and which of them, if any, are superior to the rest—the problem, that is, of the values, absolute and relative, of studies—has naturally led to much discussion.

Doubtless we all feel sure that German has a greater value than Ojibway as a school study, though we might find the fact hard to prove; but whether German has a greater or less value than Greek few would assume, to decide. The scientifically proved facts concerning just what changes are produced in pupils as a result of this or that study are so very scanty that one is left to estimate values on the basis of general knowledge of human nature and of the studies themselves. Such estimates are insecure, but can be made less so by knowledge and use of certain principles.

The first of these is that the value of any study, as a means or instrument of education, depends on how the teacher teaches it and what the pupil learns from it, not upon what the study is in and of itself. English literature has little value as a means to refining taste, broadening sympathy and deepening insight, if the teacher makes it a system of petty gossip about Carlyle's dyspepsia and Shelley's eccentricities. Geometry does little for the reasoning powers of a pupil who learns it by rote.

Two of the greatest sources of misleading in arguments about the value of studies are the false assumptions that by merely putting a subject in the course of study we can put its value into the lives of the children and that the value which a subject may have when pursued with zeal by an expert will be realized when it is studied by no matter whom. For example, it might seem that since psychology is the science of human nature and behavior, and since to learn to control oneself and live well with other human beings is man's greatest work, psychology should be a leading subject in schools for all. But, as it was taught in high schools, psychology did not have any such superior value. So, also, expert lovers of a study are likely to feel sure that, since it does so much for them, it should be studied by all. They learn their error if they observe its actual results.

The second principle is that the value of a study is complex—the resultant of several different sorts of value. Adopting the customary division into physical education, intellectual education, moral education, technical education and esthetic education, we have to test each study's effect on health, knowledge and intellectual abilities and interests, conduct, skill, and appreciation or taste. Or, considering the ultimate purposes of education, we have to measure each study's service in making man's wants better and in making him able to satisfy them. Thus it is expected that literature as a school study will increase the student's good will toward men by broadening his sympathies and inspiring him with emulation of ideal characters, will replace selfish sensory pleasures by the impersonal satisfaction of reading, and will also give him an added insight into human nature which will help him to manage himself and other men, so that his and their wants can be better satisfied. One reason for the difficulty of decisions about the relative values of studies as means is the fact that they are means to such different purposes or ends. It is hard to balance ten percent, improvement in health against four percent, improvement in morality or eight percent, improvement in intellect.

Thinkers about education tend in this respect to fall into two opposing camps—one eager to devote the energy of schools to making wants better, and the other eager to use the schools to help them get what they do want. The former favor whatever studies they think likely to improve ideals of thought and conduct, with little heed to satisfying even these ideal wants, much less those which man actually feels. The latter urge for children those subjects by studying which they may get health, escape poverty, enjoy their leisure hours, and otherwise have more of what a decent, but not very idealistic, person wants. Of course thinkers of the first group are glad to gratify wants incidentally; and those of the second group are glad to improve, incidentally, the wants which they are satisfying. But there remains a conflict between those who value primarily a study that teaches men what to want, and those who value primarily a study that helps them get what they do want.

Each study's value is complex in two further ways. It may have intrinsic value as content, and derived value as a tool. it may have a narrow or 'specific' value, by the improvement it makes in the ability specially trained by it; and a broader, or 'transfer', or 'disciplinary', value, by the improvement it makes in other abilities.

Stenography, telegraphy, handwriting, logarithms, and the Greek or German script-alphabet, contrasted with the facts of physics, chemistry, or Greek literature, exemplify tool-values *versus* content-values. In general there is cause for suspicion of a study whose sole or chief value is as a tool. There is likely to be waste in teaching such a subject, since the pupil may not realize the need which the tool is designed to meet. Also there is likely to be waste because the pupil's education may cease before he learns what to do with the tool, or because he lacks the ability or the zeal to use it. Thus those parts of algebra which are of value primarily as tools for use in advanced mathematics are to be questioned as required studies for all pupils in the first year of high school, since not one pupil in ten will study advanced mathematics, and since only very gifted pupils can use these delicate tools for quantitative thought without special training. Some of the tools of thought, such as reading, writing and simple computation, are, on the other hand, so easily and so widely usable that the value of these studies is very great. But, even with them, it is well to make sure that the tool will be used by having it acquired in connection with content of intrinsic value,—that is, by having children learn to read with matter worth reading, learn to write as a means of telling facts, making wants known and the like, and learn to add or multiply as a means to quick and sure solution of real problems.

The difference between the narrow value, due to the particular ability primarily trained, and the disciplinary value, due to the transfer of improvement to other abilities also, cannot be well illustrated by contrasted studies. For every study may have both sorts of value in some measure. But it is clear that unless the geometry of the high school has a high degree of disciplinary value by its training in rigid reasoning from general principles, it should give way to other studies in the case of many pupils. Its narrow value, as special skill and knowledge in reasoning about circles, triangles and the like, is obviously less than that of physics, biology or economics, which train pupils to reason about matter and motion, animal and plant behavior, and the motives and acts of men.

In attempting to estimate the value of a study, then, one should, if possible, secure the actual facts which measure the changes produced in students as a result of having taken that study. Where this is impossible, one can at least take account of how the subject is taught and of how it is studied, of its effect on health, knowledge, intellectual abilities and interests, conduct, skill and taste, of what improvement it makes in wants and which wants it satisfies, of its service as content and as a tool, and of its disciplinary value as well as the particular abilities that it primarily trains.

In the case of the knowledge value of the school subjects certain further principles are useful. These are stated in the next section.

What Knowledge is of most Worth

We judge the relative value of different sorts of knowledge by the extent to which each helps toward the ultimate end of education—the improvement and satisfaction of wants. Thus it is easy to see that knowledge of German is worth more than knowledge of Choctaw, that knowledge of the cause of malaria is worth more than knowledge of the cause of tickling, or that knowledge of the properties of oxygen is worth more than knowledge of the anatomy of a trilobite.

Even in such obvious cases, however, the condition, *'worth more to most people,'* ought to be added. For it may be more to the common good for a few people—government agents for Indian affairs, for instance—to know an Indian language than to know German. For a scientist, who by knowledge of the cause of tickling may be led to important discoveries, to know that rather than the cause of malaria may be best. Also the value of each fragment of knowledge depends upon what other knowledge goes with it. Knowledge of the properties of oxygen is of much less value alone than when in combination with other facts of chemistry. The difference between wisdom and pedantry is in part a difference in the arrangement of knowledge.

In the third place, the value of any knowledge is due to many factors, such as its interestingness, its utility, its moral influence, and its disciplinary effect upon the entire intellect and character of its possessor. Consequently the knowledge that is of more worth in one respect will often be of less worth in others, and many judgments concerning the values of knowledge have to be prefaced by, *other things being equal.*

With these three limitations—that better means better in most cases, better provided it has other relevant knowledge combined with it, and better in so far as concerns the particular quality under discussion—the following rules are serviceable:

Knowledge of the real is better than knowledge of the non-existent. This may seem self-evident, but the implied command has not been obeyed. Babies are told all sorts of nonsense; kindergartens abound in pleasant lies; a fourth of the reading-matter for children in the elementary schools is fiction. These choices of the false instead of the true have not been justified by proof that the fancy does little harm by being false, and much good by being interesting and stimulating to right feeling and action. The balance of value has not been proved to favor the fancy rather than the truth proposed as a substitute. In many cases the choice of the false could be justified. Red Riding Hood, Cinderella and the Three Bears, for instance, do much good by the innocent pleasure they give and by their admirable service in teaching children how to read. In many cases, too, the ostensibly fanciful account may mislead little children less than the ostensible truth. But in other cases they learn lies to no advantage.

Knowledge is of value in proportion to the number of situations to which it applies. "Knowledge of principles is better than knowledge of mere facts," and "knowledge of fundamentals is better than knowledge of derivatives," are common partial statements of this rule. It states what should oftenest be the deciding factor in the choice of the knowledge to be given to all, or nearly all, pupils alike. It governs the choice between German and Choctaw, or between oxygen and trilobites. Knowledge of means of measuring time, distance, area, volume, weight and wealth, and of performing simple computations, is by it judged to be of more value than the knowledge of geometry that could be obtained by the same pupils in the same time. Percentage is by it judged to be of more value than interest, brokerage or discount.

Knowledge is of value in proportion to the importance to human welfare of the situations to which it applies. The preference of knowledge of the cause of malaria to knowledge of the cause of tickling is an application of this principle. So also knowledge of steam-engines would be preferred to knowledge of millinery, in spite of the fact that hats figure more frequently in life. Knowledge pertaining to moral conduct is thus above knowledge pertaining to manners; knowledge pertaining to health is above knowledge pertaining to wealth; knowledge pertaining to the family and the state is above knowledge pertaining to such conventions of language as spelling and punctuation.

Knowledge of the future is of more worth than knowledge of the past. When the two are equal in respect to the intellectual pleasure, the discipline and the moral inspiration given, knowledge that can predict is better than knowledge that merely records, because it helps us better in the main business for which knowledge exists—to control the forces of nature and ourselves.

This principle has not had the recognition or influence in education which it deserves. Verification by the future is one of the best tests by which to distinguish science from false opinion. Moreover, knowledge of the past is often of value chiefly as evidence for some other knowledge, and so may be nearly as valuable to the world at large when possessed by only a few experts as when repeated in a great many students' minds. Finally when knowledge is tested to see what it will predict, it is less likely to busy itself with trifles.

8

Aims of Education

COMPUTERS AND EDUCATION AIMS

- The computer is succeeding the clock and the steam engine as the defining technology and principal technological metaphor of our time, chiefly because it can reflect the versatility of the human mind as no previous mechanism could do.
- The central issue in computer ethics during the next two decades will be the replacement of human beings by computers—most particularly in tasks that are thought to require judgment and wisdom.

There is obvious confusion, uncertainty and disagreement about the role of the computer in education. This arises, at least in part, from much more general changes in society's image of itself and of its needs, changes partly caused by the way in which computing technology has infiltrated and become part of every aspect of modern life. There is in effect a feedback loop or a form of recursion, in that the extent to which computers are used in general terms, influences the extent to which they are used in education, which in turn influences growth in use in the world generally, and so on. The fact that the best available metaphor for this process—feedback—is itself taken directly from computing, is a further symbol of the whole process.

The problem, which education must try to come to terms with, is not simply how and when and to what extent computers ought to be used in schools, but what education will mean in the new world of computer technology with all its changed assumptions and priorities. The expectations and demands made of education have never been constant, and in each age have reflected the current view of the needs of humanity. So that, for example, in primitive societies education is about learning how to survive through finding or producing food. In our own modern society education has reflected more grandiose versions of man's purpose and has included such complex and difficult aims as self-knowledge, spirituality, the education of feeling, creativity, sensitivity, and so on. At the same time it has always included, in one way or another, the need for more mundane aims thought to be of immediate use to the society, such as the training and development of specific skills. The worry which emerges most often in relation to the impact of the computer on education is about the possible demise of these higher and more complex aims and the raising to prominence of the others.

The argument takes as read the view that these higher-level aims are more worthy and more fundamental. It is in essence less concerned with technical issues as with ethical ones, such as what computers ought to be allowed to do, and 'has nothing to do with what computers can or cannot be made to do. Respect, understanding, and love are not technical problems.' (Weizenbaum, 1976, pp. 269–270). However, it can be argued that current philosopher of education are themselves of comparatively recent origin and that they represent the aspirations of a particular age and a particular intellectual climate, rather than anything final or absolute. In other words it is important to take account of the historical evolution of these matters—

> Critics of the new technology sometimes talk as if mankind always aspired to the ideal of being sensitive nature loving and creative until the computer was devised to rob it of these

> aspirations. In fact, this definition of the human condition is quite recent, the product of philosophy and psychology popular only in the last two hundred years. The values here assumed were not obvious to generations of ordinary people or philosophers.

There is also the view which is not difficult to sustain that these higher level aspirations are rarely effected in reality, and that for a great man if not the majority of pupils, education is a fairly unproductive experience, in both academic and social terms. For example, Papert (1984) writes—

> Nothing enrages me more than when people criticize my criticism of school by telling me that schools are not just places to learn maths and spelling, they are places where children learn a vaguely defined thing called socialization. I know. I think schools generally do an effective and terribly damaging job of teaching children to be infantile, dependent, intellectually dishonest, passive and disrespectful to their own developmental capacities.

It is also possible therefore to take the opposite view that computers, and the new technology generally, will make the achievement of education's current aims more and not less likely. To some observers such as Howkridge (1983) the permeation of the child's life with electronic toys and entertainments generates a level of informal and unstructured learning without precedent, and it is a situation, he believes, that schools are as yet unable to exploit. Similarly, Turkle (1984), compares the standard perception of the computer as 'rational, uniform, uniform' constrained by logic' (page 3), with her own experience of it as an 'evocative object,' an object that fascinates, disturbs equanimity, and precipitates thought' (page 3). A similar view is expressed by Papert (1984) where he goes on to argue that the computer, far from reducing the level of the school's social and academic ambitions and achievements, is likely to make them both more humanistic and more realizable.

> I think that the examples I have given of learning in a computational environment provide a glimpse of a context for learning in which socialization would be based on a potentiation of the individual, an empowering sense of one's own ability to learn anything one wants to know...As long as important bodies of knowledge (such as school mathematics and written language) are not rooted in the desires and the life experience of children schools will have to teach them artificially and by force.

Nonetheless, despite the intentions of Papert and others, the computer world is often presented as one in which the issues and problems of life are simplified into logical, structured and essentially visible patterns. The mysteries and uncertainties are thought of simply as those parts of the structure as yet undeciphered. When they are, their mysterious or spiritual quality will disappear. In such a world education becomes an easier task. Well-designed expressions of the implicit logical structures can be made available through computer technology, and nothing more will be required. All problems can be analysed and solved in logical terms, because all problems are inherently superficial once their structure is known. So education becomes a task about finding solutions to well-defined problems within strict rules. Hidden complexity and mystery are old, dead metaphors.

The causes of the movement towards and acceptance and an appreciation of this view of education must also be considered. First, there was a brief period of educational idealism and optimism, mainly in the sixties, when it was thought that education might act as midwife to a new egalitarian world. This both reflected and generated an open and liberal view of the world with such notions as child-centred education, discovery learning, and freedom of expression. The emphasis was on innovation, individuality and equality of opportunity. In retrospect it was inevitable that such ambitious expectations were bound to fail, and when they did, there was an equally inevitable and strong sense of disillusionment. Second, the emergence of such major and apparently unsolvable problems as recession, large-scale unemployment, a lowering of standards of living, and so on, all demanded that causes be identified, and education was quickly under scrutiny. It was not the only institution of society to be put in the position of scapegoat, but the conclusion was that education had failed, that its aims and procedures needed to be revised, and that its contribution to national economic and commercial life could and should be more obvious and more deliberate. For those disillusioned in this way the new technology seems to bring to education a sense of realism, with its more concrete emphasison achievable goals, usable skills, and a form of structured and measurable educational output.

However, the way in which education—or educationalists—manage to subvert what they see as simplistic responses to complex problems can be seen in the importance attached to Logo and the work of Papert, which is a model of computer education more in line with the earlier optimism. Turkle (1984) writes about a classroom using Papert models of learning as follows—

> Commonplace assumptions about what happens in schools did not hold true for the computer-rich Austen classroom: that teachers know more than students, that teachers are more interested than students, and that it is the teacher's job to design artful ways to motivate children to learn things that would not come naturally to them.

COMPONENT OF THE PROBLEM

Because of these difficult and unresolved issues, we began this book by arguing that it is impossible to be certain about the future impact of the new technology on education. The rest of the book is an attempt to examine this question by looking closely and analytically at the many issues and problems which are likely to have some level of influence on the outcome. The book identifies three essentially different major components of the problem: first the technology itself and its influence on general social issues; second the relationship, or the interface, between the technology and a variety of long-standing educational questions; and third the possible effects of the technology on educational practice.

The analysis of the first of these is concerned with the innovative and essentially unpredictable character of the technology and the speed with which it changes. These characteristics, along with its power and efficiency, ensure that it is likely to make an impact on all aspects of the modern world, and consequently on a great many social issues and on the understanding of human values. Bolter (1986) has recently argued that it makes sense to regard the computer as a technological paradigm for the science, the philosophy, even the art of the coming generation' (page xvi). For him the computer has become a sort of general metaphor for the age, and the effect of this on language, culture and philosophy is likely to be very profound—

> By promising (or threatening) to replace man, the computer is giving us a new definition of man as an 'information processor', and of nature, as 'information to be processed.'

The second component of the discussion relates to the specifically educational questions, many of them of very longstanding, and embedded in other larger issues such as human values, the structure of society, and the influence and importance of ideology and politics. These questions involve such major and complex topics as learning, curriculum and intelligence. It is becoming clear that the discussion of these must take place in the context of changes in the fundamental aims and aspirations of education, and this makes it necessary to reflect on what these new aims are likely to be. Educational questions are now being considered, for good or ill, without necessary reference to what have hitherto been seen as constant and fundamental and unchangeable aims. The values associates with the old way of educating are being challenged and the new technology is seen as both one of the causes of the change and as one of the tools that will make the new practice of education possible.

The third component with which the book concerns itself is the practice of education in the light and influence of the new technology, and such intrinsic and day-to-day problems as teaching and classroom organisation. Much of the literature and development work, produced over the past few years, has concerned itself almost wholly with this area. Included are the various forms of educational software, the means to be used to integrate these into existing classroom practice and subject content, the emergence of such techniques as home learning, data analysis and retrieval systems, word-processing, and so on. The emphasis is on the computer as just another highly complex tool, nothing more. It is, or at least has the potential to be, a more efficient means towards educational ends which are in essence unchanged. This world is sometimes criticised because of its lack of deep knowledge of, and respect for, the world of computer science: Self (1985) is particularly incensed by this and perceives it as a lack of seriousness of purpose on the part of educationalists. He writes—

> Why are teachers, alone of the professions, so insistent that only they are able to write software to meet their needs?...Could it be that teachers are sensitive to the revelation that they do not know precisely what they are trying to do or how they do it?

Criticism of this sort is often associated with the promotion of artificial intelligence as an important way (perhaps the only important way) forward in educational computing. Because, it is argued, it takes account of the complexity of learning and moves away from the superficiality of much that passes for computer-based education. But, more importantly, it makes proper use of the science of computing and of those who are experts in this, and it exploits the real potential and power of modern computers in a way that education currently does not.

There is probably some truth in this, but there are also a number of half-truths. Even if there was a certainty that the current world of computing had a great deal to offer education, very considerable resources would be necessary if advantage was to be taken of this, and these are not going to be made available. Also, the emphasis in the argument is often on the computer and on computing rather than on education. Questions about the nature of education are excluded, not because they are not important but because software can be discussed separately. Clearly, if computers are going to be important in schools, then knowledge from both domains must be exploited and it ought to be possible to do this more effectively than it is being done currently. But it is realistic to assume that the philosophical and humanistic issues of education are not likely to be the first concern of programmers. There can be little doubt that artificial intelligence will eventually have a role in education, and it will be necessary for its use and development to be carefully monitored with respect to its underlying model of education. At present it appears to be promoting a new utilitarian education which is functional, purposive, complex in its structures but simple in its human models. It raises quite starkly the question: What is education when computers do the teaching?

This book has tried to adopt an analytical approach to these problems, because we felt that there was an unsatisfied need to encourage and promote, among teachers and educationalist, a critical response to the proposed role in education of the new technology. We believe that educational innovations, especially those of a dramatic and possibly revolutionary nature, need to be constantly examined, both to assess the extent to which they represent a change in the model of education being considered, but also to measure them against existing long-term educational needs and aspirations. Currently there is little evidence of such an evaluative approach.

We are aware also that the two most salient features of the new technology are its speed and constancy of change, and the enthusiasm and excitement which it generates. The result is often a kind of breathless innovation syndrome, and an unthinking or blind faith in the quality and importance of its actual and potential contribution to education. This is to be found among educationalist, parents, third level academics, government organisations and society generally. It is clear from the resources being invested and the energy and commitment being demonstrated, that many of those concerned, including government, believe deeply in the importance of using the new technology. What is not so clear is why this should be so, and what evidence there is to support it.

FORMS OF CHANGE

There are a number of difficulties about the view that computers can improve education. These are all interrelated in various ways, and all require elaboration and thought. The first is that it is not at all clear what is meant by the improvement of education, or how such improvement would be recognized and measured. There is an implication that there can be no argument about what constitutes improvement, as though there existed some sort of unquestioned consensus. Furthermore, the level at which it is believed this change is to be effected varies a great deal. In some of the writing it is clear that what is intended is a change in the fundamental character of education itself, that is to say in the underlying aims and purposes of education. For example, the current emphasis on the needs of industry and commerce, and the demand that education should begin to supply pupils with a tool-kit of skills and techniques, represents a version of the intentions of education which is startlingly different from that of a decade ago. For some this is a retrograde step which is based on a simplification of the long-term needs of society. In this situation, where aims are changing, and are to some extent still vague and undeveloped, any notion of improving education is difficult it not impossible to measure, since there is no parallel previous state to compare it with.

However, in most of the work of educational computing it is clear that the intended improvement is to be in the means to be used to achievement existing and generally acceptable ends, arising out of some level of consensus about the aims of education. The emphasis is on such things as improving the speed and efficiency of learning, and on the understanding of ideas. In this situation improvement ought to be measurable to an extent, even thought there are still considerable difficulties. Certainly it is not enough simply to state that there has been improvement. This view is at best based on belief and some selective evidence rather than any evaluation or research. It may indeed be true that future educational practice can be improved dramatically be the new technology, but as yet we cannot say.

There are a number of reasons for a degree of hesitancy, if not pessimism, in this area. Before any real improvement can start it is necessary to transfer the proposed changes into the classroom. This is a well-known stumbling-block for all innovations. The history of attempts at curriculum innovation in the sixties and seventies suggest that, while the initial steps in the process of innovation (namely the generation of ideas and enthusiasm among academics and leaders of thought) are easily accomplished, the later stages of classroom acceptance and establishment are very difficult to achieve. In part this is to do with the essential conservatism of much of the teaching profession which has long been used to bandwagons, and which protects itself from them with some skill. So it is probably not surprising that what little evidence there is suggests that schools and teachers are not taking up the technology in any very consistent or organised way.

It is also necessary to bear in mind the current stage in the evolution of the technology. To learn to use modern small computers is not yet a simple direct task. The human-machine interface is still in a comparatively primitive state, and although the quality of the presentation of the materials available for schools is improving, it is still not very high. The experience is that getting teachers to the stage where they are comfortable with even a well-designed software package is a longer and more long-term task than is often suggested.

It must also be accepted that, however improbable, there is a possibility that some of the change which the new technology demands may turn out to be opposed to the long-term best interests of education. The technology is young, the attempt to apply it to education is recent, there has not been enough incubation time for the ideas and innovations to be properly reflected upon, and there has not been any systematic and large-scale examination and testing process.

Quality in education is a relative notion, since it depends completely on what is intended by education. In the same way, what is deemed to be a negative outcome depends on what hopes and intentions are placed in the system. Some of those who have written about the possible negative outcomes of introducing the new technology into education have made their case in terms of what they clearly consider to be unarguably important or fundamental characteristic of education (see for example the article by Baker, 1985, page 449). They argue that many of the values associated with the traditional concept of education are being challenged often unconsciously or without notice. Among these they include such things as the importance of social interaction between teachers and pupils. They would argue that the incidence of this is threatened by the one-to-one impersonality of the machine and of computer-based learning systems. Children need to be constantly in touch with other humans, especially teachers, so that they learn communication skills—not just the direct and obvious ones, but the hidden or less overt forms which are often at least as important: the 'wink and nod' of non-verbal communication; the need to learn how to use and interpret gesture, the changing pitch and volume of voice, the expression in another's eyes; and how to read intention, meaning and response in facial expression. These they argue are not open to question as of crucial importance in education, and it is necessary to make sure that any system of computer-based education does not exclude them.

There is also some evidence beginning to emerge that the use of the technology exacerbates existing intergroup performance differences. For example, use of the computer far computer-based learning seems to widen the performance gap between the sexes to the further advantage of the males. Similar results occur with respect to class differences in that the quantity of machines and software available to pupils in schools with essentially middle- class clientele is much greater than in other schools. A development of this sort is clearly retrograde in that there have been serious attempts to move educational practice in the opposite direction.

It is also argued that each individual school builds up over time a philosophy which is manifested in a great many aspects of its day-to-day running such as pupil behaviour patterns or curriculum structures. These reflect not just the views and opinions of the staff, but represent a way of working to achieve goals which has evolved out of practice and error. Such patterns are often quite delicately balanced and can only be changed carefully and slowly without the risk of doing more harm than good. The intrusion of the computer culture into this patterning with all its characteristic speed and evangelism is likely to cause confusion and to lead to the adaptation of new ways of working which are not yet known to be appropriate and which may not be designed to lead to the established and accepted school goals.

There is also the epistemological question about the way in which the computer encourages the user to think about knowledge. Obviously there is no single answer to this, but the negative side suggests that there is a tendency for computer-based learning to present knowledge in a limited form. For example, in much of the interaction between the computer and the human, knowledge is presented in a way that seems to suggest that it cannot be challenged or expanded or contradicted or restructured. By its very nature the way in which a computer represents knowledge involves structure and formalism. In its interactions with humans this structure forces it to be intractable. Consequently, for the most part the human is not encouraged to be creative or to improvise or to interpret situations. This would seem to represent a limited version of the experience of education.

Implicit in this structured form of knowledge there are also the questions of who decides what the content should be, and what content is 'true'. The danger in this comes from two different directions. On the one hand the decisions may be made by the computer experts who will control the system, and there is always danger in this sort of singular and undemocratic power. But on the other hand the decisions may be made by the pressures of the market-place. Education may well become what people are prepared to pay for and this could lead to a heavy bias towards vocational models with a content made up mainly of knowledge that is seen to be immediately valuable in the job-market. The result would be an education geared towards training, results, and singular ungeneralisable skills.

9

General Learning Issues

INTRODUCTION

There are clear indications of the beginning of a debate about the impact of the new technology on what we mean by learning. This debate is one of the public manifestations of more general anxieties about the effect of this technology on such things as the quality of life, the availability of employment, and the importance of human skills and abilities. In order to try to understand and contribute to this debate on computers and learning it is important that we look at the whole subject in some detail.

We must try to see the ways in which the technology has provided new perceptions of what learning might mean, and we must also take account of the new dimensions it has added to the subject.

Initially the value of these developments is not always clear: we can find in the literature quite vague and general phrases like: 'Logo is a language for learning'. But we can also find less obviously acceptable views which seem to suggest that computers can be used in education as a sort of cognitive engineering, or as a way of shaping children's minds.

THE MEANING OF LEARNING

The study of education has always posed great difficulties for student, teachers and researchers alike because it involves the consideration of a number of closely and yet essentially mysterious, human characteristics or facilities such as knowledge, learning, understanding, intelligence, motivation, cognition, problem-solving, and others. Because all of these 'faculties' are aspects of human behaviour and human potential their definition is not always clear or permanent. For example, it is obviously impossible to get very far with a discussion of any aspect of learning without considering motivation. For this reason it is not always easy to separate out any singly one of these issues and to try to analyse what it might mean simply by itself.

The nature and determinants of the learning process have always been central issues in education, sometimes very obviously so as in debates about psychological models such as behaviourism and stimulus-response learning. But even when the discussion is focussed on some other general organising notion such as curriculum, the problems and difficulties of learning are still crucial. The importance of trying to understand the process can be estimated by an examination of the number and variety of complex theories that have attempted to make sense of it over the past century. It is difficult to make judgments in this area, since these models or theories cannot be shown to be either valid or invalid, since proof in this area is meaningless. But some seem to have greater staying power than others, perhaps because they made the issue seem simpler than it was, or because, in the Popperian manner, they managed to explain more of the experiential data. For example, models which postulate some form of developmental sequence in learning have proved very persistent since they appear to complement the visible physical growth of the child. The most obvious example of this are the theories of Piaget, and these are described below.

It also seems clear that learning theories cannot be understood in isolation, since most have been underwritten by general philosophies about fundamental problems such as the nature of mankind, or the nature of knowledge, or the nature of human society. For example, the power of knowledge (through learning) to help people to become free, in all the senses of that word, has always been thought of by many as the justification for education. For some, the formal structure of the school system, and the power of teachers to define what is knowledge and what is learning, can become difficulties in the way of this ideal of freedom. For this reason such complementary ideals as independent judgment, freedom of speech, and the right to be wrong, have always been in some conflict with the formal structures of the educational system. It is not surprising then that when information technology, perceived by some as being to do with the mechanisation and depersonalisation of education, is introduced, into the system and becomes thought of as a part of the learning process, this can be interpreted as an additionol hazard. That is to say there is a danger that it will decrease the freedom of the learner and increase the power of the system and, perhaps, also of the teacher.

A large number of problems and unresolved issues related to learning have been common to almost all the widely held theories. These include: the relative importance to be attached to learning specific facts, learning about processes and acquiring skill in problem solving; the influence of testing both on what is learned and on how it is learned; the contrast between theories about learning and how it does or does not happen in practice; the difference between learning in a logical hierarchical imposed order, and the constant and unexplained insights and heuristic leaps of the learner; the extent to which the learner can be a passive recipient in the knowledge-acquiring process.

Whatever the theory or the underlying philosophy almost all writers have referred to the puzzles of learning, and in particular its hidden or inferable nature. The most often quoted example of this is the complex and as yet unsolved mystery of learning to talk, and the fact that young children perform this manifestly difficult task on their own. As yet, however, we do not know enough about how this natural learning occurs to be able to reproduce it in schools and with children.

MODELS OF LEARNING

Despite the wide range of theories of learning that have emerged, it might be possible to make a crude summary of them by expressing a broad dichotomy. On one side are those which emphasize, in one way or another the structural or logical nature of learning. The vocabulary associated with this uses such words as organised, hierarchical, repetition, practice, reinforcement, succession, and logic. For example, Shinner (1968) writes—

> Some promising advances have recently been made in the field of learning. Special techniques have been designed to arrange what are called contingencies of reinforcement—the relations which prevail between behavior on the one hand and the consequences of that behavior on the other—with the result that a much more effective control of behavior has been achieved.

On the other side are the theories which depict learning as a much more individual and variable interaction between a unique organism and its environment. These tend to make extensive use of words like intrinsic, natural, unstructured, spontaneous, motivated, creative, discovery, investigation and interest.

Although this 'child-centred' approach has a long history, the popularisation of Piaget's theories over the past twenty-five years has been very important in giving it a rationale. Piaget's writings, or interpretations of them, have had an enormous influence on curriculum change, and on theories and developments about classroom practice. The two basic postulates of his work are, that most children learn from experiencing concrete situations in the real world, which they then use to revise their own internal theories about the world; and that they pass through a series of stages of development in the growth of this learning. An example of the expression of these views within the context of a well-argued personal theory can be found in Bruner (1967)—

> The will to learn is an intrinsic motive, one that finds both its source and its reward in its own exercise. The will to learn becomes a 'problem' only under specialised circumstances like those of a school, where a curriculum is set, students confined, and a path fixed. The problem exists not so much in learning itself, but in the fact that what the school imposes often fails to enlist the natural energies that sustain spontaneous learning—curiosity, a desire for competence, aspiration to emulate a model, and a deep-sensed commitment to the web of social reciprocity.

These ideas have been seminal and although many people have found ways of reworking them, or disagreeing with aspects of them, their lasting achievement seems to be the introduction of scepticism about superficial and unexamined theories which purport to explain how children learn. For example, a report of a modern classroom-based research show quite clearly its heritage in Piaget—

> A theme that will recur in different forms...is the idea that at the heart of any good teaching and learning experience is a critical relationship. That is, a relationship in which teachers and learners alike seek to question each other's ideas, to reinterpret them, to adapt them and even to reject them, but not to discount them.

We will later discuss in some detail the specific issues raised by any attempt to integrate this view of learning with the use of computers (and information technology generally) in classrooms. However, it is useful at this stage, using research of this sort, to emphasize the involved and intricate nature of the set of human relationships present in any classroom. Also, it is vital to keep these relatively sophisticated models firmly in mind when we consider the impact of the new technology, since it is extremely unlikely that technological change can itself resolve the issues they raise. Certainly a view, like the one presented in the next extract, may strike a chord for many teachers but it holds out little hope that any single technological innovation will provide easy answers. Even when, in reading material like this, allowance is made for an element of enthusiasm, and an assumption that all teachers are equally gifted in classroom management, it still raises many questions about the role of technology—

> At the risk of oversimplifying a highly complex and philosophical matter, there appear to be two broadly different approaches to teaching which I shall call the transmission mode and the interpretative mode. According to the transmission mode of teaching, the teacher is seen as having, or having access to, certain knowledge and skills and as having the responsibility of transmitting these to the learner...According to this mode (i.e. the interpretative one) the process of teaching and learning is two way. It involves not only the child's attempt to interpret and assimilate the knowledge and skills offered by the teacher, but also the teacher's attempt to understand the child's growing understanding of the world...It is through such processes of reinterpretation, as teachers and learners strive to understand each other, that we gain some access and insight into the child's understanding. It is in this way also that we can evaluate the effects of our teaching.

There is, as well, the possibility of tension between this sort of classroom-based approach and the attempts to introduce the new technology into education. These two might be thought to be the most salient and powerful movements in modern education, but they can also be thought of as representing what are essentially opposed trends. One is towards the study and understanding of the practice of teaching and learning as observed and understood in the classroom, so that theory may arise out of the reality of action. This puts the teacher and the children firmly at the centre of the stage, and suggests that any general theory which does not take account of the implicit theory which their practice represents, is bound to be incomplete, at the least. The other trend tries to take account of the new technology in thinking about educational developments, on the grounds that the impact of the technology on society in general is bound to be reflected in education. The danger is that this introduces the possibility of modes of action that are essentially controlled from outside education.

To begin to make the connection between models of how children learn and the introduction of computers into classrooms, we must consider the work of Seymour Papert. His contribution represents and almost direct line with the writings of Piaget, with the added influence and perspective of the field of artificial intelligence. He has a beautifully written and highly developed theory about the effects of using computers on the way in which children think and learn. For example, he argues that children can be provided with reasoning strategies from their experience of the process of teaching computers (via programming in Logo) through such processes as debugging, developing concrete models, and heuristic problem solving. He demonstrates this in one paper, when he describes how children found out for themselves how to make the computer do what they wanted, even though this knowledge involved concepts considered by their teacher to be too hard for them—

> And when the concepts of degrees, and compass points are acquired in this way by personal appropriation, the knowledge has forever a special personal power, a special rootedness in the sense of oneself. What a contrast with how hard it is to teach children at a much later age the concept of degrees, and what a contrast with the alienated form.

Papert's views are, of course, not without their critics but what he says is original and important, and so there is a full chapter devoted to his work. For this reason we will only touch briefly on his views here. One of the criticisms made of him is that he does not take enough account of the social process in education, and he responds quite fiercely to this, although it is interesting to juxtapose his response with the quotations above from Rowland—

> Nothing enrages me more than when people criticize my criticism of schools by telling me that schools are not just

> places to learn maths and spelling, they are places where children learn a vaguely defined thing called socialization...I think schools generally do an effective and terribly by damaging job of teaching children to be infantile, dependent, intellectually dishonest, passive and disrespectful to their own developmental capacities.

It is not difficult to take a polemic like this at its face value and make nonsense of its generality and overstatement. Indeed, as already suggested, the quotations from Rowland do this very well. However, it is not necessary to agree with every line of it to experience at least a mild shock of recognition, and to accept some of the argument: the heart of this is that there is built-in to the structural world of school a model of children and of learning that is not overt and so difficult to make available for analysis or argument.

There can be little doubt that it is difficult to reflect the models and theories about children and learning developed by Piaget and his hires in the world of computer software, and indeed few current software producers would claim to do so. This will be on forms and classifications of software, but it is worth repeating that because of the speed and flurry with which computers became available to education, the models of learning which software developers, often not teachers, found easiest to adapt to were the older and apparently less complex ones of behaviourism—

Sage and Smith (1983) found this to be particularly true in America:

> [In the USA] in particular it was found that the computer had reawakened the programmed learning movement, and that a good percentage of the research effort was directed towards justification of rather simplistically behaviorist CAI materials in terms of 'cognitive gains'.

This model is of course at the opposite end of the spectrum and can be justified in a certain very well-defined learning context. There is a long history of debate about its value, and about the extent to which it reflects a limited and unsophisticated version of learning and of education generally.

THE EFFECTS OF THE NEW TECHNOLOGY

The new technology has helped to revive many of these long-standing debates on issues related to the processes of learning, but it has also moved the discussion in new directions. Two particular aspects of this will now be mentioned briefly, and each of these has a separate chapter devote to it. The first of these is the growth in the study of artificial intelligence which has led to the development of important new insights into such related areas as perception, vision, and the representation of knowledge. This has almost inevitably led to the beginning of a new style of experimentation on the nature of educationally related issues such as cognition, intelligence, memory and learning (O'Shea and Self, 1983). The second is the development in telecommunications technology which have led to an enormous growth in the use of television-based direct accessing of information systems such as national and international databases, electronic mail, bulletin boards, and so on. The effects of these on education generally, and on learning in particular, is as yet impossible to predict. It would seem likely, however, that they will influence what is learnt and also how it is learnt.

The revival of interest in matters relating to learning is reflected also in some recent publications concerning research in the area of computers in education. In 1983 the Social Science Research Council (now called the Economic and Social Research Council) published a consultative document called *Microcomputers in Education: a framework for research* by Morley Sage and David Smith. This made a number of recommendations for research, and included a proposition about the need for a major research on 'learning processes and information technology'. This 'would be directed towards the styles, strategies and processes of learning with IT'. Although this proposal arose out of the issues generated by the new technology, it was also felt to reflect a more general' need, nonetheless sharpened by the existence of the new technology—

> In any case, the development of a model of the learning process would be of the greatest consequence even to conventional education and so this general field may be held to embody problems which are of fundamental importance to education.

In the past theories of learning have usually been referred to as based on psychological studies of individual learning. They are now more likely to be referred to as arising out of what is called cognitive studies. Cognition refers to all the information-processing activities of the brain, including perception, memory, attention, problem-solving, language, thinking and imagery—

> Little or no attention has been given to the need for a fundamental understanding of learning, cognitive processes and the organisation of knowledge. Such understanding is essential to the design of learning experiences based on IT application. Indeed, the question of what is called 'Instructional Design' in the USA has been largely ignored in British initiatives...

This clearly postulates the need for new, better and more powerful theories of learning suited to the new technological age. However, apart from expressing a need, and justifying it in terms of new knowledge and new factors, it is not all clear how this might be done. Sage and Smith refer somewhat vaguely to the need for 'sound' models of learning, but it is difficult to know what they mean since all such models are bound to be partial and to reflect particular biases and particular philosophies—

> A greater awareness of the need for sound models of learning and cognitive processes to support the design and implementation of educational experiences was found in those countries than in the UK, and less tendency on the part of practitioners to dismiss theoretical considerations as irrelevant to classroom practice.

A contribution by Ruthven (in Smith, 1984) argues that this approach misunderstands the nature of theory, and goes on to argue the case for the importance and validity of 'action research' as described above.

Sage and Smith (1983) clearly have a much more structured and tightly controlled 'input–output' style of research in mind, and they describe the sort of studies that might be needed this as follows—

> studies directed towards gaining information about the direct and indirect effects of IT based educational environments on the learner and the process of learning. Such research might give particular attention to the styles, strategies and processes of learning required or facilitated by IT in different contexts. Interest might also be directed towards the effects of contact with IT devices on cognitive development and organisation, motivational dispositions, individual behaviour and social interactions. Research under this heading would provide and information base for courseware designers, for teachers wishing to design and develop new learning environments, for curriculum developers and for cognitive scientists.

It will be some time before there is much in the way of evidence, either from research or from the analysis of classroom and individual performance, about the effects of these 'IT based educational environments'. The danger is that the current situation, which is very new and very incomplete, will be used as a basis for long-term decisions long before any such decisions are warranted.

10

A Theory of Innovation

Any Process of innovation involves the following four major factors.

1. *The Change Agent,* the innovator, the person or group (e.g. the headmaster, or individual teacher, or local authority, or national government) that decides upon and initiates the innovation or educational change.

2. *The Innovation* or change itself, e.g. an integrated approach to learning-teaching; or 'new' mathematics in place of the old; or a comprehensive system of education as against the more traditional tripartite system of grammar school/secondary modern/technical education; programmed instruction; education by television etc.

3. *The User* system—the person or group at which the innovation is directed or targeted.

These three key factors answer the simple question:

- *who* (the change agent) says
- *what* (the innovation)
- to *whom* (the user).

To ignore or underestimate the importance of any one of these key factors would be courting trouble. It is important to bear in mind, too, that these three factors interact with, change and are changed by each other during the process of innovation.

4. *Time:* Innovation is essentially a social process and so takes place over a period of time.

Any change agent or innovator will obviously be involved with:

- the Process of Innovation,
- the Planning of Innovation,
- Strategies of Innovation.

Considering these under the change agent system does not imply that the user system is not involved. It sometimes happens that the change agent and the user are in opposition. But for any innovation to succeed the two must co-operate and collaborate. So, while considering what the change agent does, one must remember that, ideally, the user will also be closely involved in the change agent's activities.

THE PROCESS OF INNOVATION

Most innovation go through something approaching these logical phases.

1. There is some *problem,* some dissatisfaction, some need, that requires attention.
2. Some *possible solutions* are considered.
3. A *particular solution* (innovation) is selected as being the most likely to meet the problem.
4. This *optimum solution*is *trialled* and *evaluated.*
5. If promising, the solution is *implemented* on a wider scale.
6. The solution is absorbed into the system, it is *institutionalized.*

Havelock and Huberman point out that many innovations fail because innovators fail to appreciate the *process* of innovation, because they pay little heed to the lessons that can be learnt from the process, particularly the fact that innovation is a matter of *system change* and system building within a social context. On the other hand they show how careful diagnosis of needs, specificity of objectives, detailed organizational planning and development of competencies and materials, can be instrumental in the success of innovative projects such as, for example, the Caribbean regional teacher training and curriculum development project.

Let us consider these phases of the innovation process in some more detail.

1. *The problem:* Before any innovation process begins there must be some problem, some situation, which is causing dissatisfaction and which it is hoped some innovation will solve or at least ameliorate. Otherwise, why introduce any innovation?

The difficulty is often to identify the *real* problem, i.e. the one that is the root-cause of the dissatisfaction. If youth unemployment is the cause of concern, the real problem may have nothing to do with education and with what goes on in the schools, but rather lie in the economic and political spheres. Unless there are jobs available, changing the education system won't solve the basic problem. Only providing jobs will reduce unemployment. The job of the change agent is to assist in identifying the real problem.

2. Having identified the real problem, the next phase involves considering possible solutions, bearing in mind the economic, social and cultural limitations. The examination system often provides constraints on innovation. Parents, too, can shackle new ideas and solutions. Some parents think diplomas and certificates have magical powers: no "child-centred", "play-way" methods for their children. The change agent must constantly keep in mind the *context* in which the solution, the innovation, the educational change, will be applied. He must consider the peculiarities of the *user system* and its likely response to any innovation. An innovation is a deliberate intrusion into the fabric of a culture. Often this entails a change in the existing order of things. Any solutions, innovations, preferred must not only be feasible in

terms of costs, etc. but must also be compatible with existing values.

Havelock and Huberman give this timely warning.

> It is important to understand that innovations are not adopted by people on the basis of intrinsic value of the innovation, but rather on the basis of the adopters' perception of the changes they personally will be required to make. Those designing, administering and advising projects do not generally have to make very many changes *themselves. Their* task remains the same. It is *others* who will have to modify their behaviours and very often to modify them rapidly in fairly significant ways, and with little previous or even gradual preparation. These are typically the kinds of rapid and massive changes which planners or administrators or advisers would never plan, administer or advise for *themselves.* This is yet another example, in large-scale or centralised projects, showing the dangers in cases where the innovator is separated from his public.

Social systems (and innovation systems) ought to exist for the people and their welfare, not the other way round. And just because something is new or different it need not necessarily be better than the system it is transplanting.

Remember, too, that over-ambitious, "cloud-cuckoo", solutions seldom get into orbit.

3. *The innovation:* From the possible solutions the change agent (e.g. a Government planning unit, a Ministry, a Headmaster, etc.) will select that solution, innovation, educational change, that it considers will *best* achieve the desired results with the greatest effectiveness and at reasonable cost.

4. The next task of the change agent is to develop and introduce this innovation, this optimum solution, into the client/user system on a *trial* basis. This will involve promoting awareness and interest in the innovation, adjusting internal organisational procedures and arrangements, locating and arranging appropriate resources, providing training courses (and possibly incen-

tives), setting up monitoring and feedback procedures to assess the relevance and effectiveness of the innovation.

Schramm mentions the careful planning and trialling that went into the educational television project in Niger.

> The production team in Niger tried out all its television programmes, by closed circuit, on two experimental classes during the 1964-65 school year. At the end of this time, the team found it desirable to remake, in the whole or in part, about 80 per cent of the programmes. During the second year, the revised programmes (about 400 perschool year) were presented to 20 first grade classes (800 students), and second grade programmes were tried on the two experimental classes. In the third year, the second grade programmes, revised as necessary, were presented to the 20 classes, while new third grade programmes were tested on the two experimental ones. At this careful pace, the project moved through the five elementary grades.

5. *Implementation:* For effective planning and execution of an innovation, the implementation phase should be regarded as a distinct process from the earlier "trial" phase. It is not merely an extension of the earlier "trial" or "development" phase; implementation entails new and distinctive issues and problems that call for new and distinctive approaches. For example, the production and distribution problems for Indonesia were quite different when it decided to extent its "modular" system of instruction from eight trial schools to its 130 million people scattered over 7,000 islands.

Initial acceptance of an innovation, even enthusiasm, is not enough to ensure implementation. As Pratt points out: "more good curricula sink without trace on the shoals of implementation than on any other point." Innovation is a process, a continuous and complex negotiation between people involved in establishing new ideas and practices. Most innovations require considerable change in the usual pattern of teacher behavior. To break away from old modes of behaviour and begin to act in an entirely different way is far from easy and takes time.

All over the developing world there are graveyards of abortive pilot projects long since forgotten by those (outsiders) who first inspired them.

Many of these projects were funded from outside, and often the foreign assistance was of the show case type, totally inadequate to serve the real longer-term needs of the projects. And when the foreign funds ceased the projects usually ceased too. The instructional television station that Unesco helped build in Senegal went dark when the project ended. The reason why the Niger instructional television project stalled after reaching 20 classrooms was the recognition by the government that its budget would not support a broad expansion of the project. None of the educational television projects could have gone forward successfully without substantial support—financial, logistic and technical—from outside. One wonders whether such "forced feeding" is the best way to encourage national educational reform, or whether a simpler, less ambitious and less expensive method, supported largely by local resources, would not be more lasting, even if somewhat slower. An essential ingredient for large scale adoption and institutionalization of educational innovations is a national *capacity* and *commitment* to carry on after the initial "trial" and "development" period. El Salvador and the Ivory Coast seem able to meet the cost and technical demands of their national educational television projects, although outside help was needed to get them started.

Massive changes can rapidly be *initiated,* but they cannot rapidly be *adopted* on a stable or permanent basis. This is due to the fact that a system, be it an individual, an institution or a series of individuals or institutions, is unable to assimilate rapidly a great number and variety of new elements or behaviours which are unfamiliar. Indeed, as Havelock and Huberman point out, if the assault is too massive, there will be an attempt to reject the changes.

The final task for the manager (change agent) of an innovation process, assuming a decision to proceed with the innovation has been taken, is to take steps to stabilize or institutionalize the innovation, that is, get it absorbed and structurally integrated into the system. To do this he must make provision for continuing maintenance of the innovation, and for ensuring that the innovation can be adapted to meeting changing needs. This is where many literacy programmes failed—there was no follow-up, there was no provision for maintaining and increasing the skills already acquired. On the other hand, in the Upper Volta rural education project, wherever post-school groups had been set up, notably in Yatenga district, not only did the students not lose their skills, they enriched their knowledge. Similarly, in the successful locally-initiated Indonesian project in vocational training for out of school youth, occasions and facilities were provided for maintaining and increasing the skills learnt after the project ended.

As an illustration of the *process* of educational innovation let us consider an example from Indonesia. Indonesia is selected because of the sheer magnitude of introducing and implementing any innovation in a country as large and diverse as Indonesia. The total area of Indonesia is larger than that of Europe; it is made up of over 7,000 islands, which add considerably to the logical problems; it has a population of 110 million which will reach 130 million by the end of the century; the population comprises people of many cultures, religions, languages; it has a high rate of illiteracy and a high proportion of young people never go to school.

An Assessment, in 1969, criticised what teaching that was being done as inappropriate for a modern Indonesia. What kind of learning would be appropriate? In 1973, the National Assembly stated the general aims of education to be "to educate a 'development-oriented' man with the character of Pancasila and to develop Indonesians who are healthy, mentally and physically, having knowledge and skills, being creative and responsible, democratic and tolerant." But how does one translate the rhetoric into reality? Not by the prevailing 'chalk-and-talk' method. Besides, more than half the teaching force was unqualified. Given the size of the country, training enough teachers would take too long, and would cost too much.

1. Here was the *problem* identified, one of monumental proportions: To plan an education system from scratch for so large and populous a country, a system that would lead to national, economic, cultural and social development, having in mind the ill-equipped and insufficient teaching force. The search was on for an appropriate teaching-learning system, one that was as 'teacher proof' as possible.

2. The *solution* chosen as the most effective method of teaching/learning to be used in the schools was a form of programmed learning, 'modular instruction'. Bloom and others in the USA had argued that given:

(i) an appropriate definition of achievable learning objectives;

(ii) a logical sequence of steps geared to them; and

(iii) sufficient time,

then most (if not all) children could achieve mastery of learning. The argument had further appeal in that educational excellence, instead of being the preserve of a privileged elite, could be shared more equitably.

Basically, as its name suggests, modular instruction provides instruction through a series of teaching-learning modules. The Indonesian module writers broke down a semester's curriculum in any one subject into learning units, which were then developed into 'modules'.

Each module consisted of:

(i) a teachers' guide booklet or guide sheet;

(ii) a set of learning activities directed at achieving the set learning objectives;

(iii) a worksheet on which the student recorded his answers or solutions;

(iv) a means of evaluating how well the student had achieved the learning objectives of the module.

In addition, diagnostic sheets, remedial activities and enrichment programmes were also devised.

3. After an initial evaluation, the modules were then *tried out* in eight trial schools, called Development Schools, the beginning of the first trial being prefaced by some in-service training of the teachers.

4. After evaluation and revision, the modular instruction system was implemented on a wider scale.

THE PLANNING OF INNOVATION

The problems of innovation are very complex and nowadays can no longer be solved by mere intuitive judgment or educated guesses. If innovation is not to be a hit or miss affair it must be planned. Evidence shows that careful planning is resorted to far less than is imagined. This results in waste of scarce resources, stress, disenchantment and ultimately failure of the innovation.

President Nyerere coined the phrase "to plan is to choose". In essence, planning is an exercise in *forecasting.* As innovation is always a risky affair the effective planner (change agent) minimises the risks not only by anticipating as many future events as possible but also by providing 'fail-safe' mechanisms to cover unforeseen events and in this way help to nip in the bud any potential disasters. A good plan allows any imperfections that occur to be remedied easily.

For effective *planning* of innovation Adams and Chen enumerate eleven elements which must be considered at each of the six stages of any innovation process. These elements concern "who does what, with what, to whom, where, when, in what manner and why and with what effect."

These elements are:

1. The *personnel* to be employed (who). At all stages of an innovation process there must be people available all along the line who have the expertise and capacity to carry out their allotted tasks. No one with experience of teaching by correspondence was involved in the original planning of teaching by this method

and so there was lack of awareness of the problems that might—and did—arise.

2. The specification of what the actual *task* is (what); i.e. what has to be done, what the innovation in action will consist of, its size and its scope, the role of teachers, of researchers etc. Whether the specifications are detailed or more open depends on the capabilities of those who are to carry out the tasks. Where the teaching force is largely unqualified the curriculum materials and tasks are made as 'teacher proof' as possible. The purpose of task specification is to provide a sufficient basis for getting into the *action* of innovation.

3. The *method*—the strategy or procedure to undertake the task (how);

- ❖ is the change to be effected by a formal, legislative approach, requiring individuals to act in accordance with new regulations?
- ❖ or is change to be effected by a more natural approach, relying on the new idea diffusing and gradually catching on, the process being helped along by advisers, community developers, publicity etc?

Between these two extremes there are other approaches or strategies which are mentioned presently.

4. The *equipment* needed (with what).

5. The *plant*, buildings of environment (where). There is usually a 'critical mass' of equipment and plant needed to enable a new project to function. Too little equipment hinders action; too much may stultify (as research in the USA has shown). The trick is to determine how much is just enough. When equipment and plant are part and parcel of an innovation then means must be found for producing and delivering them.

6. The *cost* entailed. Often planning is based more on aspirations than on realistic analyses of available resources. One must face up to the costs, not only of initial trials, but also the full implementation costs of any innovation. The unit cost for producing one graduate of the Unesco World Functional Literacy

Programme in four countries worked out higher than that for six years of primary schooling in the same conditions. (John Simmons, *The Educational Dilemma*, pp. 51–52.) In Iran, the cost per successful student of the Unesco functional literacy campaign was $332. This figure would hardly encourage any government to extend the campaign on a national scale. When one has little money or time or manpower one has to cut one's innovation coat according to one's cloth, even if that turns out to be far from elegant.

7. Other people or rather *other social contexts* on which the innovation impinges. It is wise and, perhaps, essential to gain the cooperation, or at least acquiescence, of interested parties, especially if they are powerful, who might otherwise regard their territory or prerogatives as being violated or threatened. Failure to involve, or at least, inform interested sections can prove an innovation's undoing. Murphy's law states that "if something can go wrong, it will". It is here, at the interface between 'interest' groups, that things often go wrong. Whilst, as Adams and Chen say, "it is not necessary to contact all of the people all of the time", it is necessary to identify the interest groups and to enter into mutual dialogue and negotiation with them.

It is also necessary to bear in mind that the 'thalidomide syndrome' can apply in education too. The damage that some side effects of an innovation may do may far outweigh the direct benefits. (Thalidomide was a very efficient sleeping pill but it had some disastrous side effects.)

8. The *time* involved (when and for how long). Innovations take time. People and social systems are generally slow to welcome changes, which they often regard with suspicion. Beware of making haste to quickly. And remember Harrary's flippant law: "no matter how long you think it will take, it will take twice as long".

9. The *scheduling* or sequencing or co-ordinating of activities (in what manner). Time spent in planning the sequencing and co-ordinating of events is time well spent. The more precise the co-ordination, the faster the process of innovation. The IPAR

project in Cameroon on rurally-oriented applied pedagogy was held up for nearly two years because of over-ambitious estimates of the time it would take to have sufficient quantities of new teaching materials available.

10. The *rationale* for undertaking the innovation (why).

- i.e. what are the justifications for the particular approaches used in the operational phase.

11. The evaluation of the *consequences* or *effects* resulting (with what effects). This is the 'moment of truth' when either a 'thumbs up' or a 'thumbs down' decision has to be taken on whether or not to go ahead with the innovation. Whether an innovation is implemented on a wide scale depends on at least three factors:

(i) the *political climate,* in a national sense and in an institutional or local sense;

(ii) whether there is sufficient *'energy'* in the form of material and human resources to sustain it (any proposal that adds to costs is generally viewed unfavourably);

(iii) its place in the general array of priorities.

SUMMARY

Four major factors in the process of innovation are: the *change agent,* the *innovation* itself, the *user; time.*

The Process of Innovation

1. A specific problem.
2. Possible solutions considered.
3. A particular (optimum) solution selected.
4. Optimum solution trialled and evaluated.
5. Implemented on wider scale.
6. Institutionalization of solution.

Corresponding to these phases in the process of innovation the change agent using a systems approach would:

1. identify the major problems;
2. specify objectives for action,
   - analyse the tasks involved in achieving the objective,
   - thoroughly assess the total input and constraints of the system,
   - propose alternative strategies;
3. identify/design the preferred solution in a given context;
4. evaluate the preferred solution;

5 and 6 modify the components and systems operation, based on feedback data and continued evaluation.

In a nutshell, the change-agent would identify the task and what it entailed in the way of requirements, bearing in mind the needs and limitations of the learners and the socio-cultural environment in which they live.

For effective *planning of innovation* certain essential elements should be considered at each stage of the innovation process. These elements are:

(i) the *personnel* to be employed,

(ii) the specification of what the actual *task* is,

(iii) the *method* (strategy or procedure to undertake the task),

(iv) the *equipment* needed,

(v) the *plant*, buildings or environment,

(vi) the *cost* entailed,

(vii) other people or rather *other social contexts* on which the innovation impinges,

(viii) the *time* involved,

(ix) the *scheduling* or sequencing of co-ordination of activities,

(x) the *rationale* for undertaking the innovation,

(xi) the evaluation of the *consequences* or *effects* resulting.

11

Strategies of Innovation

By *strategy* is meant all the available procedures and techniques used by individuals and groups at different levels of the educational system to attain desired objectives. A strategy is a deliberate attempt to engineer innovation. R. G. Havelock identified four predominant patterns or models of how change, whether in education, or science, or agriculture, or industry, came about.

1. *The Research, Development and Diffusion Model* (R, D and D), where an innovation is conceived at the head or centre, for example, at a central planning unit, and then fed into the system.

2. *The Social Interaction Model,* where change proceeds through contacts, formal and informal, among interested individuals or groups of people.

3. *The Problem-Solving Model,* where the users themselves are involved in conceiving, initiating and developing innovation at the local level.

4. *The Linkage Model,* where intermediate agencies, e.g. teachers' centres etc., link together the centre and the users (e.g. the schools) involved in the innovation process.

Chin and Benne identified similar strategies, but gave somewhat esoteric names to their categories. Their *rational-empirical* category essential is similar to Havelock's R, D and D model but adds elements of his Social Interaction Model.

The rational-empirical strategy is based on the assumption that men are guided by reason, that they are rational and so will respond to rational explanations and demonstrations. The change agent appeals to the enlightened self-interest of the user; the appeal is to logical argument, not force or compulsion. Such strategies typically involve the use of education, of training programmes, of written material to disseminate knowledge and research findings.

Their *normative re-educative* category is similar to Havelock's Problem-Solving Model. Such strategies assume that effective innovation requires a change of attitudes, skills, value systems, norms and relationships within the user system. (As Per Dalin emphasises, "change in attitudes is just as necessary as change in products.") These strategies usually involve the activation of persons, groups, forces, within the user system to bring about such change in attitudes, values etc. The emphasis is on mutual co-operation and collaboration between change agent and client, with equal powers to each.

Chin and Benne added a new category which they called *power-coercive*—based on the application of power in some form.

Just as in planning there are two basic models—the *engineering* and the *clinical*—strategies for changing a system, such as an educational system, correspond to these two basic types. In the 'engineering' model of applied research, plans are made by the experts (change agents) to meet the needs, as they see them, of the users. After the plan (innovation) is devised, the consent of the users is obtained by effective means of persuasion. The underlying concept of this model is '*control*'.

In the 'clinical' model, experts (change agents) work collaboratively with the users in identifying and solving the problems. The underlying concept here is '*influence*', using 'people technology', that is, a knowledge of human behaviour, individual and social, to introduce and implement change.

Chin and Benne's 'rational-empirical' and 'normative re-educative' strategies are examples of the 'influence' stratagem to bring about change; whilst 'control' is typical of the 'power-coercive' strategy.

Amalgamating the categories of Havelock and of Chin and Benne we obtain:

1. Strategies based on *systematic research-oriented* and *evaluation-controlled* approaches, such as Havelock's *Research, Development and Diffusion* (R, D and D) and to some extent Chin and Benne's *rational-empirical* approach.

2. Strategies emphasising communication and *diffusion* of innovations through various channels and inter-personal networks, such as Havelock's *Social Interaction* perspective and to some extent Chin and Benne's *rational-empirical* approach.

3. Strategies involving locally participative *problem-solving* and self-help, including those of Chin and Benne's *normative re-educative* model.

4. Strategies which emphasise inside-outside (or user-change agent) co-operation and dialogue by *planned linkage.*

5. *Power-coercive* strategies, based on power, authority, administrative and legalistic directives.

6. *Open input* strategies which emphasise *openness* to all ideas.

These *strategies* are now considered in some detail.

The Research, Development and Diffusion Model

This strategy is effective where innovations have to be introduced on a large, macro scale, where ideas have to reach geographically dispersed and isolated users and where those who will be implementing the changes (usually the teachers) are often lacking in knowledge and expertise. This is the situation in many developing countries and hence the model has been used extensively in introducing innovations in these countries.

The Research, Development and Diffusion approach is a highly organised, systematic and rational approach to innovation, founded on the following logical sequence of activities:

1. Basic research (as in industry) by a central team which plans and develops the innovation;
2. Trials of the innovation in the field;
3. Planned mass dissemination or diffusion of the innovation, by conferences, workshops, courses, etc.;
4. Implementation of the innovation by the users.

Characteristic of the R, D and D approach is a development agency at the centre which produces packaged solutions for the users at the periphery (schools and teachers). Hence, this approach is also known as the 'centre-periphery' or 'top-down' approach.

One advantage of such a strategy is that the more talented and experienced teachers and experts are more likely to be found at the 'centre' of an educational system, and this expertise can then be utilised for the benefit of the whole system.

Among the disadvantages are:

(i) Users (e.g. teachers) are involved in the development process only to a limited extent; they are the passive recipients of changes proposed for them by some distant agency.

(ii) Because of the high degree of centralisation, local needs and variations are often neglected.

However, by involving users more closely in the development of the innovation they need not be left to feel that they are dancers to a tune composed and played by people remote from their problems. When others invent solutions we are less committed to implement them.

The introduction of the 'modular instruction' innovation by Indonesia mentioned a few pages earlier is an example of the R. D and D approach.

The Social Interaction/Diffusion Model

Social interaction is the usual way by which ideas and practices are diffused through society—by informal contacts between interested individuals and groups. This strategy usually takes the form of convincing people of the value and usefulness of an innovation and then enabling them to see for themselves the innovation in action. This is how 'extension agents', especially in agriculture, carry technical knowledge to the consumer. This 'extension agent' approach is used in many developing countries, for example in India with its village-level workers. The A CPO rural education project in Colombia makes extensive use of the social interaction/diffusion strategy, using the network of local parish organisations to promote its programmes through informal, personal contacts.

A great advantage of this strategy is that it is a 'natural' process.

One disadvantage is that the process can be unsystematic and unplanned (even though the original source of the innovation may be research-based). Also, the process being informal, can be slow. But any unplanned approach can be made more systematic by structuring and co-ordinating the contacts between groups and individuals interested in the innovation. This can be done by courses and conferences, by visits to schools, by setting up special agencies to stimulate diffusion.

Participative Problem-Solving

This strategy is essentially a *user-centred* one. People have within themselves most if not all the ideas, resources and energy to bring about change. Innovators at the periphery set about solving *their own problems.* The problem-solving process of innovation is carried out within the user or client system, be it a school, a community or an individual. The user identifies a *need*, the need is translated into a *problem* statement which is then diagnosed; this diagnosis leads to a *search* for a satisfactory solution;

possible solutions/innovations are considered and the *best alternative selected;* this optimum solution/innovation is *trialled* and *evaluated* for its effectiveness; if satisfactory, the solution/innovation is adopted and *implemented.* The problem-solving strategy is similar to the problem-solving systems analysis *process* mentioned earlier and which may be represented as follows:

Need
↓
Diagnosis
↓
Search for solutions
↓
Select the best alternative
↓
Try out and evaluate the innovation
↓
Implement the innovation

Whereas in the R, D and D approach the initiative for innovation comes from the 'centre' or 'top', in the participative problem-solving model the initiative comes from the 'periphery', from the user system. In contrast to the 'top-down' approach, this is a 'bottom-up' approach, grass roots innovations developing as a result of *local* initiatives. Local initiative, local responsibility, collaboration and self-help, reliance on local resources to the fullest extent, these are the driving forces behind innovation. The role of the outsider is essentially consultative. providing ideas, guidance and perhaps temporary inputs of aid.

P. T. Orata provides this example of the participative problem-solving strategy used in the Barrio high schools in the Philippines.

> The only way to start is to start, and the place to start is right here with what little we have and with even a negative quantity. In every case we did not wait for experts to come, or for money to be appropriated, or for certain things to be done for us. Had we waited, we would still be waiting. Our only capital was ourselves, our health, our determination to succeed, and of course our own resources—land, artesian wells,

> canals and some shovels, and good humour. We did not have any budget. We studied our needs, made plans, and went ahead as best we could to achieve or objectives.

The problem-solving approach offers Headteachers and teachers themselves the means to improve the organisational health and self-renewing capacities of their own schools. Using what is termed organization development (O.D.), staff members themselves carry out the assessment, diagnosis and transformation of their own schools and so help to enhance the creativity of the schools, that is, their "capacity to adopt, adapt, generate or reject innovations".

The Planned Linkage Strategy

This strategy combines aspects of the three earlier strategies by using linkage procedures and agencies intermediate between the centres of educational change and the users. These agencies mediate and link together all the parties involved in the innovation process.

These linkage agencies could be teachers' centres, regional resource centres, institutes of education, etc. which provide linkage by giving support and advice, providing resources, running in-service courses, seminars, workshops, visits, by providing support to trial schools after the main innovation development team has withdrawn, by suggesting innovations tried and tested elsewhere to users with similar or related problems. These agencies can also provide valuable feedback, thus helping to improve project administration, materials etc., and also serve to strengthen the sense of collaboration between change agent and user. Much of the success of the ACPO rural education project in Colombia was due to its extensive use of feed-back. The information fed back by listeners determined the content of its radio programmes; all correspondence was answered, either directly or over the air; the staff of letter writers drew upon the various government ministries and technical and research agencies to supply users with the information they sought. ACPO also took great care to build and maintain connections with key persons and groups. At every turn it exploited local institutions and capabilities and planned its own activities to dovetail with private and public sector efforts.

Power-Coercive Strategies

These are strategies used by persons or groups who have power to enforce innovations, e.g. governments, national or local education authorities, inspectors, headmasters, teachers, that is, people who have political, legal, administrative and economic power and resources to impose innovation. Such action is sometimes necessary, as for example, when it is necessary to co-ordinate effort, or when it is necessary to overcome inertia, or just on the grounds of greater efficiency. The highly successful rural education project in Colombia is sometimes accused of being too highly centralised, being administered from a central headquarters in Bogota and directed since its founding by Father Salcedo. However, this centralisation is defended on the grounds of the need to co-ordinate all the many aspects and activities of the programme. Often strong leaders at the 'top' can prove very effective in initiating an innovation or in cutting through all the 'red tape' of a traditional system to get it moving. This is what happened in the Jombang Youth Project in Java: the Bupati bypassed the many bureaucratic hurdles and so saved river embankments that would otherwise have been washed away. Enlightened depotism can be beneficial.

Whilst most countries use these strategies to bring about changes in the fundamental aims and structure of their educational systems, many are now doubting the effectiveness of such 'top-down' approaches for changing curriculum, methods of teaching, teachers' attitudes etc. One can take a horse to water but one cannot make it drink. One must take account of the individuality of members of the user system; the relationship between change agents and users must be characterised by respect and co-operation rather than by coercion and compliance. To instruct the staff of a school to change to a new and unfamiliar method of teaching often results only in a limited 'mechanical' or 'superficial' conformity with the directive, only in compliance with the "letter of the law"; at worst it can invite teachers to ignore the directive altogether or even defy it. Planned change is more readily accepted when a policy of assent rather than compliance is adopted. Power-coercive strategies have a propensity to stir up a divine discontent. This happened in the IPAR project in Cameroon. The administrative hierarchy dictated new behaviours required of the teachers and inspectors implementing the reform. No allowance was made for the fact that the inspectors had a traditional attitude opposed to the spirit of the reform and that time was required to change such attitudes regardless of rules or laws. The project naturally suffered.

Much the same thing happened in Indonesia when a radically new kind of education in which teachers "don't really teach" and children appear to 'play' at learning was being introduced. There was mistrust, misgivings and even opposition. Time and effort are needed to prepare the ground for public acceptance of this kind of innovation.

If innovations are to be genuinely institutionalized at school and classroom level then much more consideration has to be given to the needs and problems of the users—teachers and schools. There must be more 'power equalization', the users must be allowed to participate more in the decision-making relating to any innovation. This is happening in Sierra Leone and other countries where a 'new breed' of teachers actively assist in curriculum development, rural development, etc.

In passing, one might note that coercion can take many subtle forms, ranging from brainwashing and manipulation to 'hidden persuaders' and payola. When persons in authority have the power to withhold or withdraw incentives, this is a form of coercive sanction. When an inspector offers 'advice' to a young probationer in such a way that the latter is left in no doubt that he is not free to ignore it, such non-rejectable advice is coercion. In New Zealand a new design of school building was introduced to 'coerce' teachers into accepting a more 'open-plan' form of teaching.

Among the *advantages* of power strategies are:

(i) they are effective when there are *time* constraints; quick and dramatic results can be achieved more quickly by such strategies;

(ii) they are perhaps the easiest and cheapest to apply, but are not necessarily the best in the long run.

The disadvantages are that they can be less cost effective and less lasting, if based on coercion which generates resistance and hostility.

With 'participative' approaches, change may be effected more slowly, but resistance will be less than an 'authoritarian'—"Here it is, use it"—approach. Strategies based on 'persuasion' are generally longer lasting.

Open Input Strategy

Havelock, in a more recent study, identifies yet another strategy of innovation, which he calls the *open input* strategy. It is a very wide open, flexible, pragmatic and even opportunistic approach to innovation. The underlying philosophy seems to be "let's try anything and everything, being as open and pragmatic as possible, using power and the law where need be, and informal influence and persuasion where they can be used." The model is an 'all strategies' approach. However, as Havelock and Huberman point out, while flexibility may be the best way to counteract the mire of bureaucracy, more anchoring is needed if an innovation is to have solid and lasting accomplishments.

Mixed Strategies

Rarely are the strategies mentioned used in their pure form. Often the distinction between the various strategies of innovation is not quite as clear-cut as indicated; they often merge into one another. Often several different strategies are used effectively at the same time.

What strategies are used depends on the varying circumstances. Often 'control' strategies (like power-coercive) are combined with 'influence' strategies to 'sweeten the pill', to gain the assent of users. Rather than sanctions, incentives in the way of pay increases, promotion, enhanced status, are offered to the users.

At a 'pilot' or 'trial' stage of an innovation the change agent will not be able to include everyone. If these people are not to feel 'left out' he must develop suitable strategies to somehow give them a feeling of participation.

Developing countries often don't have the time to await detailed research findings before mass implementation of an innovation. They resort to action research and 'rolling reform' as the innovation proceeds.

Havelock and Huberman indicate how mixed strategies can be used most effectively.

> It is important for innovators to pursue a *planned* strategy which takes full account of what is known about the innovation process. This includes being *open and flexible*, being oriented towards the *user's problem-solving process and needs*, making judicious use of *power* where it is necessary and reasonable to do so, and taking full advantage of research on the *diffusion* of innovations in social systems. The optimum strategy takes account of all these elements and orchestrates them, retaining a continuing awareness of what is happening in the user system, making an effort to maintain two-way communication and, above all, remaining sensitive to the people the project is trying to help.

Whatever strategy a change agent uses he should make use of all the resources available to him e.g. the spoken word, print, radio and television for communication; micro-teaching and other techniques for training; observation, evaluative research etc. for feedback. It is these that often decide the fate of an innovation.

SUMMARY

A *strategy of innovation* refers to the planned procedures and techniques used by people to bring about change.

1. The *Research, Development and Diffusion* Model. (R. D and D.)

   - an innovation is conceived at the head or centre and then fed into the system.

2. The *Social Interaction* Model.

   - where change proceeds (diffuses) through formal and informal contacts between interested parties.

3. The *Participate Problem-Solving Strategy* is focused on the *user,* on *his* needs, and on what *he* does about satisfying these needs. The user system identifies and diagnoses *its own* needs, finds *its own* solution, tries out and evaluates the solution, and, if found satisfactory, *itself* implements the solution. The emphasis is on local initiative, self-help, self-reliance.

4. *Planned Linkage,* where intermediate agencies link together the centre and the user of the innovation.

5. *Power-coercive* strategies operate on the basis of power and coercion by those in authority, using laws, directives etc.

6. *Open Input* strategies are open, flexible, pragmatic approaches that make use of all ideas and resources from outside.

Mixed strategies. Depending on the situation and circumstances aspects of several strategies can and should be used at the same time. As a rule, a strategy should be open and flexible-oriented to the user's needs, and using 'power' or informal collaboration and 'persuasion', as the situation demands.

THE USER SYSTEM

The User System; where the 'action' is. This is the target of all the change agent's planning—the system which is trialling and possibly adopting an innovation.

> The readiness of the 'school culture' (the readiness of the community, the managerial group, the teachers and students) is more essential than the product.

> The best of intentions are likely to be frustrated if too much attention is paid to the nature of a proposed innovation, whilst too little attention is given to the nature of the innovator(s) and to the nature of the social system in which they work...

Because 'centre-periphery' or 'top-down' strategies have tended to have little impact on innovations, attention is now increasingly being paid to the user system's view of the innovation process and the accompanying problems.

Most developing countries have introduced the 'new' mathematics into their schools. S. Sarason pinpoints some of the fundamental errors that were made by the workshop trainers when introducing the 'new' mathematics in the USA. He reports that there was:

> little sensitivity to the plight of the teachers—they were being asked to learn procedures, vocabulary, and concepts that were not only new but likely to conflict with their highly overlearned attitudes and way of thinking...No one formulated the problem as one requiring teachers to *unlearn and learn.*

He goes on:

> It is extremely difficult for a teacher to state to the Principal, to other teachers or supervisors that he or she doesn't under-

> stand something. One consequence of a lack of openness, supportiveness and readiness to accept failure is the 'facade' phenomenon, the situation in which teachers, schools and inspectors present an image to each other and to outsiders, which suggests that an innovation is working extremely successfully, whereas objective observers report differently.

If teachers are ordered to set specific learning objectives for their students but are not told why or how this could be done and are excluded from any participation in developing the necessary procedures, they will not understand either what to do or how or why it should be done. They will resist doing it; and when they apply the rule they will make a mockery of the innovator's original intention. That is what happened in Cambire School, as described below.

Gross and others give this example of the failure of an innovation because of failing to give adequate attention and support to the *user system.* The innovation took the form of a major organizational change in the role of the teacher. The teachers at Cambire School, a formal, traditional inner-city elementary school in New York, were to adopt a 'new catalytic' role. The new role of the teachers was aimed at encouraging children to become increasingly self-motivated and increasingly responsible for their own learning and education. The teachers' role was to act as a catalyst in helping children learn according to their own interests, allowing them maximum freedom in choosing their own activities. The external conditions were favourable, the project had the support of a high-status and powerful external change agent (the Bureau of Education Director), and yet the innovation failed. It failed because:

(i) The teachers didn't have a clear understanding of what was expected of them in their new role. Although they had some notions of the *behavioural* changes which they should be making, they had little grasp of the *conceptual* basis underlying the change.

(ii) They didn't have the necessary skills, attitudes, values and perspectives to carry out their new role. The traditional notions they had about the teachers' role, about the nature of the child, about the learning process, about pupil discipline, were quite inadequate and inappropriate for their completely different new roles. A complete 'brainwashing' of the teachers was necessary, but it was not given them.

(iii) They didn't have the required materials and equipment.

(iv) The organisational arrangements in the school, e.g. inflexible, subject-based time-tabling, the assigning of pupils according to age, etc. were incompatible with the innovation.

(v) There were no feed-back procedures whereby some of these deficiencies could be rectified. And if there was any feed-back, it was what the innovators wanted to hear. Here again the 'face phenomenon' occurred, or what Martin Shipman calls 'fictitious implementation' of a project, where all the problems and difficulties are hidden under the disguise of success. As he points out, the only thing a teacher does learn in a situation like this is not to get involved in that kind of thing again.

(vi) As a result of these unsatisfactory experiences resistance to the innovation grew among the staff. They resented the demands which the change made on them. They shuddered at the apparent disorder of their classrooms. They felt they were being exploited by the managers who had introduced the innovation.

Among the lessons to be learnt from these examples is that the task of managing an educational innovation doesn't end with the decision to introduce an innovation. The entire process of innovation must be carefully supervised and monitored. The change agents must create and foster frank, open, climates in which things are openly recognised and discussed, in which teachers feel confident enough to admit that not only their pupils but they themselves don't understand, where they are not afraid to admit they are failing.

One needs to remember that user systems, receiving cultures, often perceive innovations very differently from the change agent. Thus a headmaster may see an innovation primarily in terms of timetabling difficulties, a teacher in terms of job prospects or status, a parent in terms of its implications for examination results.

One must bear in mind, too, that user systems are often receiving many messages simultaneously.

Despite all the good intentions of change agents, despite all their careful planning, whether innovations are successful or fail depends, to a very large extent, on their reception in the *user system.*

What are the various factors that make for success or failure? By *success* of an innovation we mean that the innovation project

(i) has attained its stated objectives;

(ii) continues to operate according to the original design after any initial supplementary energies and resources have been removed or reduced;

(iii) is fully implemented and institutionalized i.e. it is absorbed and integrated into the system.

By these criteria, the ACPO rural education project in Colombia which has survived and grown for over 30 years can certainly be rated a success.

Potential users of an innovation will be more predisposed to accepting it if:

1. it is *relevant* to them. This depends on several other factors, e.g.
2. if the innovation is seen to have some relative *advantage* over their existing practices, i.e. if it compares favourably or better with other practices, activities, keeping in mind the question of resources;
3. if the innovation is *feasible* in their particular organisational context;

4. if it is *compatible* with the practices, values, characteristics of the user system. Compatibility ensures greater security and less risk to the user and makes the innovation more meaningful to him;
5. if it is seen as posing little or *no threat* to the user group—to its identity, integrity, territory. Hence the importance of dialogue and negotiations with interested groups. The innovation must be shown as benign or tolerable, not anti. Hence, too, the importance of providing adequate information;
6. if *benefits*, material or non-material, attach to the innovation; e.g. a sense of intrinsic satisfaction in the innovation, increased learning and knowledge, a gain in status and social worth, career opportunities etc.
7. if it is flexible and *adaptable*—if it can be re-interpreted, 'creatively' adapted, if it is able to exploit to advantage any situations that arise, then the greater the likelihood that the innovation will persist.

Most studies of innovation refer to the readiness with which individuals revert back to their former habits and practices. In the traditional role the teacher knew he was transmitting knowledge successfully in an easily testable way—by examinations. He was in close contact with a class of children at regular intervals in a secure, closed classroom. This was the way he had been trained; this was the way he had taught for years; and this was what parents expected of him—no 'playing around' with education. The innovative role, on the other hand, is not so secure; the new content is strange; the new and unfamiliar techniques like team-teaching and integrated studies leave him uncertain, even vulnerable; the enquiry methods are too time-consuming; the assessment of work is difficult. The pressures on teachers involved in innovation, often with futures that are somewhat uncertain, to revert back to their old, secure, traditional habits is strong.

Having launched an educational innovation and seen it safely into orbit, the change agent must then ensure that it remains in orbit. The innovation must *persist* long enough to become established, institutionalized.

The Failure of Innovations

"To recognise the problems in advance is to *decrease* the likelihood of failure."

Study of the literature of innovations, both in developing countries, shows that they can be characterised by these features:

(i) innovations usually fail;

(ii) barriers to innovation invariably emerge;

(iii) resistance to change seems universal;

(iv) change, if any, is usually transitory;

(v) willingness to change appears related to conditions in society;

(vi) change may or may not be rational.

The sad fact about educational innovations, indeed, about any innovations, is that most of them fail. As Adams and Chen point out, at least 70 percent of educational innovations die before they achieve their stated purpose. As they say: "the road to educational development is strewn with the debris of shattered innovations."

Bhuntin Attagara of Thailand bears this out:

> how often has unrestrained excitement at the start of a project ended up, three or five years later and one or ten million dollars later, as just another project.

And Havelock and Huberman add:

> Many of the educational innovations in developing countries involve a 'major system transformation'...In spite of large investments and expectations, few of these innovations appear to make a major dent at the *national* level in the

educational or training problem which they were designed to solve. They appear in many respects to be giant pilot projects.

Not only is the road to educational reform rough; the costs of travelling it are high. And when innovations fail scarce resources have been wasted.

Resistance to Change

It is not in the nature of human beings to welcome change with open arms. All reforms inevitably clash with certain entrenched attitudes and values. Individuals tend to protect, preserve and promote their own view of the world, their own values, their own mores. In doing so they tend to resist alien views, norms and values. And any innovation, to the extent that it is *new,* will be alien to an existing system. This resistance to change is strongly related to the extent to which the people who are required to change have or have not been involved in deciding what that change should be. "The number of unsuccessful development projects masterminded from the outside or mounted by foreign 'experts' who depart prematurely testifies to this." Countries are individually unique and what happens to their innovations is often a function of their culture. The inertia of institutions is also a vital element in the evolution of innovations. Educational systems have a considerable propensity and capacity for withstanding change. The change agent is always faced with the pitfalls of extreme conservatism on the one hand, and extreme radicalism on the other. His task is to steer a sufficiently flexible path to arrive at a dynamic equilibrium between the two extremes.

Profiles of Innovations

Havelock and Huberman isolate four factors as being significant in determining the likely success or failure of innovation projects. These factors are:

I—*infrastructure*

A—*authority*

C—*consensus*

R—*resources*

I. By *infrastructure* they mean the procedural configuration of the system involved in the various phases of the innovation process. A strong infrastructure (I+) means the system is able to:

(i) correctly identify needs;

(ii) correctly analyse a problem (for example, that a high drop-out rate is partly due to lack of trained teachers);

(iii) elaborate appropriate solutions to the problems, ensuring the solutions are feasible and materially possible;

(iv) implement the solution.

One reason for the great success of the ACPO project in Colombia was that a long established intra-structure—in the religious structure of parishes and village priests—already existed in the country and was able to carry through the innovation.

When the infrastructure or procedural configuration is weak (I-), the system lacks the *procedures* for designing and implementing an innovation. When this is the case many unpredictable and usually unpleasant things happen, e.g. lack of co-ordination, of communication, of continuity; delays, confusion, wastage of resources; all causing disillusionment and finally, after lurching from crisis to crisis, failure. The Unesco assessment of its World Experimental Literacy Programme describes how in one country, agricultural extension workers, under one ministry, had no contact at all with literacy instructors who were answerable to another ministry. In several countries lack of transportation was a major obstacle hampering the promotion of adult literacy. Madagascar, or example, where no literacy zone was closer than 800 kilometres to project headquarters, had no infrastructure for distributing equipment and materials. Certain classes were several days' travel from even provincial capitals.

Speaking of the early stages of the Iranian Literacy project, the Unesco assessment talks about confusion and a lack of certainty with regard to what directions the vocational side of the functional literacy instruction should take—

> Major problems were associated with internal administration, at both the central and field levels. Unesco had a difficult time co-ordinating the travel, and identifying the specific duties, of international expert staff. Regional directors and their subsidiary colleagues were often absent, and for the first three years of the project administrative malaise was commonplace.

Lack of appropriate infrastructure caused many problems in a large-scale educational television project in Africa—

> This was a huge project, but there was no structure for managing and administering it. We had to rely on the same administrative machinery to service a massive new project. Things like visas, requests for materials, clearing budgets were all held up for months. The most useful people have been the ones who had good personnel contacts in the ministries and could make things happen faster.

At this point mention should be made of what is called the 'invasion' phenomenon. There is a limit to how much a country can take in the way of new inputs at any one time; there is a threshold of the numbers and varieties of innovations a system can withdstand, beyond which the situation becomes unmanageable. This is particularly so when countries are under-developed, when per capita income is very low, when resources are minimal, when roads and communications are poor whilst distances are long, when the climate is harsh, when the economic, governmental and educational infrastructure are minimal and often just vestiges from a colonial past. It was poverty that vitiated much of the non-formal rural education programme in Upper Volta—

> The Upper Volta farmers, burdened with poor farm land, entirely dependent on the vagaries of the weather for their next harvest, and always concerned about producing enough food for survival before taking chances with untried meth-

> ods, need far more help than just knowledge of new agricultural techniques. In a situation where the animal-drawn plough is virtually an agricultural revolution not because the farmer does not know its value, but because he cannot afford the price of the plough and the animal, the villagers can be justifiably skeptical about a programme to teach better farming practices unless the programme is linked to an overall attack on the obstacles to poor farming.

It goes without saying that any innovation is hardly likely to succeed if the wrong people are employed to execute it. Sometimes those who are to be the prime implementers of an innovation in the field are given such poor recognition and rewards as to discourage the better candidates. In India, for example, those extension workers who were to provide the technical assistance for small-scale industries occupied very junior positions in the State service, with very low rates of pay and few opportunities for promotion. A similar situation occurred in the rural education programme in Upper Volta—

> The lone teacher in the village REC is expected to supervise and carry out instruction, manage a profitable school farm, account for the produce, organize school co-operatives, act as local animateur, form a liaison with the village leaders—both to gain their assistance in running and maintaining the school and its equipment and to reciprocate by providing services to the village. In return for this variety of heavy duties he would be paid only half the salary of his counterpart in the primary school, have a more limited security of job tenure, and almost certainly have inferior housing. These conditions have made it difficult to recruit and hold good quality staff, and the poor morale in the REC structure and teaching services had led at its worst to fraud and absenteeism, and at its best to an unending uphill struggle for the rural teacher whose enthusiasm is difficult to sustain.

A. *Authority* relates to leadership. High authority (A+) means strong and able leadership—that people are available who can initiate an innovation and vigorously attend to its implementation. Discussing the experience of several countries with educational television Schramm reports—

> None of these projects could have come into existence, and none of them could have continued for very long, without strong support from the top. In Samoa, it was the vigorous backing of Governor Lee; in El Salvador, the strong support of Minister Beneke; in the Ivory Coast, the support of President Houphoet-Boigny. In Niger, President Diori's interest made possible the existence of the project.

Likewise, once the President of Sierra Leone came out in favour of the Bunumba Project, its national support and success were assured.

The opposite happens when strong leadership is lacking or lukewarm. As Grabe remarks of the rural education project in Upper Volta—

> It may safely be said that the REC does not enjoy unequivocal support of the government. The objectives and rationale of the programme, which was originally conceived in colonial days mostly by expatriates, have always been the subject of debate and the programme still remains officially labelled 'experimental' even after more than ten years of experience.

A+ frequently arises in situations where there is a strong desire for radical change. This happened in many former colonial countries after independence when they recognised that the needs of the country were urgent and enormous and that the former colonial education system was inappropriate to meet these needs. The education in Tanzania associated with self-reliance and 'ujamaa' villages could hardly have been instituted without strong political leadership. Likewise, the successful Tanzanian functional literacy project was due in good measure to the high level of government support. The barrio high schools would hardly have got off the ground without strong leadership.

Strong leadership often resides not only in political or educational hierarchies but also in the indigenous leadership existing in the informal network of connections that bind a society together. The Thailand functional literary project ran into difficulties in recruiting adult illiterates at the start. However, by using influential persons in the community, much of the early suspicions were dispelled—

> In the beginning, the programme encountered difficulties in trying to convince adult illiterates to enroll, particularly those who had no occupational need for formal credits. Many associated the new functional classes with the rigid traditional literacy and primary classes; some felt they did not need literacy; and still others felt they were too old. However, community leaders, such as village headmen, monks and respected villagers, helped the educational officers to convince potential students of the differences between functional literacy and literacy programmes in the past.

Indigenous leadership in the form of dukuns (mid-wives) was put to effective use in the National Family Programme of Indonesia (1972). Clan religious leaders were used in implementing Bimas, the mass guidance in the rice cultivation programme in Western Sumatra (1971). Much of the success of the ACPO multimedia rural education programme in Colombo stems from its involvement of the village priests, who are the influential members of the peasant communities.

Teachers exercise authority; and innovations can founder at the chalk-face due to the opposition and resistance, often subtle, of teachers, who, because they exercise effective control of what goes on in the classroom, constitute a source of relevant power.

In 'crusade' forms of innovation, a particular 'doctrine' ideology is the driving force motivating and sustaining the innovation. In the case of Tanzania such a philosophy was the one of 'self-reliance' and 'ujamaa'. China and Cuba use socialist-collectivist doctrines, emphasising self-help and self-sacrifice rather than external 'hand-outs', as the power behind their development policies. In the rural education project in Colombia the ideology which inspired and which now sustains the programme is that of development of the *whole man.* As Brumberg remarks—

> In a mass education programme that seeks to treat the 'whole man', a clear ideological stance is important. It lends cohesion to the programme, serves to establish clear objectives, and lends authenticity to spiritual and motivational messages. ACPO has fostered a developmental mystique among its workers and its audience, and evidence suggests that this has resulted in greater dedication among staff within the organization and a considerable degree of voluntary action on the part of campesinos.

It is strong leadership and strong motivation on the part of the users that accounts for the success of 'crusades'. Since in a crusade any disagreements with an innovation and its objectives are unacceptable, local foot-dragging and other substle forms of sabotage are uncommon. Users strive to achieve the high standards of performance expected of them. This, in turn, entails that the leadership must be both *inspiring* and demanding.

C. *Consensus:* C+ means that the users of an innovation agree with its objectives and the way it is being or is to be implemented. It goes without saying that consensus is a critical component at user level both to initiate and to implement an innovation. If an innovation responds to a real need, consensus will usually be gained readily; and motivation for learning or for risk-taking will be increased. One secret to obtaining consensus is to demonstrate the merits and benefits of an innovation, rather than using political or administrative authority to gain co-operation. In the rural education programme in Colombia the campesinos could see the benefits to themselves of the programme; they co-operated enthusiastically.

Lack of consensus—resistance—(C–) comes about when people are asked to behave in ways that are radically different from their customary behaviour. This explains why many birth control programmes don't succeed. Likewise, courses for experienced farmers on new agricultural techniques often are less successful than they might be. Havelock and Huberman describe an African rural education project where there was almost immediate resistance from both within and without. The school inspectors delegated to supervise the execution of the project were not in agreement with the plan formulated at the ministry by foreign 'experts'; and the local inhabitants perceived the rural education centres as a cheap substitute for the primary schools; this was discrimination against them, the rural people. Moreover, the villagers neither understood nor approved of the teacher's new role as teacher-farmer. There were other reasons for resistance. Teachers were told they must integrate the basic skills of literacy and numeracy with practical exercises such as cultivating plots of land. But they were not told *how* to achieve such integration. The teachers had no training as farmers, and the soil on the school grounds was poor. Not surprisingly, they soon reverted to their customary teaching ways.

Invariably such projects undergo substle deformation or 'sabotage' causing them to be continually modified until they take on a form more acceptable to the users. Thus, the rural education centres came to look more and more like the primary schools they were meant to replace. In the same way, new forms of out-of-school entrepreneural training came to resemblè the conventional in-school curricula or the traditional apprenticeship schemes. Havelock and Huberman point out that—

> people who are unwilling to do something (C-) find innumerable ways of conforming superficially to the requests or orders of their superiors (assuming A+) even while they resist those orders or take up their former behaviour patterns when not being supervised...Teachers are invisible to outsiders 90 percent of the time in their classroom...this form of passive resistance is difficult to detect, much less change.

In teacher education programmes student teachers go to great lengths preparing 'model' lessons, but these are soon forgotten as soon as the teacher leaves the programme. Micro-teaching 'clinics' for in-service teachers also follow this pattern.

It was due to the passive resistance of the educational establishment that the Niger educational television project never went beyond the pilot project stage. Since the educational establishment has almost limitless power to obstruct, delay, distort, sidetrack and undermine the efforts of innovators, it is essential to involve it in any innovative enterprise. Teacher participation and co-operation are essential for any successful innovation. Yet the literature from several Unesco projects suggests that this important group is often ignored at the time key decisions are made.

R. *Resources*—funds, materials, equipment, facilities, premises, personnel, trained cadres, technicians such as electricians etc, able to maintain and repair equipment—all these are necessary in some measure for successful innovations. Often the lack of *technical* infrastructure hampers the smooth functioning of innovations. The Unesco assessment of a Latin American literacy project states that the major shortcoming of the project

> was the lack of government financial and logistical support...The most graphic demonstration of this was the project's inability to recruit and maintain a skilled (local) teaching staff and other professional personnel at competitive salaries. High staff turnover resulted in a strain on the training machinery which ultimely diluted the quality of the project's teachers.

One reason why the rural education programme in Upper Volta could not achieve its full potential was "the crushing poverty of the Voltaique rural families."

Lack of resources is not always a bad thing. Lack of equipment proved a blessing in the development of the barrio high schools in that it forced students to improvise with whatever little they had, thus learning the basis of modern technology without becoming dependent on supplies of complex technical equipment and paraphernalia from outside sources. Sometimes too much resources can prove harmful. As Havelock and Huberman point out—

> an overabundance of a certain kind of resource or the introduction of an inappropriate technology may actually do considerable harm to a project, to the project's clients and even to the host culture; in other words, sometimes resources from outside can act as an invading virus, damaging and scarring

the social organism the way a real virus damages and destroys the body.

Profiles of Innovation

Using these basic ingredients I, A, C, and R, one can build up profiles of innovation that can point to the likely success or failure of an innovation. If, for example, an innovation has a good infrastruce (I+), strong and stable leadership (A+), popular support (C+) and adequate resources (R+), then everything bodes well for success. Countries attempting major breakthroughs, quantitative and qualitative, in their educational systems would need such I+, A+, C+, R+ profiles. Unfortunately, all four are seldom present together. Often one or other of the ingredients is missing. If the infrastructure is weak (I—), it is still possible to compensate for this deficiency with strong leadership (A+) and widespread support (C+). Literacy projects in Tanzania, Cuba and Algeria have used this formula with success: popular enthusiasm (C+) and a powerful social doctrine (A+) have carried the projects over the logistical obstacles.

The Time Dimension

Innovation is a dynamic, social process which occurs over a period of time during which it may be modified as a result of that social process. That time can often be longer than imagined. Professor Mort of Teachers' College, Columbia University, has estimated that there is a 50 year time lag between recognition of a need or problem in education and the invention of an innovation to meet the need. Then there is a further elapse of 15 years before the innovation is adopted by 3 percent of the schools. The concept of the comprehensive school was suggested in Sweden in the 1880's. But it was not till the 1930's that the educational change was put into practice.

Time, however, is a commodity which Third World countries are desperately short of.

Even so, there is a danger in making haste too quickly. Maybe the introduction of some innovations should be paced more realistically. Instead of insisting on or expecting great changes in the shortest possible time, there is merit in moving ahead a step at a time, building at a pace within the capabilities of the user system. Unesco came to this conclusion concerning its Experimental World Literacy Programme—

> Perhaps it would be wise—if international programming is to suit national needs (and not vice versa)—to impose no time limit on future world efforts in this field. EWLP's experience suggests that the tortoise may be more likely than the hare to cross the finishing line first. At the international level, illiteracy may prove more vulnerable to persistent long-term action adapted to diverse national paces than to occasional short sprints which all participants are expected to run at the same speed.

Bolam analyses the time dimension in terms of three major stages:

(i) *The antecedent (prior) stage:* At this stage the three innovation systems—change agent, innovation and user—exist separately of each other though each will probably have some relationship with the other. As Bolam points out, it is vital to have a clear understanding of the situation and of the characteristics and peculiarities of the change agent, innovation and user, before any innovation process begins.

(ii) *The interactive stage:* This is the time from the beginning of a project to its completion, during which period the three systems interact with each other.

(iii) *The consequent (after) stage:* When the innovation process is over, when the three systems separate again and some assessment can be made of the interactive experience on all three systems.

During the interactive and consequent stages the user system will respond to the innovation in a variety of ways: it may reject the innovation for one or more reasons, it may resist it, it may adapt it (sometimes to the dismay of the change agent) or it may accept it fully and the innovation becomes institutionalized as a fully integrated part of the user system.

SUMMARY

The User System: where the 'action is:

Conditions for success of an innovation

It must:

(i) be *relevant* to the user,

(ii) have some *advantage* over other practices,

(iii) be *feasible,*

(iv) be *compatible* with existing values, practices, etc.,

(v) pose *no threat,*

(vi) have some *benefits,* materials or non-material,

(vii) be *flexible* and *adaptable.*

An innovation must *persist* long enough if it is to become established.

Profiles of Innovation

By considering these four factors:

I— infrastructure or procedural configuration of the user system;

A— authority, leadership;

C— consensus, agreement with the innovation;

R— resources, available

one is able to get a 'profile' of the health of any particular innovative project and the likelihood of its success or failure.

Time

Innovation is a social process and so take *time.* Bolam recognises three phases of this time dimension:

(i) the situation *before* innovation,

(ii) the *interactions* between change agent and user and the innovation itself during the innovation period,

(iii) *after* the innovation.

12

Some Old Themes

Before considering the more spectacular innovations in education such as educational television, satellite communication, etc., it is worth considering some innovations within the traditional structures of education that can provide the same or better education for more children at no increase in time, resources or costs. In a situation when the population explosion, inadequate resources both in personnel and money, and galloping costs are vitiating so many commendable efforts to provide education for more and more of the population, any innovations that can help to do this are worth investigating.

REDUCTION IN THE YEARS OF SCHOOLING

Tests in the USSR and other countries have shown that as a result of advances in pedagogy, psychology, educational technology, etc., it is possible to reduce the normal four year primary course to three years without any loss in quality. In the same way, research studies show that teacher training courses of two or three years produce results no better than courses of one year. Simmons makes a further statement that will come as a surprise: that students who have access to well-stocked libraries and well-equipped laboratories in schools perform little better than students with poor facilities.

With a view to doubling the number of children that can receive education some countries have experimented with reducing the four year primary course to two years. But it seems there is a *critical mass* of four years of education below which the effects of any schooling soon evaporate. Unesco has found that a minimum of four years of primary schooling is necessary to achieve adequate literacy. Data from Tunisia suggests that even six grades of primary education may not be enough for a large percentage of students to reach a level adequate for reading and understanding a newspaper. Reading tests in other countries seem to bear out this conclusion.

Many planners argue that when resources are scarce they would be more wisely, efficiently and equitably spent it they were concentrated at the lower end of the educational system. Thus, instead of trying to achieve primary education of six or seven or more years for some of the people, provision should rather be made for four years of basic primary education for all, with more selective education for the fewer numbers able and needed nationally to go beyond that. But at a time when governments are trying to meet the demand for more and longer education, it is a brave government that talks of cutting back on the number of years of education. Indonesia is one such. It plans to compress its primary schooling from six years to five years.

Reduction in the Daily Hours of Schooling: 'Shorter-time' Attendance

According to research in Chile and Venezuela the time of the day spent in school (whether morning, or afternoon, or the whole day) or the number of hours of schooling (beyond six hours daily) does not make any significant difference in student achievement. If attending school for five hours a day rather than six hours does not make much difference to student achievement, then this lower threshold limit could permit several possible ways of extending education to many more students, whilst using the same physical facilities. Thus a five hour daily programme, four times a week (in a school working a six day schedule) could serve a third group of 50 percent more students. If it is found that the threshold point could be reduced to five fours a day three times a week *twice* as many students could be served with no additional resources. Even if this did result in a slight reduction in the quality of performance of the students, the entire demand for school places in most developing countries would be met by such an innovation.

Dr. Schiefelbein argues that once these threshold limits or minimum levels for effectiveness for each of the main inputs into the educational system have been ascertained and reached, then resources should not be used to increase facilities beyond that point but rather should be used to expand the number of students served by the educational system.

The strategy of reducing the hours of schooling is used in several countries.

Short time attendance is also adopted to counteract the inefficient learning that results when schools are massively overcrowded, when the noise and restriction to movement are such that learning becomes impossible.

The Shift-system

Especially in areas of high population density, the *shift-system* is another way of getting more children into school without building additional schools and of improving the effective teacher/student ratio without a commensurate increase in costs. It takes various forms: two sessions a day, attendance on alternate days, and staggered and overlapping school terms, so that three groups can use facilities designed to accommodate two. In the *double-shift* system children spend half the time in school and then another group of children takes their place. In the second shift, children follow the same curriculum but with either the same or different set of teachers. If a different set of teachers is used for a second shift, this involves an increase in the number of teachers. One way of not increasing the teaching force would be to use a form of monitorial system—where pupils in the higher classes, especially secondary school students, teach those in the lower classes. This system is used in many countries; in Cuba, for example.

Double-shifting generally involves fewer hours of class time. This may result in loss of learning efficiency but recent findings in EI Salvador indicate that the performance of students in double-session rural schools was superior to that in single-session schools. There is a tendency to view second shifts as inferior and less effective than 'regular' morning shifts. These and other disadvantages are, however, offset by the resultant gains in educational opportunity for many more children.

Class Size

In many developing countries 90 percent or more of the recurrent educational expenditure is taken up on teachers' salaries. Naturally, savings can be achieved by increasing the size of classes taught by teachers. A study, carried out in Chile, based on actual budget data, showed that an increase of 15 percent in average class size produced a reduction of 5 percent in the annual educational budget. On the other hand, increasing class size can defeat the whole purpose of the exercise by causing a reduction in the quality of education. But within certain limits, increasing class size does not necessarily imply a reduction in educational quality. World Bank studies in Brazil, Chile, Puerto Rico and Venezuela show that any variation in class size between 20 to 40 makes little or no difference in average achievement. Conversely, decrease in class size does not imply improvement in educational quality. In fact, some studies associate larger classes with better performance by pupils.

Though increasing the size of classes would understandably not please the teachers' unions, increasing classes from 35 to 45 students would means that the total enrolment could be increased by one third at little extra cost. By adopting this simple strategy no student in many developing countries who was willing to study would be denied the opportunity of doing so. Dr. Schiefelbein argues that classes can be increased to up to sixty with the provision of minimal facilities.

Paring, or Cutting Down, the Curriculum

In the early 1970's the South East Asian Ministers of Education Organisation set up a Regional Centre for Educational Innovation and Technology (Innotech) to devise strategies that would provide quality primary education at a significantly lower cost. One solution advocated by Innotech for mass education was the paring down of the curriculum to *'life skills'* only—to what is relevant and absolutely essential: forget the frills and fancies. They ask: are eight or ten or twelve subjects really necessary in a school curriculum? No. This is hang-over from the medieval days of scholasticism when the educated few went through the trivium and quadrivium of subjects.

INNOVATIONS IN AREAS OF LOW POPULATION DENSITY

In areas of low population density where pupils within an acceptable range of distance from school are not numerous enough to fill individual classes, student/teacher ratios and the use of space can be significantly improved by organisational changes, such as biennial intake, multi-grade teaching, and nuclear-satellite networks.

Biennial intake

Biennial intake means that entry in Grade I occurs every *other* (i.e. second) year. In a six-year primary-school system, only three classroom and three teachers are needed. In the sparsely populated areas of Sweden children go to school every *second* year—hence the phrase 'biennial intake' These children attend school for only three years—every second year between the ages of 7 and 13. It has been shown that this stratagem pays of almost as mush as if they had six years full-time schooling. The assumption underlying this strategy is the it is not the number of years of schooling that is critical but the *quality* of the schooling that matters.

Multi-Grade Teaching

This grouping children of different ages and grades in one room to be taught by the same teacher. This grouping may involve only two adjacent grades or, in the case of the one-teacher school, all children in all grades. Another name for multi-grade or *plural-class* teaching. Despite evidence to suggest that multi-grade or plural-class teaching can be as effective academically as single- grade teaching, its success depends largely on the quality, dedication, and specific training of teachers.

In *nuclear-satellite arrangement smaller 3– or 4– or 5– grade schools feed into a larger school, say a 7-grade school, in the same catchment area. Such arrangements often involve boarding or transport facilities as well.*

Maximum use of Existing Facilities

Educational expansion involves high capital (e.g. building) costs. In most countries schools are not utilised full-time, being closed for 25 percent of the year and generally not used during the evenings. Intensive rotation of classes and staggered scheduling of classes can optimise the use of classrooms and specialised facilities.

While staff are needed and must be paid for working outside regular hours, it is quicker and less expensive to arrange timetables to permit full-time utilisation as against struggling to provide additional facilities. Facilities could be made available in the summers for repeaters and for those who fail to qualify in the regular times, thus allowing more school-age children to enter or remain in school. In Bahia, Brazil, schools are used all the year round.

SUMMARY

Some of the innovations used to secure the same or better education for more children with no increase in time or cost are:

Reduction in the years of schooling, e.g. three years of primary schooling instead of four.

Reduction in the hours of schooling, where, for example, children attend school for $2 \times \frac{1}{2}$ hours a day instead of 5 hours.

Shift system: there are many versions of this, e.g.

- *double-shift system* where one shift of children spend the morning in school, and another shift attends in the afternoon. This allows the teacher to give his services to double the number of children.
- *in-school/out-of-school system,* where one group of children attends school for some time and then another group takes their place. Class size.

One can economise on the number of teachers by increasing the size of classes. Within limits, increasing class size does not mean the quality of education necessarily suffers.

Paring down the curriculum to 'life-skills' only—to what is relevant and absolutely essential.

In areas of low population density student/teacher ratios and use of space can be maximised by:

Bi-ennial entake—entry to Grade I takes place every second year; thus only 3 teachers and 3 classrooms would be needed in a sixty-year primary school system.

Multi-grade (or plural class) teaching, where one teacher teaches children different grades and ages. The use as *monitors* of more able children in higher classes to teach lower classes can be effective. Making maximum use of facilities such as school building etc. which are often under-used.

13

Non-Formal (Out-of-School) Education

The stakes are too great, the dimensions of under-development too staggering, the vicious circles it generates too implacable, for further patience and forbearance. in the life and death struggle against the interlocking stranglehold of ignorance and poverty, the mission of education is clear. It is to awaken men and nations to the infinite possibilities of growth and change that exist within them. But education must itself grow and change to carry out that mission. It must set its house in order. It must forge its ploughshares into swords.

Non-formal education, as the term suggests, is organised education provided outside the formal educational system, e.g. upgrading the proficiency of agricultural extension workers through short courses, or raising the awareness of poor adults about the sources of their problems and how to organise to overcome them. (Learning that is not organised is often termed *informal* education) Non-formal education takes many forms: 'adult education', 'continuing education', 'on-the-job training', 'accelerated training', 'farmer or work training', 'functional literacy', 'extension services', 'second-chance schools', ètc. It provides education to those many millions of people who, by accident of birth and place, would otherwise be deprived of the stuff of learning. Formal and non-formal education: not two rival systems, but two branches each supporting the other; neither by itself can solve the world's educational crisis; as supplements to each other they can begin to make some headway in doing so.

WHY NON-FORMAL EDUCATION?

In the past two decades developing countries have strained to put more and more of their budgets into education, regarded by governments and parents alike as the 'open Sesame' to progress and prosperity. For governments, investment in formal education was considered a vehicle of economic growth; the more schooling per person the better. For poor parents more schooling was seen as the only hope for their children to climb out of the morass of helplessness and hopelessness and join the urban middle class. It was widely believed that expanded schooling would break the human resource bottlenecks in the development process and undercut entrenched privilege as well. More and more schools have been built; more and more teachers have been trained; more and more children have been enrolled in school. But these immense efforts have not been enough for these countries to do little more than just hold their own, if that. The massive investments in education have not made the contributions to either growth or development that had been expected. Millions and millions of children remain who will never get more than a minimum of primary schooling, if that. For generations to come there will be adults who will have had no education at all.

For most developing countries the problems that constrained their educational systems twenty five years ago have not been overcome; if anything, they are more pronounced now. These problems may be listed as:

(a) the rising total and unit costs of education;

(b) the relatively poor access to education for rural children;

(c) poor quality instruction;

(d) slow response in providing education relevant to development goals;

(e) adverse effect on income distribution, in part because children from high income families tend to receive a disproportionate share of the educational and economic opportunities.

For half his life Adam Curle, formerly Director of International Education at Harvard University, supported the view that formal education would open men's minds, shape their skills, and would thus become a great force of social equality and economic development. However, looking back on his experience he now recognises that 'education, as it is mostly practised, does not so much free men from ignorance, tradition and servility, as fetter them to the values and aspirations of a middle class which many of them are unlikely to join'.

The World Bank reported in 1974, that formal education systems had been 'irrelevant to the needs of developing countries for the past two decades'. More and more planners and educators came to realise that more of the same quality and quantity of schooling was unlikely to meet national objectives for social equality and mobility, nor the manpower development needed for growth. Disillusioned and wiser, they turned away from schools and looked instead to non-formal education as an alternative means of alleviating the world's educational crisis. They argued for a vast expansion of non-formal education as more likely to deliver the development goods than the traditional panoply of primary, secondary and tertiary institutions. They turned to a non-formal basic education—rural based, vocationally oriented, terminal—as an inexpensive alternative to universal primary education and as a means of solving the educational ills formal education failed to cure. Many argued that some of the resources made available to higher and secondary education should be diverted to non-formal education. This is what China and Cuba have done. These countries strictly limit the number of students who get more than 10 year's schooling to those for whom jobs requiring such higher education are available. The funds saved are allocated to non-formal education, to the priority needs of the rural poor, educating them to help themselves. The same strategy is adopted in health. Instead of putting resources into kidney machines and the like, they are put into rural health centres and into training thousands of paramedical personnel rather than few heart surgeons; they are concentrating on a broad build up of overall health standards. Likewise in education. Of course, there are those who argue that providing funds for non-formal education will cut into funds allocated for formal education, which is more prestigious and in greater demand. One difference between China and Cuba and other countries where defence of privilege so often obstructs educational progress in that China and Cuba have the political will and the organisation to implement such reforms. In terms of a 'profile' of innovation they have strong A (leadership and political determination) and strong I (infra-structure).

The basic goal of any national development programme is to provide an education for all its citizens. At the moment, hundreds of millions of people are deprived of education. Over 870 million people have never been to school at all. The world illiteracy rate is 20 percent. Even where universal primary education has nearly been achieved there are the educationally underprivileged, those who have been to primary school but who 'dropped out' or 'failed' the examinations. The data from Latin America and Africa suggest that more than 50 percent of the students who start primary school drop-out before finishing. Africa has the highest rate at primary level, with 20 to 54 percent all students repeating. In Tropical South America, only 29 percent of the enrolment in Grade I reach Grade 4.

It is the objective that non-formal education will serve these two groups: that it will provide a chance to acquire the skills of learning from scratch for those who have never been to school, at the same time offering those who already have the basic skills of reading, writing and counting to practice and improve them, to build on what they have learned, to unlearn what they have mislearned. Those with some schooling, while themselves continuing to be students for part of the time, can become the monitors and group leaders and literacy and numeracy tutors for those who are just starting.

One strategy employed to achieve these objectives of providing education to those children and adults who have never been to school and to those children and adults who have acquired something of the 3R's is that of *basic education.*

BASIC EDUCATION

Basic education is not so much a matter of so many years of schooling or so much content covered, but rather the acquisition by the individual, whether young or old, whether in school or out, of certain *basic* skills, knowledge and attitudes which will enable the individual not only to improve the quality of his life but to continue his education to the best of his abilities. The Faure report argues that 'basic education must be many-sided, designed not only for children and adolescents but also for adults who, at any age, may have need of it. While dispensing fundamental knowledge such education aims at learning how to perceive and comprehend the world'.

Just as basic education is not terminal, neither is it rural education as opposed to urbanised education. There is no one path to this core curriculum of basic skills and knowledge; the core can be covered in different ways and by different paths. As Hawes shows, different countries interpret the concept of basic education in different ways.

In some countries basic education is:

- synonymous with the first part of the first cycle of schooling and shorter than the conventional primary schooling (say three, four or five years instead of six, seven or eight)—(USSR, Ethiopia, Sierra Leone);
- an alternative structure parallel to conventional primary education—(Brazil);

- the acquisition of basic knowledge, attitudes and skills, by all citizens in school or out—(Tanzania).

Hawes goes on to point out that the notion of basic education is particularly attractive to politicians—

> because they seem to offer a direct and politically acceptable way out of the impasse of attempting to do more with less. Hence the greatest of good sense and maturity are needed, on the one hand to accept the implications of the basic education message, on the other to resist the temptation to give worse schooling to more people and call it basic education.

The Bunumbu Project in Sierra Leone, designed to 'improve rural living through education', provides a good example of the *process* of the innovation of basic education in action. The Bunumbu Community Teacher's College was developed in 1974 as an education centre and as a community centre for the area. Teachers were trained to provide both children and adults with basic education.

1. *Diagnosis/Needs:* Sierra Leone's rural dwellers constituted 90 percent of the three million population. The rate of migration from the country areas was mounting as children left the family plot to seek their fortunes in towns. Not only did this reduce the labour force where it was most needed—in the country, but it increased it where it was least needed—in towns. The consequence was a decline in social and economic conditions throughout the country.

2. *The problems:* Two main problems were inherent in this state of affairs:

(i) the economic development problem of how to best use the agricultural resources to the benefit of the nation;

(ii) the human, social problem of young people displaced and disaffected with no present to speak of and no promise of a better future.

Furthermore, 90 percent of the adults in the rural areas were illiterate.

3. *Search for solution:* The view was taken that education could be made relevant to local (especially rural) conditions, and that education could come to cater for society's needs better, primarily by producing school leavers who were prepared for the work opportunities that did exist in the community rather than for imagined ones that did not exist.

4. *Solution:* A Government White Paper, in 1970, aimed to provide a literate work force and primary education with a rural bias. This involved specifically:

- the development of a basic education curriculum with special reference to adults living in rural areas;
- development of a new primary curriculum with a rural bias, giving greater emphasis to practical activities and community participation;
- conversion of existing primary schools in rural areas into multipurpose community education centres, providing education and training, formal and non-formal, to young people and adults in rural areas.
- development of new teacher training curricula and training materials.

5. *Strategy:* A distinctive feature of the Bunumbu Project was the use of a mixture of strategies—participative problem-solving, social interaction, planned linkage—to ensure the 'users' were heavily involved. All appropriate networks were contacted, palliated and incorporated into the project. A vital link between 'the halls of power' and the 'work place' was established. With the enlistment of the support of the Paramount Chief the most essential ingredient of community participation was secured. The headteachers of the 20 pilot schools were given a one-year orientation to familiarise them with the underlying philosophy of the innovation. Having the principals involved in helping create the general strategy and tactics for the project was a particularly shrewd move: it ensured their constructive and committed involvement. The pre-service and in-service programmes and workshops were held, not only for the craftsmen and craftswomen. Thus every-

one—Paramount Chief, civic leaders, teachers, extension workers, health and agriculture officials, community developers, craftsmen—were involved.

6. *Trials and Evaluation:* Twenty pilot schools, designated Community Development Centres, were involved in the first trials of this innovation in basic education.

The first year rolls increased radically, and the drop-out rate between the first year and second year decreased dramatically. The adult classes escalated in popularity. The intensive community involvement in the whole array of project activities has been striking and perhaps its most significant achievement to date.

7. *Further implementation and institutionalization:* The benefits of the project have been seen and extended beyond Bunumbu. Community development is pursued aggressively in numerous areas.

8. *Further difficulties:* Problems of the basic necessities of life still remain. As Adams and Chen say, matters like water-supply, electricity, roads, may be the straws that break the camel's back.

Frequently, projects fail because they are launched in the least economically successful parts of a country. This may be where they are most needed, but also where the chances of success are minimal.

LIFE-LONG EDUCATION

I grow old learning some new thing each day. (Solon. Fifth century B.C.)

The Commission is really arguing for an extension of the very concept of education—in space by breaking through the school walls and taking enlightenment to the people in their homes, in factories and in the fields, and in time by encouraging the development of education from the pre-school infant stage through to maturity and old age—and so bringing closer their ideal of a learning society.

Life-long education is more than just the practice of adult education, usually in the form of night classes. The concept of life-long education rejects the view of a formal schooling which occurs once and only once in a person's lifetime. Schooling is just part of education, which is life itself. Education is life and life is education. The concept of primary or elementary education is today giving way to the notion of a *basic cycle of education of flexible duration.* In many countries of Africa, Asia and Latin America the demand is growing for a *basic education for the masses* as a first phase in life-long education.

The concept of life-long education, that education must be conceived of as an existential continuum as long as life, will call for drastic reform and restructuration in curricula and programmes of study and training at all levels and in all forms of education.

Deriving from the notion of life-long education are the massive functional literacy projects, combining agricultural, health, social welfare, civic and other development programmes with a built-in literacy element, that have been launched by many developing countries.

In the literacy and education campaigns modelled after Paulo Freire's 'conscientization' method in Brazil and later in Chile, learning to read and write are not merely ends in themselves but the means of personal liberation and of development of Privileged groups. Freire defines conscientization as the 'process in which men, not as recipients, but as knowing subjects, achieve a deepening awareness both of the socio-cultural reality which shapes their lives and of their capacity to transform that reality.' (*Pedagogy of the Oppressed*, Penguin, 1970.) The learning content is not the usual education subject matter, but incorporates interdisciplinary responses to personal concrete problems about conditions of life, the tools needed to change these conditions and the ability to use them. These concrete problems and situations are represented on display panels or on lantern slides and then discussed by the pupils. The pupils meet in small groups, often in the house of one of their own number, to form a 'culture centre'.

Usually by the end of 30 sessions the peasants have learned to read and write and have also acquired a political consciousness, even if rudimentary. More generally, in functional literacy programmes the elements of literacy training are integrated with vocational and technical training and with socio-economic components. In Honduras, the ACPH (Accion Cultural Popular Honduras) curriculum is based on the conviction that education for liberation must be built round peasant awareness of the forces which promote poverty and dependency and how, by co-operative organisation, these can be overcome. The curriculum demonstrates in practical ways the connection between education, development and political liberation.

Another South American educational revolutionary is Ivan Illich of Mexico.

Illich argues that the formal educational system as we know it today is fundamentally wrong, especially with reference to developing countries. He says—

> the 'problem' of education in developing countries (such as drop-outs, inefficiency of schools, non-employability of school leavers) are but the natural effects of the elitist type of Western education introduced into countries which are not in need of this system but of something quite different. In the present system the primary school is preparatory secondary, the secondary school is preparatory university education; the system is therefore irrelevant to over 95 percent of the schoolgoers. Moreover, the school system restricts education to the youngsters, whereas adolescents and adults are at least in as great a need for information, guidance and training. Finally, and most relevant to the masses, is that they should be mobilised for their own development, motivated to seek relevant information, guidance and skills, including those of reading, writing and arithmetic. The present school system is far from attaining such a 'mobilisation' effect.

Accordingly, the present formal system could and should be scrapped. In *The Futility of Learning*, he argues that the length of obligatory formal schooling should be cut to two months a year and that this type of schooling should be spread out over 20–30 years of a man's life. In-service apprenticeship and the like would provide most of what we call 'instruction' and the two months each year would provide leisure for the pursuit of 'insight'. 'Most learning is not the result of instruction. It is rather the result of unhampered participation in a meaningful setting.'

For Illich education is a lifelong process to which all experiences, all the institutions of society, contribute. In *Deschooling Society,* (1971), he recommends the setting up of 'skill centres' where those who possessed special skills would make them available to others in the community. For Illich, education *for* all means education *by* all. Everyone has the right to teach, not only the special elite with paper qualifications who now monopolise this right. He believes that every human being is entitled to an 'educational credit', an 'educredit', a ration card of mental nourishment, that may be cashed in at any stage of as lifetime. In these 'skill centres', which would generally be attached to the place of work itself, employers and employees would 'supply instruction as well as jobs to those who chose to use their educational credits this way.'

This means, Illich argues, we have to rid ourselves of the idea that 'manpower qualification must precede employment, schooling must precede productive work'. The recent educational reforms drafted in Peru reflect not a little of Illich's thinking. Article 26 of the Peruvian General Law on Education (1972) enacts that 'the State will develop a policy of lifelong education.' It proclaims that *all* people have the right to education and guarantees each individual's right freely to choose the form his education shall take. In order to effect such a scheme all the country's educational services and programmes will be split into communal (community) educational 'nuclei' or 'cells'.

The authors of *Learning to Be* propose 'lifelong education as the master concept for educational policies in the years to come both for developed and developing countries.'

Many countries have already begun to implement such a policy. The government of Indonesia has taken the concept of life-long education as a master concept in reorganising and reforming its educational system. The 'village polytechnics' of Kenya are training young people in the rural areas not only to acquire skills to transform them from 'job-seekers' into 'job-makers' but also to face the changes they will meet in the course of their lifetimes.

The following quotation from Coombs applies to all changing societies, developed or developing.

> Life long education is essential in a rapidly progressing and changing society of three primary reasons: (1) to ensure the employment mobility of individuals, and to make unemployable 'drop-outs' of the past employable; (2) to keep already well-trained people abreast of new knowledge and technologies essential to their continued high productivity in their respective fields; and (3) to improve the quality and satisfaction of individual lives through culturally enriching their expanding leisure time. In this perspective, the continuing education of teachers at all levels is of special strategic significance; if they fail to keep up with the frontiers of knowledge they will be giving yesterday's education to tomorrow's citizens.

SUMMARY

Despite the high hopes and expectations of the expansion of education and despite the enormous investment in education—building schools, training teachers, providing more facilities for more children, these high hopes have not materialised. If anything the situation has grown worse. So a solution was sought in another direction—non-formal education—to make up what the formal system was unable to do. Non-formal education takes various forms—-adult education, on-the-job training, extension services, functional literacy etc.

The *objectives* of non-formal education are:

(i) for those who have never been to school—the chance to acquire the skills of learning;

(ii) for those who have acquired some basic skills of reading, writing and counting—the chance to improve and go further.

Basic education is not so much a question of so many years of schooling but rather the acquisition of a set of basic skills and knowledge which will enable the young and the old to improve their individual lives, whether rural or urban. The basic 'core' of knowledge and skills may be gained in a number of alternative ways. Basic education is not terminal but continues for life.

Lifelong education all through life and not only during childhood and adolescence for those who get it. 'Education is life and life is education'. Functional literacy programmes emphasise learning to read and write not as ends in themselves but as the means of personal liberation, concentrating on the concrete problems and conditions of life.

QUESTIONS

1. What forms of non-formal education are practised in your country? What were the main reasons for introducing these?
2. In your country is non-formal education achieving its objectives? Explain.
3. Mention some of the reasons that explain the success or failure of non-formal education in your country.
4. Can you suggest any other forms of non-formal education that would help to achieve some of your country's education and development objectives?
5. In terms of innovation theory what strategy or strategies would prove most likely to succeed in introducing this form of non-formal education?

6. Do you think that some of the resources spent on secondary and higher education should rather be spent on non-formal education? Say why.
7. Describe any form of life-long education that exists in your country.

14

MOBRAL: The Brazilian Literacy Experiment

In 1970 there were 783 million illiterates over the age of 15 in the world. This number has continued to increase to 814 million illiterates ages 15 and over in 1980 and is expected to reach 884 million by 1990. In Brazil one-third of the population aged 15 years and over was illiterate, comprising a total of some 18 million illiterates.

The immediate cause of this is the lack of schooling for the entire school-age population. Brazil is faced with an enormous problem with an extraordinary increase in the number of school-age children each year as evidenced from these Tables.

Year	*Number of School-age Children*
1920	1,250,000
1930	2,084,000
1940	3,302,000
1950	5,240,000
1960	7,458,000
1970	12,144,306

The dramatic dimensions of the illiteracy problem which is common to all developing countries is emphasised by these figures in the case of Brazil.

While the illiteracy rates have fallen progressively these have not been enough to compensate for the demographic (birth-rate) explosion with the result that the absolute number of illiterates has steadily increased, presenting Brazil with the most serious problem in the whole of Latin America.

Year	*Population*	*Illiterates 15 years and over*	*Percentage of total Population*
1940	23,600,000	13,280,000	56 per cent
1950	30,200,000	15,272,000	50 per cent
1960	40,200,000	15,816,000	39 per cent
1970	54,300,000	17,937,000	33 per cent

In 1970 the Brazilian Government decided that a shock treatment was the only solution to the illiteracy problem. It assigned the task of reducing the illiteracy rate from 33 percent to below 10 percent by the end of the decade to the MOBRAL Foundation (Movimento Brasileiro de Alfabetizacão)-Brazilian Literacy Movement. This was to be done by producing over 2 million new literates each year; the programme being aimed primarily at the 15–35 year old group.

The *financial resources* for this massive undertaking were to be obtained through the Federal Soccer Pool (Loteria esportiva). Thirty percent of the net income of the Pool was allocated to the literacy programme. In 1972 MOBRAL received more than 14 million dollars from this source.

The *organisational structure* was one of *decentralisation*, making use of the federal administrative network at *municipal level*.

The idea behind the creation of MOBRAL was to set up a low cost educational system for adults, using available classroom space, a volunteer teacher body and the co-operation of publishing firms to produce the educational materials. In 1972, the unit cost per pupil was about $ 8, which compares favourably with

Unesco's estimated $20 per pupil for this kind of project. Over 2 million adults learned to read and write between 1970 and 1972 and the adults illiteracy rate fell from 35 percent in 1970 to 26 percent in 1973.

In Brazil there are 4,000 municipalities throughout the country. The *Municipal Committees* were created as *executive agents* of MOBRAL'S programmes, thus learning the MOBRAL Central Office free to concern itself with essential problems involved in mobilising more than 4 million Brazilian each year. The task of the Municipal Committees was to mobilize the illiterates, engage teachers, procure classrooms and organise the Literacy Classes. These Committees are composed of municipal administrators, businessmen, clergymen, as well as volunteer service organisations, in this way uniting community efforts in support of the literacy programme.

THE FUNCTIONAL LITERACY PROGRAMME

The first task is to persuade the illiterate, particularly the younger among them, to follow the literacy classes for a period from five to six months in order to obtain a literacy certificate. Such a certificate can bring beneficial results to the holder. In one follow-up study it was found that 35 percent of the participants had been promoted since becoming literate.

The daily sessions last approximately two hours and the time-tables are adjusted to fit in with the time available to the students. The courses are given by monitors whose cultural level varies greatly but who have been given elementary training. About half the literacy teachers have themselves only attended school for barely four years. In the rural areas especially it is difficult to recruit more qualified teachers.

The groups consist of 25 to 30 students, whose degree of homogeneity varies greatly with the milieu. Each month the literacy teacher completes and submits attendance sheets on the strength of which the MOBRAL Central Office pays them through the Municipal Committees. Instructors receive about $4 for each adult attending his classes for the fourth month. About 100,000 literacy teachers were thus engaged by the municipal committees.

During the 5 month period (approximately 200 hours) of classroom activity the pupils are taught reading, writing and elementary arithmetic. In addition, general information for everyday living completes the programme. The teaching of reading, writing and elementary arithmetic are not ends in themselves but an integral part of broader training processes *determined* by the interests and needs of the adult, mainly those related to productive work—hence the name 'functional literacy.' The course covers matters relating to health, hygiene, nutrition, national economy, human relations, local development, civic education, skills required in everyday life, thus opening up a wide range of possibilities for dealing in educational terms with the interests of the group. With a view to retaining a high proportion of students, the literacy programmes treat them as adults. The teaching material is designed for grown-ups with family and social responsibilities. The training of the literacy teachers includes notions of adult psychology and the techniques of group activities. This approach is maintained and strengthened in the integrated education and community development follow-up courses. The work reflects the determination to bring the illiterate person to deal with his own problems, in his own environment and that he should be encouraged to act in accordance with his own solution. It is because of this wide interdisciplinary approach that the staff are not restricted to the educational field. Instead of philosophical educational considerations the essence of the programmes is on basic, effective ideas.

MOBRAL has not created a particular method of literacy teaching. The teaching of reading, writing and arithmetic is based on the different methods proposed by the firms which publish the educational material. The production of the educational materials, vast quantities of which, running into millions, are needed, is left to the publishing firms. The materials, produced at cost, are distributed by the firms to the State and

Regional Co-ordination Bodies from where they are picked up by the Municipal Committees and distributed free to local centres.

The Teaching Materials

A fundamental precept of MOBRAL is that both students and teachers have plentiful printed material at their disposal. In 1972, more than one-third of MOBRAL's budget was ear-marked for the purchase of educational material.

For the literacy teaching there is a didactic kit consisting of three textbooks for the student, one of learning to read, another for exercises in writing and a third for arithmetic, and a manual for the teacher. Students are taught to read by the use of analytical and synthetic methods, starting with key-words chosen from the vocabulary and prevailing interests of people throughout the whole country, breaking them down into syllables of progressively greater linguistic difficulty and building up new words ands sentences. Each publishing firm has compiled a manual to help the literacy teacher to recognise the fundamental characteristics of the adult, organise the teaching-learning process, mater group-work techniques and teach reading, writing and arithmetic along the lines which will suit the type of student.

As a supplement to the literacy course, two books for further use in reading are given to the students after the third month of the course. They deal with questions of citizenship, health and home economics, simple skills applicable to daily life and guidance for life and work in the community.

In order to encourage regular use of printed material, MOBRAL publishes a fortnightly Newsletter. Written in simple language, with plentiful illustrations, it conveys national and international news which help the learner reader to find his bearings in the world of today.

When he begins his teaching, the literacy teacher is given a set of posters which he can use to supplement the teaching of the various key-words, to enliven his dialogue with his pupils and to decorate the classroom.

The national effort to eradicate illiteracy from Brazil has caught the public's imagination and the public supports the programme in a variety of ways. In the town of Riberirão Preto in the State of Sao Paulo, the distributors of bottle-gas undertook to make a house-to-house collection of old magazines and books and delivered them to the Municipal Committee, who then distributed them in a vehicle specially fitted as a mini-library to literacy classes and reading rooms.

MOBRAL goes to great lengths to avoid holding literacy classes in school buildings. The reason for this is that the school is the symbol of the infant stage of education and may remind the adult of the difficulties and frustrations he experienced as a child. The Municipal Committees arrange, wherever possible, to hold literacy classes in clubs, trade union centres, factories, churches. But when no such premises are available, use is made of schools.

In 1972, out of 100 adults who began the literacy classes, 42 became literate by the end of the fifth month. This was not considered satisfactory and led to the organisation of supplementary classes held during the sixth month. This enabled 10 more pupils out of every 100 to pass the test for recognition as a literate. A pupils is considered literate when, with relative ease, he can:

- read and write his own name and address and those of his entire family;
- write short notes, send telegrams, make out receipts and draft petitions addressed to the correct destinations;
- add up and check bills for purchases;
- calculate the quantity of foodstuffs he needs to buy for his family;
- give change in paper money and coins;
- estimate the time required for trips and daily travel;
- express himself on various subjects verbally and in writing, in a simple but comprehensible way;

- read and understand excerpts from newspapers, magazines and letters as well as consult telephone directories or street guides; and
- read and carry out written instructions.

In the North and North-East regions, 26 percent pupils in the literacy classes are under 14 years of age. These children attend these classes because of lack of schools or because they are already in employment. MOBRAL aims to make them literate and, if possible, make them enter or return to school or to MOBRAL's follow-up programmes such as the integrated primary education course.

There are many Brazilian primary school teachers who, for want of something better, use the MOBRAL materials for teaching their pupils to read and write.

Follow-up-Programmes

The Brazilian literacy campaign was conceived on a scale much more than merely learning to read and write. The organisers were convinced that literacy acquired in courses lasting six month or less were inadequate for the needs of modern man. There was the likelihood, too, of the new literates lapsing back into illiteracy. The literacy programme was considered in the light of life-long education. The literacy skills acquired in five or six months needed to be consolidated and enhanced by further studies. That is why MOBRAL organised follow-up programmes for its functional literacy programme. There follow-up courses embrace the Integrated Education, the Curriculum Development and the Cultural MOBRAL programmes and also courses to guide those who have completed their literacy course towards vocational training institutions.

In 1973 agreements were signed between MOBRAL and several training agencies—the Programme for Intensive Preparation of Labour (PIPMO), the Brazilian Legion of Assistance (LBA) and the National Department of Labour (DNMO)—for intensive training courses for MOBRAL's new literates, thus providing them with ample opportunities for continuing education and integration within the labour market. In many places women who have just become literate go straight on to take domestic science courses.

During the first few months of the literacy programme the determination to complete the course is not very strong. When the literacy stage has been successfully completed most students wish to attend the follow-up courses, such as the integrated education courses, hoping, when they have completed these, to find new opportunities. Between 50 and 72 percent of those interviewed stated they wished to go on studying and to pass on to the stage previously known as the 'gymnasium' (secondary education).

The Integrated Education Programme

This is a follow-up programme for persons who had recently become literate. The programme was a broad programme of integrated education lasting 12 consecutive months (approximately 720 hours) and with a curriculum equivalent to that of the second to fourth years of primary education. Students who complete the course receive a primary school leaving certificate and can enter the first form of secondary school. Or they can pursue some form of vocational training. They generally prefer to do this in institutions which follow the MOBRAL system.

For the programme MOBRAL provides technical guidance, teaching material and training for the teaching staff. The Secretariats of Education are, for their part, responsible for recruiting and paying the teachers, providing teaching premises and evaluating students' work. Such evaluation is made every four months. A student who shows that, in any of the four-month periods, he has learned as much as would be learned in the fourth year of the formal school system automatically receives his primary school leaving certificate. The teaching is not divided into subjects; rather, the abundant teaching material is grouped round integrated themes. The techniques of group work, discussions and research are frequently used in these courses.

In 1973 over one million people attended these courses.

Three publishing houses have supplied MOBRAL with teaching kits for its Integrated Education Programme. The kits contain:

- one book of key passages which, by dealing with the many different aspects of the life of the individual in Brazil, lend support to the educational endeavour;
- a mathematics textbook;
- a vocabulary book, arranged alphabetically, which facilitates self-teaching; and
- a teachers' guide, which takes into account the fact that most of the teachers are not highly qualified professionally.

Each student receive two additional books, which, in addition to reading practice, help him to acquire knowledge of himself as a human being, knowledge of his country and knowledge of the world. Every month a million copies of the periodical *integration (Integracàò)* are distribute which keep the students abreast of national and world events. The National Book Institute supplies abundant reading material free to students of the integrated education course. A student who follows the courses as far as the Integrated Education course has at least ten books and various periodicals to form a small beginner's library. The graphic productions of the reading materials are excellent, being lavishly illustrated with colour.

Another literacy follow-up programme is the *Community Development Programme.* This is a two-month course which offers the new literate activities which lead to greater participation in the community, to develop skills that maximise local resources, to reinforce the ability to communicate verbally and in writing and to fully integrate the individual in his local environment.

The participants are divided into groups of 20 to 30 adults; the group leaders explore with them the problems of the community and the means for solving them. They engage in cultural, artistic, social and recreational activities and carry out in the field simple projects to improve the life of the community.

A booklet, entitled You are *Important (Voce è Importante)*, teaches the adult students to feel that they belong to a community with a variety of different needs and how to act together in order to meet these needs in an organised manner.

The scientific information given in the reading material, although elementary, relates to the most recent discoveries and adventures of mankind. The material takes into account the diversity of the geographical, economic and cultural resources of Brazil.

Yet another post-literacy programme is *Cultural MOBRAL*. This is designed, not only to ensure the retention of literacy in adults, but to widen their cultural horizons. The activities include programmes of literature, theatre, cinema, music, popular art and folk-lore, visual arts, radio, publications, and appreciation and preservation of the historical and cultural heritage. The programmes operate through fixed and mobile centres and libraries (Mobraltecas), covering the entire country. These are usually equipped with vehicles, a library, a television receiver, videotapes, sound equipment, projectors etc. The Mobraltecas of the Amazon region move about in boats so as to cover the widespread river network. Itinerant theatrical groups may also accompany the mobraltecas.

The Training of the Literacy Programme Teachers

The results achieved by MOBRAL depend on the quality of its teachers. One Brazilian out of every thousand is doing teaching work under the MOBRAL programme. MOBRAL insists that *training is a permanent necessity for all its staff.* No one can do without training; training is never completed. In line with this principle training programmes are arranged for the higher technical staff, the field staff and the community leaders.

The largest training activity has been the courses for literacy teachers and teachers involved with the integrated education programme. Between 1970 and 1972, the MOBRAL Central Office trained directly 785 persons who, in turn, passed on their training to 43,829 front-line literacy workers throughout the country. There was no evidence to suggest conventional teacher training courses would ensure better results than crash training programmes. The crash training programme consisted of courses lasting from 5 to 10 days based on an instruction manual. For literacy teachers the manual dealt with the theory of functional literacy teaching, working methods and techniques and features of the MOBRAL assessment system, with suggestions for helping students with special difficulties, along with various techniques for use by group-leaders.

The part of the manual concerning teachers of the integrated education programme covered a wider field, including the basis features and techniques of accelerated education of adults, the psychological bases of the education process, motivation, the role of the teacher, the characteristics of adult students, techniques of group work, evaluation and teaching materials.

Training by Radio

Owing to the considerable expansion of the programme by 1972 MOBRAL decided to use, in addition, other more economical and more effective means for training the large number of literacy teachers required, especially for the rural areas. It was necessary to adopt a large-scale training operation for up to 100,000 literacy teaches and to organise this nation-wide undertaking so that its execution took place at the same time and covered the same ground everywhere. Recourse was made to radio (and later television), in co-operation with the *Minerva Project*. This was the Basic Education Movement which provided formal and informal educational programmes by radio for young and adults in the rural areas where schools and transportation were still under-developed. This scheme, pioneered in the north-east of the country almost as soon as the transistor radio was invented, consists of evening courses broadcast by regional radio stations which are picked up by villages in the interior. Soon there were over 15,000 village radio schools in Brazil and some adults and children who began their schooling in this way have succeeded in getting to university. It is now possibly among the biggest operation of its kind in the world. MOBRAL's integrated education programme now makes use of radio. Broadcasts last for thirty minutes each day and the subsequent work of the teacher for ninety minutes. In this latter part of the programme the teacher is encouraged to make use of the creative participation of his pupils.

The course for literacy teachers consisted of 12 broadcast lessons as follows:

Lesson 1 Functional literacy training

Lesson 2 The role of the literacy teacher and of the pupil.

Lesson 3 Motivation.

Lesson 4 and 5 Working methods and techniques.

Lesson 6 Evaluation

Lesson 7 Mechanics of functional literacy training.

Lesson 8 Key-words; the study of phonemes.

Lesson 9 Reading and writing.

Lesson10, 11 and 12 The new mathematics.

The Minerva Project broadcast 10 thirty-minute and two 60 minute programmes on the national network, with organised listening at 5,300 radio posts, each with 20 to 25 literacy teachers. The broadcasts were supplemented by teaching material and teachers' manuals with similar content. In this way 90,500 literacy teachers were trained. In some outlying areas where normal reception of the broadcasts was difficult, the lessons were given using tape recorders.

MOBRAL intends to extend its training of literacy teachers by making use of colour television, which is very widespread in the country. Programmes will be transmitted by the national television network on open circuit, while the same material will be shown by video-cassettes and cinema films in places not reached by television channels. Each lesson will include a real-life demonstration of how to teach a group of illiterates to read and writ, and in the second part of the programme the methodological situations which arise in the process will be analysed. Such a programme will have two-fold value: it will be seen by literacy teachers for training purposes; it will also be seen by illiterates who wish to learn to read and write.

Television will also be used for the training of craftsmen and workers with poor qualifications by demonstrating certain skills and techniques.

Correspondence courses and programmed learning are also being considered by MOBRAL as techniques to be utilised in the future.

Among some of the factors that affect the effectiveness of MOBRAL's teaching force is the very great turn-over of the literacy teachers. In the municipality of Sao Paulo, 32 percent of the literacy teachers changed in one year. Another factor is the youth of the teachers, 35 percent of the literacy teachers in Sao Paulo were between 18 and 24 years old. This shows that MOBRAL certainly awakens the social consciousness of the young, even if for only a short time.

The Saci Project

The Saci Project provides mass media educational programmes direct to schools by means of satellite. In 1972 1,600 teachers and 14,000 students in 500 schools in the north-east of the country were trained by use of a Brazilian domestic communication satellite. This project, called the Saci Project, is carried out by the Brazilian space agency (INPE).

Operation Rondon

Not unlike MOBRAL's philosophy and associated activities are those of *Operation Rondon*. Operation Rondon is another pioneer organisation, named after the pioneer General Rondon who opened up the interior and established communication with the

Indian settlements. Under this government-sponsored scheme every year several thousand student volunteers spend their summer vacations visiting and helping the small, scatted communities of the Amazon Basin. With the co-operation of the Ministry of Education and university authorities, and with transport supplied by the Brazilian Air Force, so much valuable work has been done by these volunteers that the scheme has been extended to the hinterland areas in the north-east and the Mato Grosso. the success of Operation Rondon has inspired the Ministry of Transport to mount Operation Maua (named after one of Brazil's early industrial pioneers) to enable young engineering students to spend their vacations teaching and helping workers to build new highways, bridges, ports and airfields.

Evaluation

MOBRAL's programmes and activities are evaluated by the System of Global Supervision. This System ensures better utilisation of human resources, integrates procedures and programmes on all levels, and evaluates results, leading to greater flexibility, efficiency and dynamism 4,000 supervisors from the three levels of the System are prepared by in-service training programmes to use new methods and techniques in pedagogy, mobilisation, finance and supporting activities. The System promotes closer liaison ad co-operation between those in the System and anticipates problems which may jeopardise programmes.

Evaluation of MOBRAL's activities is made from information channelled through the formal structure incorporated in MOBRAL's organisation.

MOBRAL's activities and achievements, which are not limited to the classroom only but which extend much further and encompass community efforts nationwide, make impressive reading. In the three years from September 1970 to September 1973 MOBRAL taught 5 million people to read and write. By 1973 MOBRAL had reached all of Brazil's 3,953 municipalities, covering an area of 8.5 million square km., and was operating more than 130,000 literacy education units. This means that in any area of the country there will be a school, a teacher and a community teaching organisation engaged in the struggle to eradicate illiteracy. By the end of 1972 MOBRAL's activities had catered for 8,812,000 people; 7,354,000 in literacy courses, 95,000 in integrated education courses, and 508,000 in community development activities. This means that one in every six Brazilians aged 15 or over had benefitted from the educational activities of MOBRAL. Literacy training given to more than two million adults each year evidences Brazil's acceptance of the challenges of change and its determination not to leave one-third of its adult population outside the fringe of culture. It is not surprising that in 1972 MOBRAL received an honourable mention in connection with the Mohammand Reza Pahlavi Prize, a prize awarded annually for outstanding contributions in the field of literacy.

The Brazilian masses have responded very positively to the educational opportunities offered by MOBRAL. Adults and adolescents of both sexes have enrolled in the literacy classes on a scale which in certain regions is more than the educational system could cope with.

From an economic view point MOBRAL has contributed to the increase in Gross National Product since few investments can compare with the social rentability of literacy. It has also contributed to a better distribution of income, since inequality among individual incomes is largely the result of differences in levels of education.

Not surprisingly, the success of the Brazilian literacy experiment has attracted international attention. The work done by MOBRAL has rightly become a field for profitable study by other countries faces, like Brazil, with the monumental task of eradication illiteracy. Under the Brazil-Senegal Cultural Agreement, MOBRAL cooperated with the Government of Senegal in the field of literacy teaching. A training course of a month was held in Brazil for Senegalese technicians and representatives from other African countries in mid–1973.

Summary

In many developing countries, whilst illiteracy rates have been falling, the increasing birth rates mean that the absolute number of illiterates steadily increases. In Brazil, illiteracy had reached alarming proportions.

The Mobral Illiteracy Experiment was started in 1970 to alleviate the problem. The funds came from the football pools lottery. The organisation was carried out by Municipal Committees. The programme was aimed at the 15–35 age group.

The teaching was for about two hours a day and lasted five to six months after which successful students were awarded a certificate. The classes consisted of 25–30 pupils. Rather than hold the classes in schools (which carried overtones of infant and primary education) they were held in clubs, factories and churches.

The subjects embraced the 3 R's, but related to productive work, and included health, hygiene, nutrition, local development. The aim of this functional literacy was to teach the illiterates to deal with their own problems in their own environments, using their own solutions.

The literacy teachers were monitors, many of whom had only four years primary education themselves. So training of these teachers was considered imperative. This was often done by short crash programmes. In order to prevent the new literates from relapsing into illiteracy several follow-up programmes were instituted.

The literacy programme was viewed in the light of life-long education. The Integrated Education Programme, where the curriculum was grouped round themes rather than subjects, provided an education equivalent to the second to fourth years of primary education, and opened the door to secondary education and vocational training.

The community Development Programme explored the problems of the local community. Another follow-up programme concentrated on cultural matters—music, art, folk-lore etc. As the programme grew, recourse was made to use of radio and television and even satellite communication. By means such as these Brazil has made a massive effort towards seeing that more than one third of its adult population does not remain educationally deprived. Other countries with similar massive illiteracy problems could learn much from the Brazilian effort.

15

Mass Primary Education

The almost insurmountable task of making primary education available to all children in developing countries has already been referred to. Dr. Santoso Hamijoyo, the Director-General of primary and secondary schools in Indonesia, reported that in 1972 whilst there were about thirteen million children between the ages of seven and twelve enrolled in primary schools another seven million children in this age group were not in school at all and, even more significantly, this formidable gap was widening each year.

Dr. Liceria Soriano, Director of the South East Asia Regional centre for Educational Innovation and Technology (Innotech), highlights the situation.

There is a strange paradox here, isn't there? So much of the wealth of these (developing) countries lies in the vigour and enthusiasm of their young people. This is what government planners tend to call 'human resources'...Yet more than half this wealth is cast aside because there is no money to provide school places or teachers for them. And then they become, not an asset as part of the dynamo of the country, but a major liability: out-of-school youth, unemployed and often unemployable.

What is to be done? The linked problems of ballooning populations of school age children, and of education budgets bursting the seams of the national purse, are common throughout the Third World—and are sure to worsen in the next decades. They are not likely to be solved by the conventional mathematics of educational budgeting, in which most of the operating budget goes to pay teachers' salaries.

In the early 1970s the South East Asian Ministers of Education Organisation (SEAMEO) gave special priority to 'the development of an effective and economical delivery system for mass primary education'. Project Impact (instructional management by parents, community and teachers) was one outcome of this search for a system that would provide every child in the community with an effective education at reasonable cost. The Project was launched in 1974 in a few villages in the Naga district of Cebu Island in the central Philippines and the companion Proyek Pamong in two villages near Solo in central Java, Indonesia. Since the resources, both human and material, are not available to achieve universal primary education by conventional systems of education, recourse was made to alternative systems. Unlike the advocates of 'de-schooling', such as Ivan Illich and his followers, who would abolish conventional schools altogether in their pursuit of flexibility in education, Project Impact introduces as much flexibility as possible without jettisoning what has proved of value in the more formal, conventional systems of education. Among the more notable innovations may be mentioned:

(i) The use of short, simple, inexpensive self-instructional modules or booklets and self-learning kits, in place of textbooks, thus saving considerably in costs.

(ii) The materials used in the modules are 'programmed', thus allowing students to proceed at their own pace. This has the additional advantage of enabling people who might have left school to re-enter the learning system, even after an interval of years, to study in their own time and at their own speed.

(iii) The pupils work on the modules in a room or in some shady corner of the school grounds, at a learning kiosk or, in the afternoon, at home.

(iv) the changed role of the class teacher to being more an 'instructional supervisor', with responsibility for four or more times as many students. This reduces considerably the number of teachers required.

(v) The tutors and instructors are drawn from among the students themselves.

(iv) The use of the school more as a community Learning Centre (C.L.C.) rather than as a school in the conventional sense. In the Community Learning Centre the dividing walls of the traditional type of school have been dispensed with—resulting in savings in building and material costs—so as to allow students free movement and easy access to where the modules are kept and where the simple equipment for subjects such as science are stored

(vii) Maximum utilisation of the resources of the community to produce a learning society.

THE MODULES

The use of modules rather than textbooks as basic learning materials in the primary schools has the great advantage in that they are neither bulky nor expensive. Modules run from 32 to 100 pages long, with just a few lines of material on each page. They are sub-devided into 'chunks' of learning which can be completed in a couple of hours in a student's own time. They are written in the simplest possible language, making use of dialogue, story-telling, illustrations and pictures, to eleven the learning. The modules contain built-in tests to ensure the student masters the particular topic or 'chunk'. Correct answers are provided on the following and reverse pages so that a student has a sense of completeness when he finishes the module.

The modules are based on the technique of 'programmed learning'. The first modules were written along linear model lines, usually referred to as 'Skinnerian' lines. B.S. Skinner was the founder of the linear or sequential type of programming in which small discrete facts of information are presented, followed by questions that are so cued as to elicit correct responses that can be verified immediately. This immediate reinforcement draws the pupil on to the next stage of the programme. Prior to the writing of the first modules Michael Nathensen, of the American Institute of Research, was invited to the area and wrote a sample module on how to plan the link frames and review frames and their sequences etc. In view of the success of this method of instruction, a dozen colleges in the Philippines now offer courses on learning the skills involved in writing programmed materials.

A variation on the linear model is the employing 'branching' in which the student is given a choice of answers and approaches. The team of module writers experimented with some elements of branching in their modules but later abandoned this technique as causing too much complexity and confusion. Their modules now all adhere to the simpler, linear approach, in which the student proceeds step by step.

Every module begins with a clear statement of the objective of the module: 'Why is this module important?' And the answer is given: 'You will get more vegetables to grow', for example. This is followed by a readiness test to ensure the student has the prerequisite skills and understands the words that will be used in the module. The section would be headed something like; 'Are you ready? Let's find out'. After each 'chunk' of information the student tests himself and so works his way through the module, as indicated by this flow-chart.

The post-tests are usually corrected and marked within each peer group, being exchanged among each other. It is found that the peer-group members mark each other's work more keenly and accurately than the teacher.

In addition to information modules, performance modules, dealing with applied skills and activities such as drawing, cooking etc. have been produced.

Since the students work through the modules at their own pace and since this pace differs from individual to individual it has been found that a quota of one module to six students is quite adequate, again resulting in considerable cost savings.

THE TEACHING

The expectation is that our population will double in a period of 23 years, and our school population will more than double in that time. Unfortunately, we do not have double the funds that we are spending now to meet the needs of education by them. So we are looking for ways by which we can increase the efficiency of the teacher. As of now, they are teaching only 40 children at a time. It may be possible to double, or treble, or ever quadruple that number, thus reducing the cost in aggregate terms of delivering elementary education.

Apart from this, we cannot expect the schools, during the period that a child is in a school, to teach everything that should be learned by him. What we expect them to do is to equip the child with the skills of communication, so that he can do the learning by himself. And that is one of the visible reported accomplishments of the Project Impact. (Dr. Jaun Manuel, Secretary for Education and Culture, Government of the Phillippines.)

Another great advantage of the self-instructional booklets is that they enable a student to progress step by step with a minimum of supervision, freeing the class teacher from his or her normal role to the broader one of the *Instructional Supervisor (IS),* with responsibility for a much larger number of children. With much of the routine clerical and administrative chores lifted off her shoulders, the teacher is able to devote more time to the real business of teaching, to giving assistance to those children who are struggling with their work.

Diagram showing typical pattern of work of a level 4, 5 or 6 student with self-instructional modules; also showing the points at which an IS (Instructional Supervisor) is involved.

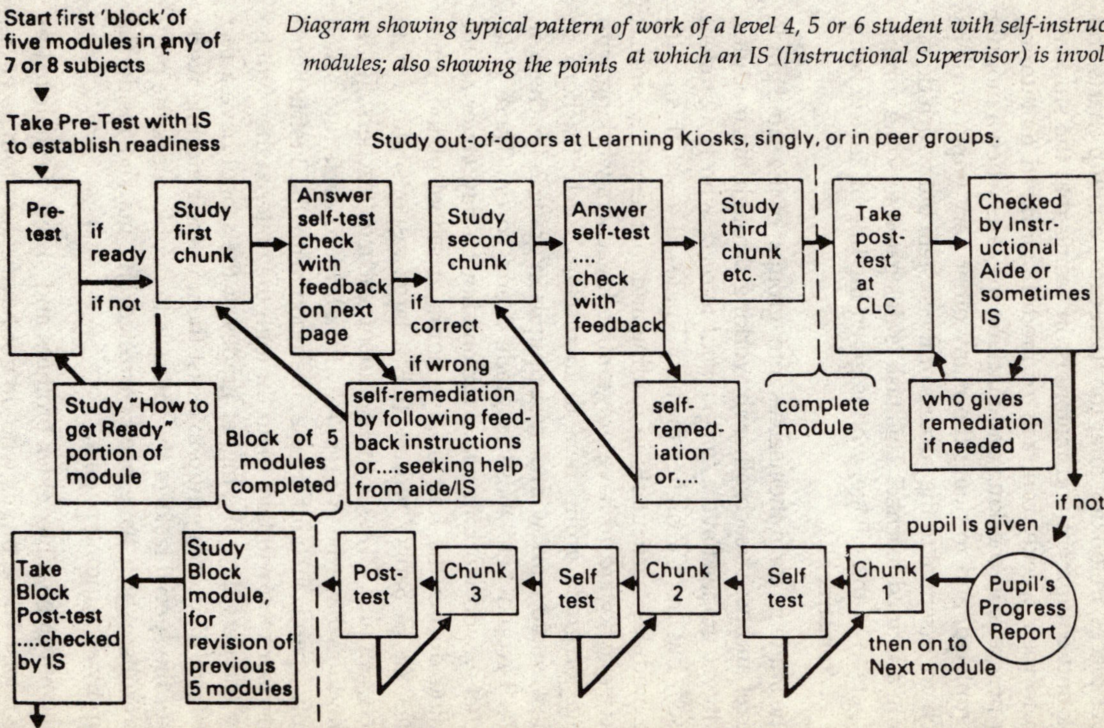

and so on, for four more 'blocks' until the year's course (25 ordinary modules + 5 block modules in all) in the particular subject is completed. If the student has completed all the subjects in that Level before the year's end, she/he can move on to the next Level.

But who, then, is going to do the routine tasks involved in keeping the Community Learning Centre running smoothly and efficiently, in seeing that modules are returned and stored in their proper places, in looking after the flash cards and flip charts and chalk and equipment and materials, in seeing that the students keep to their weekly contracts of module work, in monitoring their progress, in checking and marking the tests when a module is completed, and in doing the many other very important jobs which are essential to the success of the system but which do not require a trained teacher? This task is delegated to some competent person in the village, who is given the title of 'instructional aide' or 'registrar'.

The students form themselves into 'groups' of the same grade or level and assist each other in working through the modules. The lower grades have a '*programmed teacher*', who is a student himself, but from a higher primary grade, to assist them with their modules, particularly in reading and mathematics. Since it could be awkward to have programmed teachers working with an age or grade group next to themselves, such 'teachers' in grade 4 would work with or assist pupils in grade 2, 'teachers' in grade 5 would help those in grade 3 and so on. These older 'teachers', who work in relays for one hour a day, cover all the learning during the four or five hours at school of the junior grades. As C. Sanger writes: 'It is a large responsibility for an eleven year old'. To assist these student teachers 'teachers' guides or modules have been prepared. In addition, such tutors will usually spend an hour in the afternoon with the Instructional Supervisor who will take them through the material they will be using the next day. The higher grades of the school have a *peer tutor* from their own group to assist them in their module work. One of the special tasks of the tutors is to double-check the post-test results, which have been corrected and marked inside the group by exchanging papers.

Whenever possible, elder brothers and sisters are enlisted as *home tutors.* Those pupils who do not have elder brothers or sisters are attached to classmates who do.

Efforts have also been made to recruit *high school students* as tutors. A monthly roster has been drawn up of the high school students living in a village. Two or more of these students report to the school as tutors for one day a month. As an inducement to the high school students to undertake such work they are given credits towards the activities high school students are obliged to carry out under the Youth Civic Action programme.

As the booklet describing Project Impact emphasises: 'Community participation is the heart of Impact. Education is made a total community effort'. So members of the community who have special skills to offer are enlisted to teach the students, either in the C.L.C. or at their places or work. Thus the local carpenter instructs the boys in his trade, whilst the girls receive training from the local tailor or dressmaker.

One of the major educational and sociological problems in developing countries is the large number of drop-outs', or unemployed and unemployable youth. One of the purposes of Project Impact is to make re-entry into the learning system so simple that one can hardly talk about out-of-school youth. Young people who have left the system temporarily can re-enter it at any time.

They merely continue with their self-instructional work with modules from where they left off. But people who have been away from school for long would understandably be reluctant to return if it meant 'going back to school' with all its juvenile paraphernalia.

This gave rise to the idea of a 'learning post' in a more adult setting in the village. A 'learning post' is simply a room in someone's house which the owner has handed over for Pamong purposes. The room will contain tables and chairs and a cupboard full of modules. The old pupils come and go as they please. They usually sign up to come to the learning post twice a week.

Project Impact has only been in operation a 'few years yet its example is steadily spreading.

Summary

Project Impact is an attempt in mass primary education designed to provide every child in the community with an effective education at reasonable cost. It makes use of such strategies as:

(i) Short, simple, inexpensive self-instructional booklets or modules and self-learning kits instead of more costly textbook;

(ii) the teaching materials are 'programmed', allowing pupils to proceed at their own pace;

(iii) learning is not confined to a classroom but can be done almost anywhere;

(iv) the teacher's role is more that of an 'instructional supervisor', responsible for many more students;

(v) older students acting as tutors to younger pupils;

(vi) the school being used more as a Community Learning Centre;

(vii) making maximum use of the community's resources;

(viii) pupils who have left the education system at any time are enabled to re-enter it, continuing from where they left off.

16

Do-it-yourself Schools

The Swanson Survey of Public Schools of the Philippines, 1960, revealed that almost two million young people, four-fifths of the population in the age range 13–16 years, were not in school. This out-of-school group represented a tremendous waste of human resources. The figures for other age groups were equally staggering. How could education be provided for children at all levels as quickly as possible, especially for children living in remote areas, without additional cost to the government since additional funds were just not available? Community self-help was the only answer. Undaunted by lack of buildings and other resources, communities, rich only in imagination, ingenuity and determination, have gone ahead and set up self-help pre-schools, multigrade schools, with first to sixth grade classes under one teacher, community colleges, barrio (village) high schools. These projects were started in 1945, immediately after World War II. Today, throughout the Philippines, classrooms and schools have been set up that are used in rotation throughout the day for primary, secondary and higher education.

Dr. Pedro Orata, the founder of the barrio (village) education movement in the Philippines for which work he was awarded the Ramon Magsaysay award, an award likened to a Noble Prize, given to Asian leader for outstanding contributions of public service described the humble beginnings of this work—

> We began with a survey of the situation in order to find out what was good about it; what, in fact, should and could be continued and extended? we did not start by asking for additional funds, equipment and personnel, but did what we could to make better use of what was available. In some cases, we had nothing with which to begin but the will to do what we believed needed to be done, and so we went ahead the best we could.

The first high school outside a provincial capital was established at Urdaneta, Pangasinan, in a roofless church, without books, pencils or paper, or money to pay teachers' salaries.

As Dr. Pedro Orata states:

> The aim was to give every boy and girl a chance to go to school by bringing the school to within walking or commuting distance of their homes, and to help them and their parents (as part of their education for daily life) to earn more by improving the productivity of their farms or plots of land and through the acquisition of new skills to enable them to help support their own schools.

We started from where the people were with what they had, with existing school facilities, equipment and personnel, and proceeded one step forward—or even half a step—at a time, the people themselves (children and adults) helping to make the decisions, formulate the plans, carry them out and assess their performance, on the basis of which they helped revise the programme.

The purpose of this positive approach was to avoid to all too common practice in the Philippines, and perhaps elsewhere as well, of starting with a recital of a long list of problems and difficulties, after which everybody is discouraged and no one dares make a start. We started by doing things that were possible with existing facilities and personnel, after which there was ample time to do the other things that required more money, time and effort. We found that the best preparation for the more elaborate operations is success in undertaking simpler projects requiring little or no extra fun or training abroad. Once simple projects have been undertaken successfully, the more difficult ones are more easily handled than would at first have seemed possible.

The barrio high school brings the chance of secondary education to children in villages who could not otherwise benefit from the education provided by high schools established in the capitals or urban areas. As Dr. Orata puts it:

> the philosophy of the barrio high schools is the same as that of all schools; namely, to give every Filipino the opportunity to develop his capacities to the utmost by enabling him to go further than the elementary grades to high school—and to college, too—that are within walking or commuting distance from homes, and which they and their parents are willing to support. This right, which is part of the Universal Declaration of Human Rights, is as important as the right for life and food…

The barrio high school is an extension or branch of an existing government high school located in a more populous 'poblacion' or town. It makes use of the facilities, such as buildings and equipment, of the barrio (village) primary school where this is established and when not being used by elementary classes. Some enthusiastic parents have constructed additional buildings with funds and materials provide by themselves and others. Additional classrooms are not needed, as it is possible to get along with the existing rooms by staggering attendance of high school classes. Teachers of the elementary school who have the necessary qualifications are employed as part-time teachers in the barrio high school, being paid a small honorarium. A full-time teacher is also required for every class organised.

The subjects offered in barrio high schools are similar to those in the regular, government-provided, high schools, both the curriculum and instruction are given a strong community-centred and rurally-oriented bias. The vocational courses are adapted to the natural resources an industries in the community. The activities of the students are such as to prepare them for their future roles as farmers and as rural leaders.

What about improving the relevance and quality of education? We have not gone far on this either, but we have taken a few steps forward.

We extended the teaching of science beyond the learning of memorizing of scientific facts and discovering principles by the so-called 'process' or 'discovery approach. We asked the question; 'After the discovery of a scientific principle, what follows?' We went two steps further; first, we made an effort to lead the pupils to apply the principle in very simple and practical ways—to select seeds for planting or to lay out a bamboo irrigation scheme from an artesian well; and second, we guided them to share what they knew and the benefit of what they did to apply scientific principles, with their classmates and neighbours.

We guided science students to improvise scientific equipment, to save money, which was not available, and more importantly, to make science learning more meaningful and interesting, as well as useful, to them.

In schools, in hospitals, in chemists' shops, and in the homes of students there are innumerable objects that are discarded and thrown away: burned out electric bulbs, empty cans and bottles, worn-out tyres and inner tubes, broken glasses, corn husks, bamboo and wood. These were used to improvise science equipment for high school and college classes and play equipment for preschool children:

In the social studies programme,

> the social studies courses were designed to prevent students from ever becoming criminals or victims of crime. They not only learned what was good but practised doing it as well.

The aim was to reduce if not eradicate juvenile delinquency by having the young people usefully occupied all the time.

Students are taught to work and to earn money to pay their school expenses.

Before a high school class is opened in a barrio (village) elementary school this applies also to pre-school and community college classes—the parents and would-be students sign an agreement that they will, by working more to earn extra income, support the barrio high school, community college or pre-school classes, pay the teachers' salaries, buy the textbooks or pay the rentals on them, purchase additional library books or equipment (that cannot be improvised), etc.

The students and their parents are assisted in their effort to earn more by raising the productivity of their plots of land and farms or to start a new business or project to earn extra cash. This is not extra-curricular, but is made part of the school curriculum to prepare the students for life and self-employment, and to give their parents, who may be awarded a certificate of proficiency in recognition of their newly acquired competence, useful continuing education. The students are given high school or college credit for doing these things to help themselves and each other.

As for the motivations of barrio high schools, it goes without saying, that once the people discover that they can have their own high school where all their children go without asking the government to provide it for them, they will do everything in their power as indeed thousands of them do now, to open the same, and to operate and maintain it.

In this way, it has been possible within the last seven years to enroll at little or no additional government expense, more than a quarter of a million children and youths in barrio high schools, community colleges, and pre-schools. Whilst in 1964 there were only four barrio high schools, today there are well over 415, established in 41 provinces, with an enrolment approaching 40,000. By and large they have achieved their ambitious objectives. In general the academic achievements of their pupils have been higher than in the corresponding high schools of the formal system. There has been considerable improvement in environmental sanitation of communities, including an increase in the number of toilets, better cleanliness in home yards, more privacy in the homes, and the construction of 'blind drainage' students and parents have learned the importance and uses of compost. The holding power of the barrio high schools was significantly higher than that of the main high school.

In the economic field, or 126 students at the Cabauran barrio high school, 72 were engaged in poultry raising, 31 in piggery, 118 in home gardening, 31 in cattle raising, and 23 in other projects such as bag making, slipper making, and basketry.

In Bactad-Cabuloan, 23 had mudfish and 'gourami' projects; 31 had orchards; 30 had piggeries; 37 had poultry; 38 had home gardens; and 37 made baracbac bags and slippers. The farms were producing eggplants, tomatoes, corn or mongo.

Among parents, 112 were using some of the modern methods of farming, and had increased production.

Piglets given to indigent students had been sold and the profits distributed.

All the female goats bore kids. Some of them were sold, and half the profit went to the students.

In the social field, the problem of juvenile delinquency in the barrios has been definitely solved. According to the authorities of Urdaneta, not a single crime was committed in the three barrios by young people during the year.

The success of the barrio high school movement is due, among other things, to the strong involvement and participation of both community and students. This is one example—a road building project—

> The schoolchildren were asked if they were willing to help in the construction of the road according to their physical ability to do so. Even third-grade pupils could carry half a pond or kilo of earth to place on the road bed, and nearly 400 pupils could do a great deal if they did nothing but this. The point is that we wanted them to have a part in the making of the road so that they will later appreciate and take good care it, and not do anything to damage it. Of course every little thing

> would help, and one or two hours a week in lieu of physical education at an appropriate hour—when it is not too hot—would not be detrimental to their health, and it would certainly add to their moral character.

The experience of the barrio high schools has proved the correctness of the adage that 'where there's a will, there's a way'.

When considering profiles of innovation, the need for inspiring leadership (A+) was mentioned. Orata, a living, visible model of what he expected from his followers, provided such leadership.

We tired, in every situation, to live by the principle that a good leader must be a good follower. There is not a single activity in which we, the leaders, acted in the capacity of overseers. when there was digging to do, we had our own shovels and used them. The leader must be willing and able to do what he asks his followers to do. He must live among them and with their problems. I stayed in the village most of the time, going to town only when I needed to work in the high school.

Orata rejects any suggestion that the schools should be nationalised or financed out of the government budget. He feels this would result in the loss of the sense of local ownership and pride in local accomplishment and that the students would lose the 'work-earn' experience which he considers to be a vital part of the programme.

SUMMARY

With a view to providing education for children, especially those in remote areas, who would not otherwise receive any communities (barrios) in the Philippines set up their own 'do-it-yourself' schools. Using only what facilities were already available (often little, or none) and relying instead on their imagination, ingenuity and determination, communities have succeeded in bringing schools to within walking distance of the homes of pupils. The curriculum is given a strong community-centred, rurally-oriented bias. Courses are adapted to the natural resources and industries at hand. Student activities are geared to their future roles as farmers and workers in the community. Being short of resources, considerable recourse is made to improvisation of facilities.

QUESTIONS

1 What were the main reasons for setting up 'do-it-yourself' schools in the Philippines?

2 Do you think such schools have been successful in reaching their objectives? Explain.

3 What do you consider to the main reasons for any such success or lack of success?

4 Give an example of similar 'do-it-yourself' community project that operates in your country.

5 What are the main reasons for it being successful or otherwise?

6 Can you think of another 'do-it-yourself' community project that would benefit your people?

7 Which strategies of innovation do you think would be the most likely to succeed in 'do-it-yourself' community projects? Why?

8 Which strategy would be the least likely to succeed? Why?

17

The Problem of Mass Youth Unemployment

One of the major problem facing developing (and developed) countries is that of mass youth unemployment, especially in urban areas. In all countries a growing army of failures and drop-outs and unemployed give rise to the 'employment crisis.' The reason for this employment crisis is simple: there are fewer jobs than people capable of filling them. India can count its jobless who have technical degrees in tens of thousands. And the reasons why there are not enough jobs is because owners and managers of capital prefer to invest in physical capital rather than in labour; they prefer technologies which employ as little labour as possible. The problems of unemployment are primarily economic and political; education by itself can make little contribution towards reducing unemployment. As Martin Carnoy, Professor of Education and Economics at Stanford University, points out—

> unemployment is not a function of the amount of schooling or type of schooling of the labour force.... If capitalist decisionmakers will employ only a certain number of workers, that number will not be raised by making education more relevant.... The demand for labour in a capitalist economy is

based on the number of workers that capitalists want to employ.

As long as population growth continues unabated, there will always be more people than jobs to fill. Providing more education will not provide more jobs—except of teachers. In fact, providing more education often aggravates an already socially frustrating and politically dangerous situation. Since popular demands for more and more education can't resisted forever, many educational systems end up by producing more graduates than are necessary for filling the jobs, leading to an oversupply of schooled workers and so to the problem of graduate youth unemployment.

Just how does one solve the problem of mass youth unemployment? This chapter looks at two attempts to solve the problem.

1 *The Village Polytechnic Movement in Kenya*—which is essentially education or self-employment, and

2 *The Brigade Movement in Bostswana*—essentially a form of vocational training.

THE VILLAGE POLYTECHNIC MOVEMENT IN KENYA

In Kenya about one eight of the urban population are frustrated job seekers. The village polytechnic movement was an attempt to overcome this problem. Primary school leavers, instead of being left to join the scrap-heap of urban unemployed, were to be absorbed into vocational training institutions in their own rural communities i.e. in village polytechnics.

Linked to the problem of mass youth unemployment is the mass migration of people to the towns in search of jobs and a better life. In Africa, as against Asia, the problem is not so much one of overpopulation as of *urban* over-population; with its attendant health and other hazards. Today 22 percent of Africa's population live in towns and cities. This is double what is was twenty yeas ago.

Most young people who have a job that is paying well do not want to go to town. So long as they have work and money enough for a decent living they prefer to stay at home. Thus, the key to the whole situation is employment. The village polytechnics were seen as a way of stemming the flow of educated talent from the countryside. At the same time they were seen as catalysts to trigger off the upward spiral of rural village development by involving the whole community in the building, staffing and managing of its own polytechnic.

In essence the village polytechnic is an attempt to provide an education/training for young people in the rural and depressed rural/urban transitional areas of Kenya. The aim of the polytechnic movement is education for self-employment. Since the economy was unable to provide jobs, they would create their own jobs.

It was assumed parents and young people would want some academic education as well as practical training and so this was included in many village polytechnics. Many polytechnics include course of commercial training and agriculture to the basic skill training. Most courses last for two years and are selected on the basis of local need. Students are expected to become self-employed within their community once they leave the polytechnic.

Many parents, in awe of academic education, looked on the village polytechnic as a second or third class affair. However, the immediate problems of having unemployed sons and daughters often caused them to swallow their reservations.

THE BRIGADE MOVEMENT IN BOTSWANA

Botswana turned to vocational training as a means of solving the problem of school leavers unable to find employment. It inaugurated its Brigade Movement in 1963: this was a programme of training, teaching and productive work. In 1965 a group of 25 primary school leavers was recruited into the first Builders Brigade at Swaneng. The three-year programme consisted of:

- productive work and 'on-the-job' training;
- classroom instruction in vocational subjects;
- classroom instruction in academic subjects.

The work produced by the trainees was sold and the proceeds used to defray the cost of their boarding and instruction. The brigade was thus something of a mixture of training establishment, educational institute and commercial enterprise. It was, in effect, an 'institution offering primary school leavers a worthwhile technical or vocational training, in such a way as to cover the recurrent cost of that training.'

The builders' brigade was followed by a carpenters' brigade—making school desks etc. Today there are well over two dozen brigades in several centres, providing training in several different crafts.

However, the movement does not have the full support that it would need to become 'institutionalised'. Whilst it does provide a useful and interesting alternative secondary route for thousands of children, it is just about tolerated within the school system. Both children and parents alike see it as a second best for those who failed to get into regular secondary schools.

In conclusion it must be noted that providing vocational education does not really solve the problem of youth unemployment; it might salve the conscience, but it does not solve the problem. The Federal Republic of Germany (West Germany) is one of the wealthiest and most industrialised countries in the world. It, too, has a massive youth unemployment problem. The region of Nordrhein–Westfalen sought to solve the problem by gibing all school leavers who were unable to find employment the opportunity to return to school for one more year to study vocationally oriented courses. Admittedly, the programme offered the children a chance of acquiring further skills and something preferable to life on the streets, but if the jobs are not there then the objective of reducing unemployment cannot be achieved. Producing an educated and trained supply of labour will not solve the unemployment problem unless, at the same time, the demand for jobs is increased. All that happens is that children (with perhaps some more education) replace others in the job queue.

SUMMARY

One of the major problems facing developing (and developed) countries is that of mass youth unemployment, especially in rural areas. This is due to there not being enough jobs to fill. The industrial and business sectors of most countries are unable to absorb all those seeking employment.

Since governments and industry are unable to provide sufficient jobs some people are striving to overcome the problem of mass unemployment by creating their own jobs—through self employment and vocational training.

The *Village Polytechnic Movement* Kenya in essentially education for self-employment. The village polytechnics are basically vocational training institutions in rural areas, designed to absorb primary school leavers who would otherwise be unemployed. Their aim is education (essentially craft and technical skills) for self-employment in their home areas. They are built, supported and managed by the local community.

The *Brigade Movement* in Botswana is essentially a form of vocational training, combining work and learning for secondary age children. It provides and alternative secondary route for thousands of children who would otherwise go without.

Providing vocational education does not necessarily help solve the problem of youth unemployment. If the jobs are not there, unemployment will continue.

18

Ruralization of Education

When I refer to the ruralization of education I do not mean a cut-price education for peasant's children. Ruralization means the adaptation of education to the actual conditions of this country, which is essentially agricultural...The aim is to give the young people who go through this education an inclination to work on the land, a sense of the dignity of that work and an opportunity of living better in the villages and satisfying many of their aspirations...Though ruralized education prepares the Cameroonian school child to fit into his environment and to transform it, it is by no means an agricultural education.

(Address by His Excellency El Adj Ahmadou Ahidjo, President of the Federal Republic of Cameroon, on presenting the third five-year development plan to the National Assembly on 11 August, 1971.)

It is depressing to see that agriculture, the backbone of our economy, is looked down upon the younger generation and left to old people who know nothing about modern farming techniques.

(Address by the Head of State, Yaoundè, 13 June, 1970, at IPAR graduation ceremony.)

It is, after all, through environmental studies that it is hoped to educate young Cameroonians able to integrate with their environment in order to transform it; so it is on environmental studies that the meaning and future of ruralized education depend.

(*La rèforme de l'enseignement au Cameroun. 1970*)

The Cameroon Republic was spending 20 percent of its national budget on education yet the returns in terms of efficiency and productivity of the education system were discouraging to say the least. A very small number of children were completing their primary education: an even smaller proportion obtained the primary school certificate. There was a high dropout rate and a large number of children repeating grades. Of those who completed school and who obtained the leaving certificate, few were able to integrate in and take effective roles in society. These were just some of the symptoms of the low cost-benefit ratio of education. Classes in the lower grades of the primary school often contained more than 100 children. The problems of over-crowding were aggravated by inadequate premises and lack of adequate classroom furniture and materials. The wide age disparities among the pupils further impeded efficiency. It was recognised, too, that the main reason for the poor performance of the education system was the low training of the vast majority of the primary school teachers.

In 1967, 72 percent of the primary teachers in East Cameroon responsible for preparing pupils for the primary school certificate had themselves not passed the examination. Only 16 percent of the teachers could be considered adequately qualified. The situation was not much better in West Cameroon. The situation could have been helped by an adequate cadre of school inspectors. But these were in short supply: in 1965/66 one inspector was responsible on average for more than 250 teachers. Not only were there too few inspectors; they lacked financial and transport facilities and were overburdened with administrative work.

In addition to the low standard of primary education, much of it was irrelevant and unsuitable to the pupils receiving it, to their circumstances and way of life, and also to the social and economic needs of the country. The education system was ill-adapted to the realities of life in Cameroon. This maladjustment cut the school off from the natural and human environment, which was essentially rural, thus making school work abstract, boring and meaningless, only absorbed by dint of mindless repetition and memorization. Education was valued only to the extent that it was regarded as a means of social advancement, albeit one which took the pupil outside his own environment. In this way primary education was neither an adequate preparation for secondary education nor for those very many who would not continue their studies but who would need to fit into their rural environment, work on it, master it, transform and develop it.

The call went out clear and strong for *'ruralization'* of education; the old type of school and the traditional teacher had to be replaced by a *rural* school and a *rural* teacher, adjusted to the prevailing social and economic conditions. The basic concern was to replace the traditional school measures by measures which closely linked *education* and *development.* The task was:

(i) to give those who were to continue their studies a proper foundation for secondary education, and

(ii) to prepare the rest—the overwhelming majority—to integrate with their environment and improve it.

THE RURAL SCHOOL

In the new *'rural'* primary school pupils would first be taught the basic skills—the 3 R's—but these would be rooted in the setting of Cameroonian life and culture. The children must be able to put these skills to good use in the surroundings in which they live and move, in real life situations. The school would not only awaken the children's interest in doing practical tasks in the neighbourhood but would also take the responsibility for cultivating and tending a field or an orchard. In this way the child would not only learn the rudiments of agriculture in the context of local conditions but would be using modern agricultural techniques. This type of education could thus open the way for the industrialisation of agriculture. Such industrialisation could well be a preparation for other forms of industry and form a useful bridge or transition from a rural way of life to patterns of behaviour more typical of industrial society proper. Transferability was to be characteristic of what was learned under the new education, which would develop the aptitude for change and for adjustment to new circumstances. In towns, basic education would include an introduction to manual skills connected with crafts which would teach the pupils how to use basic tools. In short, the new education would take its bearings from the rural environment, encourage a taste and respect for manual work and introduce the child to such work. Its main task would be the dual one of communicating useful basic knowledge and giving the intellectual training which would make it possible to acquire further knowledge.

The rural primary school was to be the only primary school, whether in town or in the country. It was to be attended by all children, both those going on to secondary schooling and those going immediately into employment.

With a view to 'getting the pupil to know his environment well with a view to transforming it' the traditional compartmentalization of subjects was to be replaced by an interdisciplinary approach. The *study of the environment* is made the cornerstone of this interdisciplinarity. The environment is made a subject of study 'based on observation first of the local environment, then of a broader environment and replacing the formerly separate subjects of history, geography, science, civics, hygiene, child care, economics (home or otherwise), crop and stock framing, study of social groups and so forth. Knowledge will be directed towards practical applications. The aim is no longer knowledge for its own sake. The new school is ridding itself of those encyclopaedic pretensions which transformed the pupil into a memory machine and dissociated culture from life. Henceforth there are two sides to each lesson: the pupil acquires a certain item or items of knowledge, and the practical work sessions add to this a certain know-how. The school thereby naturally finds its place again within the village.'

The Methods, Curricula and Work Corresponding to Study of the Environment

Environmental studies are begun at the start of the third year of the primary school. During the third and fourth years the study of the environment forms the pivot around which the children's knowledge is integrated. During the last two years (the fifth and sixth) 50 percent of the time-table is devoted to study of the environment and to practical work oriented towards 'the better life' (agriculture, health, housing, nutrition, child care, hygiene, home economics, etc.)

The Syllabus in More Detail

The *third year* syllabus is expressly concerned with the learning of three things. The child will be taught to situate himself in time, which has hitherto only existed for him as time spent on doing something. To achieve this, he will practise telling the time of day (day, night, morning, evening, etc.), will note what distinguishes one part of the day from another and prepare a timetable for his various activities. Similarly, he will learn to situate himself in space by means of exercises involving the notions of right and left and of direction, etc. Finally, these two types of exercise will facilitate the third, which makes use of the preceding ideas to give the child practice in situating living creatures in the scheme of life. Having been helped to perceive the broad scheme of life, he will be trained to observe the life cycles of plants and animals. He will also acquire the vocabulary and instruments for studying life whilst being helped to understand the idea of the family. These studies will be combined with drawing and manual and community leadership work.

This third year syllabus is less devoted to studying the local environment than to acquiring the basis and tools needed for such a study. The exercises are designed mainly to complete the learning of the rules and instruments needed to study the environment, which is done proper in the succeeding years.

The *fourth year* is planned as a prolongation of the third year, as a study of the same material in greater depth. It is, in fact, reserved for a study of the local environment, and the methods used are found again in the last years of primary education. Integration is achieved through a syllabus based on topics and this knowledge is 'usually acquired by personal investigation in the natural and social environment as well as from information leaflets regularly distributed to the schools'...The topics are identical from one year to the next but, having begun by studying the local environment, pupils then pass on to the regional environment in their *fifth year* and finally to the Cameroonian nation, Africa and the world in their *sixth year.* In the fifth and sixth years, the study of the environment is accompanied by practical work conductive to a better life. In the 'school environment' gardens and plantations are to be cultivated, water supply laid on and filters built, deep latrines dug and buildings such as the school workshop put up and maintained.

The Rural School and the Community

However, if on leaving the rural school the pupil finds hostility to his ideas for progress, if he encounters the inertia of an uncooperative adult community which does not allow him to apply his knowledge and skills, he will soon lose any enthusiasm engendered at school. If the young school pupil is to play an active role in his home community, it is essential that the community itself should also develop along parallel lines. By making the village or the neighbourhood a real structure into which the young people can fit the ruralized primary school can become a significant point for community promotion, which is essential to the country's development. This means educating and involving the community to the full. The new rural school thus has a twofold function:

(i) an academic function to provide its pupils with the 'new education'; and

(ii) an out-of-school function to educate and provide leadership to the adult community in such a way that it will accept and encourage the new generations graduating from the rural school and the new ideas they will be bringing with them.

To realise its expectations to the full, the ruralized primary school must become a *model* to the entire community; the example given by the school should encourage the adults to seek changes; it should become a model to emulate. The school must become a *co-operative for* thought and action. From this standpoint 'ruralization' is a radical reform in the spirit and style of education. The adults will gradually *imitate* the school if it provides them with *familiar, everyday examples of action* which they see can change their environment and also satisfy their desire for profit, health and amusement. Such examples could be, for instance, a poultry-house, garden, plantation, canteen, latrines, clean water supply, etc. *By the example of its achievements* the school can become the focal point of leadership of the community. If the teacher is to provide leadership to a community he must gain its respect and co-operation. He can often win the people over spontaneously by the psychological effect of the activities he organises at school.

If the local community is to follow and emulate the lead of the ruralized primary school, it must be able to see what the school is doing. This implies '*open*' schools, which the local people can not only see at work but in which they can come and go as they please. The school must cease to be the closed preserve for the teacher and his pupils.

The education reforms require that each school should have a plot of land and also a supply of tools kept in a small workshop.

To serve as an *example* the 'school environment' must be constantly cared for. In the case of livestock units or gardens, plantations, water sources, filters, etc., this does not mean just maintaining equipment in sound working order; 'caring for' fields means the work involved in sowing, trimming, planting out, harvesting and so on.

Another thing that the adult community could copy from the rural school is the way in which its work is planned, decided on, organised and carried out, whereby the school becomes a 'co-operative for thought and action'.

In short, if the rural primary school is to be the 'centre of influence in the community' it must not confine its activities only to school children, but all the resources of the country must be exploited, the whole population, young and old.

But to implement this new education a new breed of teachers was essential. We saw how the new ruralized primary school was to have two functions:

(i) an in-school function: to educate its pupils according to the new perspectives; and

(ii) an out-of-school function: to spearhead adult community activities. The new breed of teacher will have a three-fold task:

   (a) as a specialist in ruralized education;

   (b) as a certificated teacher he will be a permanent advisor to his less qualified colleagues;

   (c) he will act as a permanent intermediary in the organisation of local community activities.

To emphasise his new role the primary school teacher is now called a 'teacher—community leader' (*instituteur—animateur*).

He will no longer be the 'school-master' from whom the pupils receive orders and knowledge more or less passively. His mission is rather to stimulate their minds and provide them with the instruments which they will put to use themselves in order to think, learn, act and create. By extension, the concept designates a new field of action, a vocation to educate, through community leadership, sectors of the population other than school children, for example, adolescents who have already left school but who have not yet begun an active working life, or working adults with families. The teacher will no longer lead a double life, shutting himself up in his school to teach children and only emerging to lose himself in the anonymous mass of citizens. His role does not stop at the school gate. Outside school and after school, he is still a teacher; within school, during school hours he is already a community leader.

All this involves an extensive training programme. How else is a teacher to derive his authority and expertise for community leadership? It is particularly difficult to be a community leader in a village where, very often, habits are ingrained and long- established. Teachers must be taught how to arouse interest among the adult section of the community in economic development and socio-cultural advancement so that it will welcome and encourage the activities of pupils leaving school. If his school is to really become a centre of influence and if he is to win the respect of the community to the extent that he will be asked to guide and organise its efforts to achieve a better life, he will need to be trained. He will be able to provide community leadership if he trained to do so in a teacher training institute which is itself a living model of this concept, a living model for organisation of activities in the rural school, which in turn will become the model for organization of village activities.

The concept of ruralized primary education implies a new way of teaching, new attitudes and a new style of training. To produce this new brand of teachers it was decided to establish a new, rurally oriented, primary teacher training institute, which would train teachers to play a new key role in a specifically rural context. A request to set up a teacher training college was made to the United Nations Development Programme in April 1967, and shortly afterwards such a rurally oriented primary teacher training college, ENIR, (Ecole normale d'instituteurs de plein exercise á vocation rurale), was set up in temporary premises in Yaoundé, with a first intake of 70 teachers. The purpose of ENIR was to develop a new type of primary school teacher who would also promote social and economic development. The course was a three year course, following the BEPC (Brevet d'etudes du premier cycle) (Certificate of lower secondary studies), leading to an examination and diploma, the higher certificate of proficiency (*Brevet superieur de capacité*). In the basic subjects, emphasis was placed on the works of black African authors, especially such works as had a rural setting. A crash course on theoretical and practical educational psychology laid stress on the psychology of the African child. Considerable importance was given to the practical applications of science in the spheres of health, hygiene and agriculture.

The trainee teachers are not given instruction as specialists in agriculture, health or crafts, One might well ask how the primary teacher is going to be able to build up a 'school environment' and transform the school into a 'model' for the community. The reason for not giving the student teachers such training is that their pupils in the primary school are too young to be receiving vocational training as such. In any case, the idea is not to make the rural school into a technical or vocational school. Moreover, in the adult community the teacher will not replace the technicians, who in this respect will provide leadership for the adults, the teacher acting more as an 'intermediary' for such specialists from the departments of health, youth, rural development, planning etc. In any case, no special advanced technical training is needed for many agricultural practices, such as the application of fertilisers to increase yields, the diversification of crops etc. The teacher graduating from the teacher training institute may, given fairly simple device, usefully take such initiatives.

In addition to pre-service courses for teachers, in-service courses for the primary school inspectors and educational advisers, lasting three months, are held. The participants are expected not only to study but also to lecture.

But if the country was to achieve its objective under the 'new' education, it was obvious it was not going to do so by relying solely on the pre-service output of 70 teachers a year. The teacher training institute was called on to extend and expand its activities to include *in-service* training as well. There were large numbers of primary teachers who had to be trained quickly. Of the 15,000 serving teachers, 13,000 were only 'monitors' with the primary certificate their only qualification. A ten-year programme of in-service training was envisaged. To carry out this massive in-service programme another teacher training institute, IPAR, (Institute of Rurally Oriented Applied Education—*Institute de Pédagogie Appliqâe a Vocation Rurale*) was established at Búea, in the former West Cameroon, similar to but distinct from the teacher training institute in Yaoundé. By establishing a second institute in another part of the country the government was not only respecting the identity of the different regions but was adapting education to the context fashioned by history and geography.

It was expecting too much to ask the teachers who had not yet been trained to use the new curricula and methods to work out by themselves the form of the lessons in the various subjects using the new approach. Accordingly, the teacher training institutes at Yaoundé and Búea had to go beyond preparing and drafting model lessons and producing prototypes. They began to prepare *all* the lessons in the various subjects, along with support material.

CHANGES IN SECONDARY EDUCATION

Reform of the education and teacher training system could not be limited to the primary level alone. Any education system must be seen as an integrated whole and if one of its parts is modified the whole system will feel the repercussions and be affected. It was not possible to 'ruralize' primary education and at the same time maintain its unity while leaving secondary education unchanged. General and technical secondary education and higher education must take cognizance of the considerable changes affecting pupil's primary education. When a child leaves the primary school he is too young to start his working life; hence the need to develop post-primary education and training in order to offer the young Cameroonian the facilities he needs, not only so that he does not lose the benefits of the education he has already received but also so that he may turn it to account in active, working life.

Postscript

These changes in the Cameroonian education system were readily affected largely because they had the full backing of the highest authorities in the land, from the Head of State down. As Lallez states—

> it only needs the highest authority in the land and his government to place their trust in those concerned and show their attachment to the reform, as happened, for a change to occur. A deep commitment of men in key positions is important.

SUMMARY

- Because of its existing low standard of primary education, much of which was irrelevant and an inadequate preparation for life in the predominantly rural environment, the Cameroons turned to the 'ruralization' of education, linking education and development, as a remedy. In the new ruralized primary school would be taught not only the 3 R's but also the basic skills necessary to life in a rural environment. The interdisciplinary approach, centred round the study of the environment, emphasised the practical applications of knowledge oriented towards 'the better life'. The ruralised primary school also has an out-of-school function to provide education and leadership to the adult community so that it will accept the new ideas and techniques which the graduates from the new schools will bring into the community. The school was to spearhead community activities. It must be a model, an example, to the community. To do so, instead of being a closed preserve of teachers and pupils, it had to be 'open' so that local people could see, and copy, the work being done. The school was to be a 'co-operative' for thought and action. If it is to be the centre of influence in the community it must extend its activities beyond its pupils to all the population, young and old.

Such a ruralised primary school implies a new way of teaching, new attitudes and hence, a new style of teacher training. The teacher's role becomes that of 'teacher-community leader'. His role does not stop at the school-gate; he has responsibilities to the whole community. He must be trained to promote social and economic development, attaching considerable importance to the practical applications of science in the spheres of health, hygiene, agriculture. (It should be borne in mind, however, that such a school is *not* just another vocational or technical school.)

19

Education in Iran

For people who are always on the move, never long in one place, education becomes a difficult proposition. This is the case with the nomadic, migratory tribes that exist in Iran, Northern Kenya and many other regions of the developing world. In Iran, for example, there are tribes who migrate to the warmer areas in the winter and to the cooler areas in summer. Understandably, provision of education for them has been very difficult, if not impossible, in the past. Until two decades ago these tribal people were deprived of all educational and training facilities and for years had lived in ignorance and lack of information.

About 25 years ago, Mohammed Bahmanbequi started a scheme to bring literacy to the children of the different tribes of Fars province and to establish mobile tribal schools. The school was established in a large tent; and when the tribe moved the school went with it. Education was made free and often supplies and textbooks were also provided free. The mobile school was easily distinguishable in the tribal encampment—a white tent, with an Iranian flag above, in the midst of black tents.

But finding teachers for these mobile schools was not easy. Teachers from the city were not prepared to teach in rural areas, and educated individuals were not to be found among the tribai people. The few urban diploma-holding teachers who did come out to the tribes did not stay for long: the primitive, basic conveniences for even a low standard of living in the city were non-existent among the tribes. Every inducement was made to attract and hold such teachers, but with little success. The only solution was to go to the half-educated people in the tribes themselves. Tribal youths who had acquired some education in the recent past and had completed an elementary school course were recruited as teachers for the tent schools. In 1957 a Tribal Teacher Training School was founded in Shiraz to increase the basic knowledge of these tribal youths and to familiarise them with teaching methodologies and techniques. The course of training was for twelve months. The young tribesman then returned to has tribe as a mobile school teacher. When the season arrived for the tribe to move the teacher would fold up his school—a large tent—and travel with his tribe and pupils as they made their migrations, thus not interrupting the school work of his pupils.

Over the past 20 years the Tribal Teacher Training School has graduated nearly 5,000 teachers.

As a result of the success of this programme in bringing literacy and education to the tribal children of Fars province the Office of Tribal Education has established similar tribal schools in all parts of the country. In 1976 a boarding high school was established in Shiraz for those needy but talented tribes-children who had completed primary education and wished go on with their studies.

MIDWIFERY AND PARA-MEDICAL TRAINING

For many centuries tribal have given birth without the benefit of midwives or medical facilities. The urban-education midwives were neither able nor willing to go to the tribal areas to assist young mothers. Thus girls who had graduated from the tribal primary schools were used as midwives. However, with the co-operation of the Ministry of Health, a tribal midwifery training programme was started in Shiraz.

Likewise, with the co-operation of Pahlavi University, a programme was started to train tribal school graduates as para-medics and veterinarians for service in tribal areas.

CARPET WEAVING SCHOOL

For a long time weaving has been an important source of income for the tribal people. However, the tendency to settle down in the rural areas or in the cities has gradually discouraged the women of the tribes from continuing this art. Thus, the techniques of tribal handicrafts such as jajim, gelim and carpet weaving were threatened with extinction as the elderly, skilled, and experienced craftswomen died.

In order to revive this valuable art, which was on the verge of dying out, the office of Tribal Education established a girls' vocational centre in Shiraz in 1970. Each year the centre accepts 50 girls and young women from among the applicants of different tribes. At this centre the girls learn wool spinning, jajim and gelim weaving, vegetable and natural dyeing, carpet weaving, and other tribal handicrafts.

The teachers for this centre are selected from the elderly tribal women well-skilled in these traditional crafts. The apprentices become skillful craftswomen in the handicrafts within a period of 12 months. They then return to their villages or tribal areas and start private workshops. The Office of Tribal Education assists the graduates in establishing their workshops by providing the initial capital. Within the last few years, 150 students have completed training at this centre.

20

Population Education

Today there are over 4,300 million of us. It has taken all of time to reach this figure. If present trends continue, this figure will double in only another forty years.

Population education is an essentially new curriculum area which has emerged in the past fifteen to twenty years and refers to all the various educational activities in the formal school system dealing directly or indirectly with population issues. The basic purpose of the activities is to aid young people in school to understand the potential significance of population factors for their own lives and for the family, nation and for the world in general and to develop values and attitudes based on this understanding.

In existing school programmes the exclusion of population education forms a crucial gap in the curriculum. The introduction of population education into the educational systems of a number of countries of the Third World is among the most significant curriculum innovations of our time.

It is estimated that the population of the world reached the first billion mark about the year AD 1825; the second billion mark about 1930, the third billion in 1960, the fourth billion in 1975. In all probability another 2 billion more people will be born into a world of 4.3 billion in the next 20 years.

It is a sobering thought that each day over 170,000 babies begin life on planet Earth. Every five days the world population increases by one million; this means an increase of some 2,000 million by the end of the century, more than the global population in the first two decades of the century. Moreover, nine-tenths of this increase, which will take the population from 4,300 million to perhaps 6,500 million, will be in the developing countries.

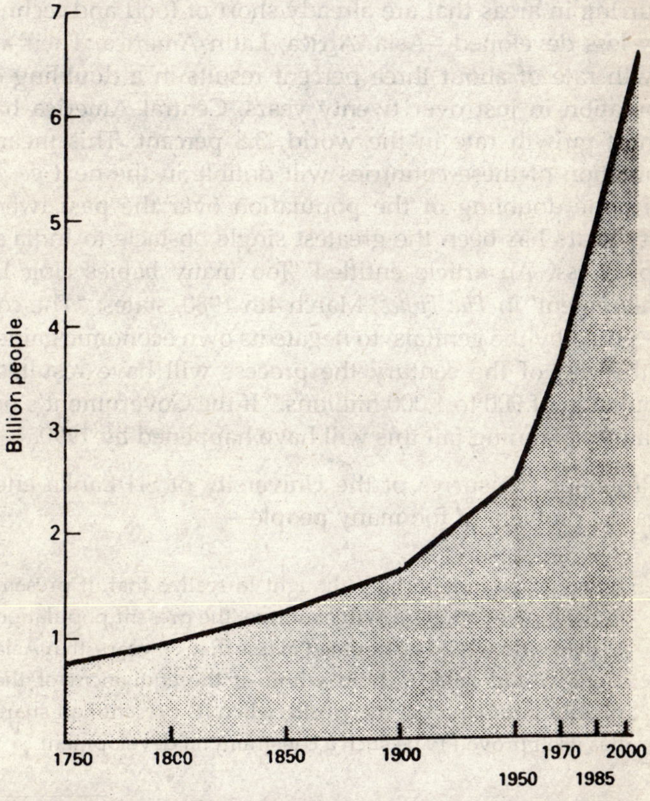

Estimated Rate of Population Growth AD *1750–2000.*
Source: Information, Volume 8, Number 5, International Labour Organisation, October 1972.

This exponential growth in population, rightly called the 'vital revolution', brings with it enormous problems not only for individuals and families, countries and nations, but for the entire world.

Concomitant with the 'population explosion' is the phenomenon of 'exploding cities'. In the next twenty years alone there will be 32 million people in Mexico City; Calcutta and Bombay will have 20 millions each.

To aggravate the position the greatest population increases are occurring in areas that are already short of food and technologically less developed—Asia, Africa, Latin America. Their annual growth rate of about three percent results in a doubling of the population in just over twenty years. Central America has the highest growth rate in the world, 3.8 percent. This means the population of these countries will double in the next *decade*. In India, the doubling of the population over the past twenty to thirty years has been the greatest single obstacle to India's path to progress. An article entitled 'Too many babies clog India's development' in *The Times*, March 4th 1980, states: "The country has 'voted by the genitals' to negate its own economic gains. And by the end of the century the process will have resulted in a population of 900 to 1,000 millions." If the Government's policies of family planning fail this will have happened by 1990.

Professor Jayasuriya of the University of Sri Lanka encapsulates the problem of too many people—

> It should be a disturbing thought to realize that, if present rates of population growth continue, the present population of the world would be doubled in less than 30 years, that Asia alone would have to hold within it the equivalent of the present population of the world, when its present half share has itself proved to be such a constraint on development.
>
> In spite of massive inputs into education, Asia has more illiterates, aged 15 and above, today than ten years ago, more children between 5 and 19 out of school today than ten years ago... Concurrently with the absolute growth in numbers,

> there has been an increasing degree of urbanization, with its attendant problems. Shortages of housing, water supply and sanitation have combined with water and air pollution to make urban living increasingly hazardous...Assuming, with some degree of over-simplification, that the key problems which countries face in this field are the rapid growth of population and urbanization, each requires a national strategy for coping with it.

Recent World Bank surveys show that the birth rate in the developing world is falling faster than anticipated. In Costa Rica, for example, the average size of family has dropped by 40 percent in one generation: today's mother is expected to have four children, not seven as before. Similar declines in birth rate are reported from Sri Lanka and other Asian countries where the age of marriage has risen sharply. The age of marriage among young women has risen from 18 to 23 and is possibly even higher among males. In Kerala and Sri Lanka there are clear indications that the sharp fall in birth rates is directly, though not exclusively, attributable to the spread of female literacy, and the resulting access of women to information not to mention their ability to read and understand family planning literature, and to their participation in social and economic life. Women who are given educational opportunities tend to have, on average two less children than those who lack such opportunities. Development is evidently the most effective form of family planning for our time.

However, not everybody agrees that merely raising the level of education of men and women will reduce fertility levels, that the more educated the people the fewer children they have. In fact, there is some evidence to show that in some cases, for example, Israel, especially at the higher levels of education, increase in education raises fertility levels. Michael Todaro argues that creating more full-time jobs for women is a much more realistic policy than increasing their level of education. Women in employment stand to lose in terms of wages by raising children, and this would act as a deterrent to large families.

As the World Bank warns, the problem of improving the quality of life of teeming millions engaged in the seemingly losing struggle for bare survival haunts the world. President Nyerere pointed out in his Address—'The Economic Challenge'—to the Royal Commonwealth Society in London, November 1975, more than half of the world's population lives in countries with a per capita GNP of less than $200 per annum. And Professor Tinbergen, the Dutch Nobel Prize economist, has estimated that the wealthy 10 percent of mankind consumes 25 times as much as the remaining 90 percent of the world's population. About 800 million people still live in absolute poverty. These are people living at the very margin of existence—with inadequate food, shelter, education and health care.

The Brandt Commission has warned that even with declining fertility, most developing countries are at least likely to double their populations; Nigeria and Bangladesh are expected to have as many people as the United States and the Soviet Union today; India will have at least 1,200 million people.

Till quite recently, epidemics, famines and chronic malnutrition each year killed off nearly as many people as were born. However, within the last hundred years developments in medicine have brought many of the 'killer' disease—smallpox, yellow fever, plague, typhoid, cholera, diptheria, tuberculosis, malaria—under control. Penicillin alone is estimated to have saved more lives than were lost in the two World Wars. As a result death rates have decreased, while the expectancy of life at birth has been greatly increased. These two factors have not only fostered the growth of population but also influenced the age structure of the population, resulting in significant increases within the younger and the older age groups. Factors such as these have to a large extent vitiated the spectacular advances made in the quantitative provision of education in many countries of the Third World. More is spent on education, but there remain more and more to be educated.

The Korean Educational Development Institute suggests a way of breaking the vicious circle—

> In connection with curriculum, considering that rapid population growth and increasing urbanization are seen to act as

> constraints on the provision of education in quantitative and qualitative terms, an essential response of education to this state of affairs should be to include in the curriculum a strong component of population education that would provide insight into the interrelationships between population change and development at the micro-level of the individual, and at the macro-level of the nation. All in all, the essential need is for new developmental, educational and population perspectives that are supportive of each other and can lead mankind to a life of richness and serenity.

India has a population of 600 million; every seventh person in the world is Indian. The Government of India resorted to power-coercive strategies to curb its growing population. It introduced compulsory sterilization. But that failed. Sterilization was then made optional. That failed too: the man offered a vasectomy feared for his impotence, and if his wife was offered a tubectomy he feared for her fidelity. Free condoms were handed out to the peasants. That failed too. Dom Moraes, who made a study of population problems on behalf of the UN Fund for population Activities remarks—

> In a remote village, a government official is godlike. When the government officer tells a villager that he should have fewer children, the villager says, yes, indeed, he has always thought so himself. The government officer departs; he will not return for a long while. Meanwhile, the condoms he has generously distributed shrivel on a dusty shelf or are bequeathed to the children as balloons.

Cash incentives and rewards were offered. That also failed. People are no longer being paid cash to have operations. Rather, in some countries, benefits are being *removed* from those who do not limit the number of their children. Singapore is aiming for zero population growth, i.e. not more than two children per family, so that when the parents die the children replace them in society. In Singapore tax relief could once be claimed for 'up to five children'. Tax relief can now be claimed only for up to three children. Hospital fees for pregnant women are low for the first child but rise steadily for every subsequent pregnancy. Paid maternity leave used to be available up to the third or fourth confinement. Now it stops after the second. In the scramble for subsidized housing, priority is given to couples who have three children or less.

The failure of power-coercive strategies in India emphasises the need to consider the *user* system if any innovation is to be successful. *Their* wishes, beliefs, customs, etc. must be respected. Before one starts to explore how to resculpture the lives and minds of people one must first explore how those minds think and work. Traditions are the hardest windmills to tilt at.

Most parents in developing countries look to their families, especially sons, as a means of security in their old age. The peasant knows babies are apt to die, and he wants to be sure that if one son dies there will be a replacement; and so he wants four to five children. As with money, when you have a lot you want more, as insurance for the future. To the peasant family limitation is unacceptable; unless he can be sure his children will last, he wants more—to have more hands to work, to provide security. Fertility has a direct correlation with insecurity. One way of overcoming this ingrained attitude is to strive to lower the infant mortality rate: then the villager doesn't have to store up children like a squirrel storing up nuts for winter. In many traditional societies, as part of their religious beliefs, tremendous importance has always been attached to procreation. As India has discovered, it is easy to tell the peasant, entrenched in tradition, how to limit his family; it is not so easy to tell him why he should.

But even with more educated groups selling the idea of family limitation is difficult. The number of State members elected to the central Lok Sabha (Parliament) in India depends on the size of the state population; so, too, does the size of government subsidies to the states. A situation where larger populations mean more parliamentary members and more state subsidies offers little incentives to programmes for population control. Maybe this is a case where politicians need to be educated before the people.

In Malaysia, as in many developing countries, there is opposition in certain quarters to population control. Some Malays oppose it because they think the Koran is opposed to it although there is nothing in the Koran against contraception. In addition to religious scruples, some Malays believe that birth control will decimate their numbers thus enabling the Chinese to gain the upper hand in Malaysia. Some Chinese have a similar fear in reverse. Moraes give examples of several countries in Africa where the local people believed family planning was a white plot to wipe out the Africans.

Instead of coercion, the policy in India has now changed from 'Don't do this, don't do that', to persuasion, to 'it's a great joy to have children, but only if they are healthy and happy'. However illiterate, the message reaches the masses. So family planning was introduced under the guise of mother and child care; as Moraes says:

> 'the family planning pill was wrapped up within the scented capsule of mother and child care'.

Family planning was not birth control. Family planning is a means of ensuring the health of mother and child; its main purpose is health care, and this includes spacing of children for the sake of parents and child. Posters appeared all over India showing happy parents with their two beaming children and bearing the message, *Dho Ya Theen Bacche Bas* (Two or three children are enough). Another poster proclaimed 'Better one leopard than ten jackals'. The inverted red triangle (the family planning symbol) became a feature of the landscape. But family planning also failed for a variety of reasons.

Young educated unmarried women were recruited as field agents. But the village women, when lectured about childbirth by an unmarried girl, tended to tell her to marry and have children before talking about them. Women tended to feel embarrassed if their neighbours knew they had accepted family planning.

HOW COULD EDUCATION SOLVE THE PROBLEM?

In brief, the problem is to be solved not in the uterus but in the human mind.

T. S. Mehta, an educator from India, puts forward these arguments for including 'population education' in the school curricula:

(i) Rapid population growth is a threat to economic development, specially with respect to per capita economic growth.

(ii) India is facing the crucial problem of providing adequate food for more and more people.

(iii) Rapid population growth in the last half century has made the Indian population a young population whose needs for more schools, more job opportunities, more health facilities, more transport facilities, more housing and so on put the economy under great pressure.

Professor Jayasuriya would have as the *goals* of population education to assist the individual, with due regard to maturity,

(a) to acquire an understanding of the factors affecting selected aspects of quality of life in their bearing upon the individual and upon society, and to appreciate in particular the pervasive nature of population change as one of the most important of these factors;

(b) to acquire the ability to assess the quality of life implications, now and in the future, for oneself and others, of alternative actions, most especially those related to population;

(c) to develop attitudes, values and skills conducive to responsible decision making and action with a view to enhancing quality of life for oneself and for others, now and in the future;

(d) to take such action in the immediate present as would lead to the enhancement of quality of life in those spheres of life in which such action is immediately possible. For example,

> "he can be an immediate activist by not wasting water, helping to avert soil erosion, participating in the care of plants and in weeding, preparing compost manure, improving his nutritional knowledge, not wasting food etc." And in other matters, such as population related behaviour regarding which immediate action is not possible, to resolve to act with due regard to the enhancement of quality of life when time and opportunity for such action come.

India held its first seminar on population education in 1969. The Report of this National Seminar on Population Education, held in Bombay, laid down the main objectives of population education.

The objectives of population education should be to enable the students to understand that the family size is controllable, that population limitations can facilitate the development of a higher quality of life in the nation and that a small family size can contribute materially to the quality of living for the individual family.

Students at all levels have a right to accurate information about the effect of changes in family and national population size on the individual, the family and the nation so that this body of knowledge is utilised to control family size and national population with beneficial impact on the economic development of the nation and the welfare of the individual families.

On the basis of these overall objectives a Draft Syllabus was drawn up around the following areas:

(i) Population growth (determinants and demographic situation);

(ii) Economic development and population growth (consequences);

(iii) Social development and population growth (consequences);

(iv) Health, nutrition and population;

(v) Biological factors (family life and population);

(vi) Population programmes (national and international).

A National Workshop on Population Education was held in Kuala Lumpur, Malaysia, in 1971. The Report of this Workshop outlines the goals of population education for Malaysia as follows—

> The goals of population education are, on the macro level, to impart to the students knowledge and information concerning population characteristics and the causes and consequences of population change so that they will the better understand the effects of these characteristics and processes on wide range of public policies. Also, they might gain an understanding of the effect of public policy on population issues. Thus, the goal is to create an informed citizenry capable of making responsible decisions with regard to population policy matters. On the micro level, the goal of population education is to develop responsible fertility behaviour as might be defined by the norms and the needs of the society.

Hosts of seminars in many countries have followed, but implementation, apart from a few sporadic instances has not been significant. It is perhaps in the Republics of Indonesia, of Korea and of the Philippines that the most successful nationwide programmes of population education have been undertaken, helped by some generous funding by the United Nations Fund for Population Activities (UNFPA) in the case of Korea and the Philippines.

The Korean Educational Development Institute wisely advises against embarking on a programme of population education in a country until there is a firm prospect of support from a wide cross-section of the political, administrative, social, religious and educational elite of that country. Many parents, community leaders, social groups, who might otherwise accept population education would object if it included topics such as sex education, family planning, birth control, contraception education. In some cultures, a woman's status is related to her fertility, subfertility being looked on almost as something of a personal tragedy. In some cultures the tradition is for girls to get married as soon as menstruation starts. There are traditions that place a high value on the birth of sons. The safe birth of a son is the supreme achievement of every Hindu married couple.

Edward Pohlman and Seshagiri Rao argue that while an understanding of sex education is not essential. As they point out:

> One can teach about (1) population dynamics and the problems of overpopulation, (2) the advantages of small families and (3) the advantages of late marriage without discussing sex or contraception in any way.

They point out that 'the population crisis is a matter of life-or-death urgency' and as such demands priority. They do not want to risk population education becoming embroiled in controversies about sex or contraception education. Thus they advocate a population education programme which is 'clearly and loudly divorced from sex education, family life education and contraception education'.

Harold Howe also argues that—

> the consequences of a rapidly growing population can be taught in an objective, non-sectarian manner without examining areas likely to raise governmental and parental opposition or to create discomfort among instructors.

He also points out that—

> population education is not family planning or birth control education although these topics are related and relevant. Population education is merely instruction in the dynamics of population without the emotionally charged areas of sex, birth control and family planning.

W. H. Southworth, in his book *Curriculum Planning and Some Current Health Problems* also points out that

> Population education is not necessarily school instruction about the use of contraceptives. Neither is it a programme in

> sex education as has been developed in some European and American schools. As defined by the Population Reference Bureau, 'Population education is an attempt to create a deep, universal, action-guiding perception of the consequences of demographic change. It seeks to bring about a realization of the individual, family social and environmental effects of the explosive increase in human population, the rapid shifts in the concentration and distribution of people, the implications of changing age and other demographic patterns and the conceivable options that may be open to mankind to cope with the consequent problems'.

Southworth's little book is very helpful in that it goes beyond generalities and deals with specific items of content in a programme of population education:

> The specific form which population education takes in any particular setting needs to reflect consideration of the population policies, the demographic features, and the educational system of that country or area. Some possible foci of attention include:

1. *Population dynamics*: Pupils can be instructed in the pattern of population growth with attention to birth and death rates and rates of population increase in their own countries. As pupils progress through the grades, the world-wide picture of population growth can be examined. In national, regional, or world history classes, in health education classes, in geography and in civics, the significance of population growth can be studied. Using population data, routine problems in arithmetic can provide incidental learnings.

2. *Human reproduction*: This topic can be studied progressively at different grade levels as the interests and maturity of pupils permit. Specific methods and mechanisms of contraception need not be presented, but factors which facilitate or impede reproduction in various forms of life can be identified. The science curriculum is a natural setting for this instruction. For some age levels

and in some schools, health education and home economics classes may be appropriate allocations.

3. *Health problems associated with childbearing*: Several well established clinical findings could be examined here concerning the risks of maternal morbidity and mortality associated with:

(a) Pregnancy of the young mother and the older mother;

(b) Short intervals between pregnancies; and

(c) High parity.

From this study, the health values for the mother and children involved in marriage at a mature age, of adequate spacing, and of limitation in the size of the family could be shown. The concepts here are sufficiently simple to be considered in health education classes in the lower grades, but could also be examined in more detail in high level health education, home economics and science classes. The problems of the illegitimate child and the unwanted child might be studied in a health context and in relation to population growth. Again, it is important that both boys and girls be reached, since the future father's stake in the health of his wife and children is no less important than that of the future mother.

4. *Family size and its quality of life*: Consideration needs to be given to the economic and social consequences of a family with a large number of children. With a given level of resources and earning power, the larger the family, the smaller the share per child. This idea is particularly true for the town and city family. The consequences are felt not only in matters of housing and food, but in the family's ability to provide for the education, health, and other needs of its children. The pressure of these problems can be viewed as they influence both the individual family and the community or total society. At the upper primary or elementary schools, health classes and social studies may be an appropriate place; civics classes, home economics classes, and geography classes in the middle and secondary schools may be the best locations.

5. *Population characteristics and their relation to policies for social and economic development:* Of special interest to a number of countries is the problem of an adequate food supply which will not only permit a minimum diet for all, but make possible some progress toward improvement in the quality of the diet. Adequate nutrition is not only a health need, it is basic for a population which wants to be more energetic and productive economically.

In the secondary schools, where national history and current development problems are considered, adequate study of population is appropriate. Similarly, in geography, more detailed instruction about population is possible. In the lower grades a selected set of basic ideas could be included with emphasis on the local community, particularly in social studies classes.

6. *Population policies and family planning programmes*: In the context of becoming socialized for responsible adult citizenship roles, each pupil can be informed about the national population policies and the family planning programme in his own country. In the lower or middle grades, the presence of family planning facilities and symbols can be treated along with other community resources. A fuller explanation of the factors which have led to the development of current policies and programmes can be taught in increasing depth at the upper school levels.

It is desirable for secondary pupils to know enough about the purpose and resources of local family planning clinics, public and private, so that they will be ready to take advantage of these facilities when they reach the stage of being"at risk of pregnancy." Knowledge of the purpose and availability of clinics can be transmitted without teaching about specific contraception methods, if necessary.

Professor Jayasuriya suggests the following as representing the content in population education a learner might be expected to have covered by the time tertiary education is completed:

(i) An overview, in a rudimentary form, of population dynamics as a part of the total social and economic development process, in order to give a perspective to the study of population education.

(ii) Population change as a result of the processes of fertility, mortality and migration.
Fertility.
Measures of fertility.
Factors influencing fertility.
Fertility trends, past and present. Likely trends in the future.
Mortality.
Measures of mortality.
Factors influencing mortality.
Mortality trends, past and present. Likely trends in the future.
Measures of migration.
Factors influencing migration.
Migration trends, past and present. Likely trends in the future.

(*iii*) Population size, growth and distribution.
Population size.
Rate of growth.
Population trends, past and present.
Likely trends in the future.
Doubling time.
Age and sex distribution.
Dependency.
Age-sex pyramids.
Rural de-population.
Urbanization.

(iv) An analysis of macro-level relationships between population change and nutrition, housing, education, employment, socio-economic development.

(v) An analysis of micro-level relationships between population change (including family size), and quality of life (same areas as (iv)).

(vi) Inter-relationships between population and resources, population and environment.

(vii) Inter-relationships between population change and political issues (e.g. perceptions of and effects on minority religious and ethnic groups).

(viii) Population policies of own country and other selected countries.

A regional Workshop on Population and Family Education held in Bangkok in 1970 made the first systematic and comprehensive attempt to develop a *conceptual* structure for population education. It identified four areas: namely, population growth; economic development and population growth; social development and population growth; health, nutrition and population growth; and broke down each of these areas into concepts appropriate for three levels of schooling—primary, lower secondary and higher secondary. To cite an example, in the area 'economic development and population growth' the following concepts were listed for the lower secondary level:

(a) Food, clothing and shelter are basic necessities of life.

(b) Availability of these basic necessities varies from place to place, and country to country.

(c) Rapid increase in population leads to inadequate supply of goods and rise in prices.

(d) The standard of living is the sum total of amenities and facilities a man enjoys in a community or country.

(e) The standard of living of the people in a country depends on the total national income and population of that country.

(f) Standard of living differs from country to country depending on the stage of economic development.

(g) A poor standard of living affects adversely the consumption level of people with reference to food, clothing, education, medical facilities etc.

The population education project of the Republic of Korea identifies 31 concepts in five areas, namely: human reproduction and family planning; family size and standard of living; population and the environment; the effects of population phenomena on human life; population policies and programmes. In the area of the effects of population phenomena on human life, there were five 'generalizations' as follows:

(a) So long as man lives within the limits of resources on the earth, he must reasonably limit his desires;

(b) Population congestion exerts a direct influence on the quality of individual and collective lives;

(c) The people living in densely populated countries always face the problems of illiteracy, diseases and poverty.

(d) Today, population problems have become a global concern as the development of communication and transportation brings together many nations more closely, and the need for economic co-operation.

(e) National development has close relationship with the resources available and population size.

These suggested syllabi illustrate the multi-disciplinary nature of population education, its content being drawn from several subject areas and organised around unifying themes.

Whilst most national and international seminars have favoured the fusion and integration of population education concepts throughout the entire school programme, there are those who argue that if the imparting of population education is of such crucial importance to the welfare of humanity, then it should be accorded the status of a 'compulsory subject' in its own right, with its own special courses and with modification of the school programme to make room for it.

A satisfactory compromise would seem to be the infusion of population education concepts into the existing curricula whenever possible together with a short (or long) term compulsory core course for all students. But here there is a danger of overloading the school curriculum. The context of school syllabi tend, like entropy, always to increase. Bits and pieces are tagged on to the curriculum but nothing is ever discarded as redundant. If change does come it tends to be incremental not substitutional: the total amount of content to be studied grows apace.

Southworth rightly points out that 'there are no perfect models of population education in any part of the world' and notes that 'the availability and variety of instructional materials is limited'. The Korean Educational Development Institute warns against the introduction of over-ambitious plans for population education that require all kinds of sophisticated gadgets and equipment. It states:

> Schools and classrooms in Third World countries are a far cry from what obtains in the U.S.A. Film and slide projectors, encyclopaedias and other reference materials, dittoing or mimeographing machines etc., are found in less than one percent of classrooms in Third World countries. Class sizes are large, often shortages of desks and chairs for students; in many classrooms not even a chalk board, or if there is one, there is no chalk to write with unless the children themselves contribute money to buy supplies. The conditions for the use of certain methods of teaching do not exist, even if they are indisputably the right methods to use.

Even so, despite shortages of materials and other problems, some countries have gone ahead imaginatively with their programmes for population education. For example in the Philippines, the following methods have been used in the teaching of population education:

Role-playing	Confrontation
Brainstorming	Small group discussions
Use of spring boards	Interviews
Buzz sessions	Surveys
Case studies	Graphs

The charts appended illustrate how population growth impinges on a variety of social and economic factors. Simple charts like these can be the jumping off point for a whole series of lessons to illustrate how standards of living etc. are affected by population size.

Swaziland
Population Growth Under Three Fertility Assumptions, 1975–2025

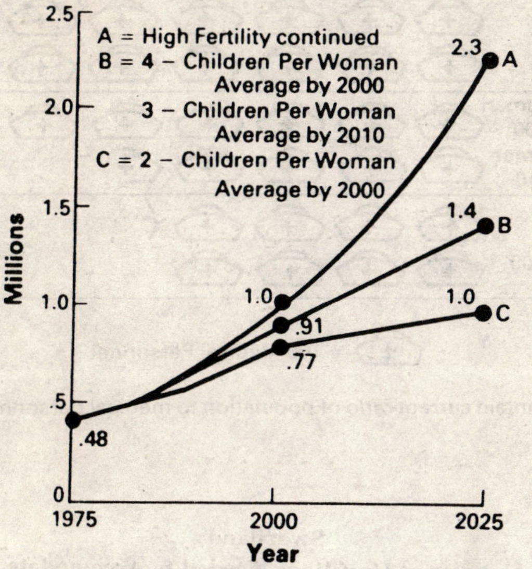

Swaziland
Average Size of Homesteads 1980–2010
Under Three Fertility Assumptions

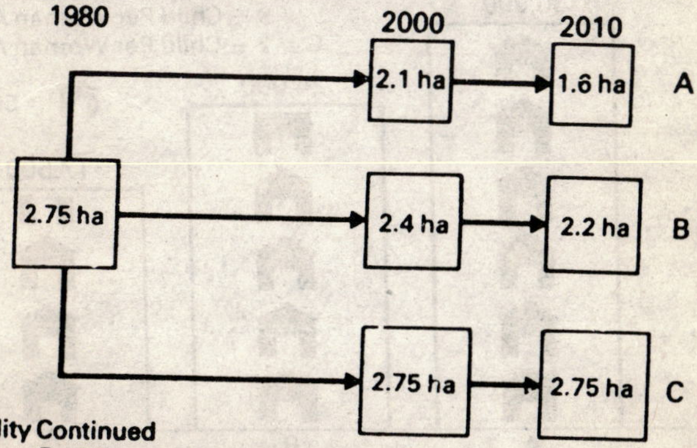

A = High Fertility Continued
B = 4 – Children Per Woman Average by 2000
3 – Children Per Woman Average by 2010
C = 2 – Children Per Woman Average by 2000

Swaziland

Additional Medical Personnel Required, 1980–2010*

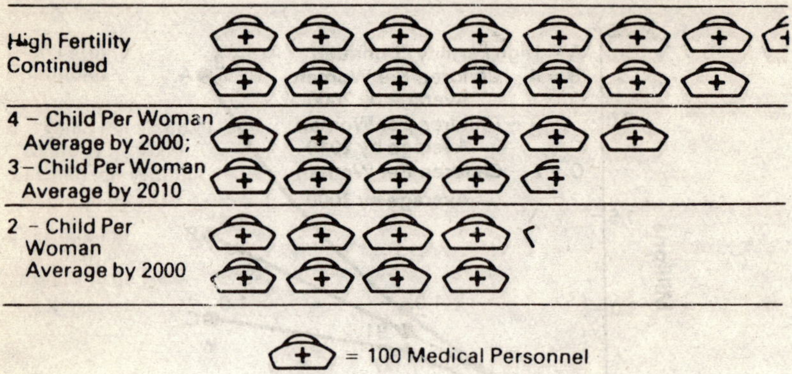

* To maintain current ratio of population to medical personnel.

Swaziland

Number of Dwellings Needed to Accomodate Urban Population Growth, 1980–2000*

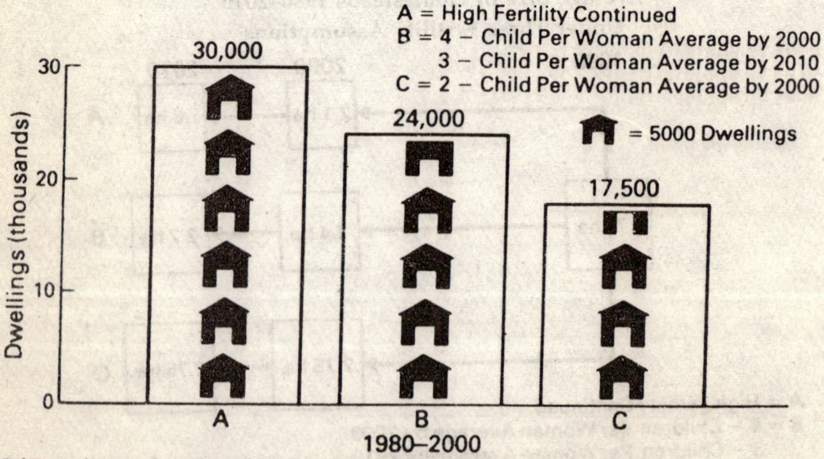

* Assuming an Average of 4.5 Persons Per Dwelling in Urban Areas

Swaziland
Size of the Urban Population, 1980–2010

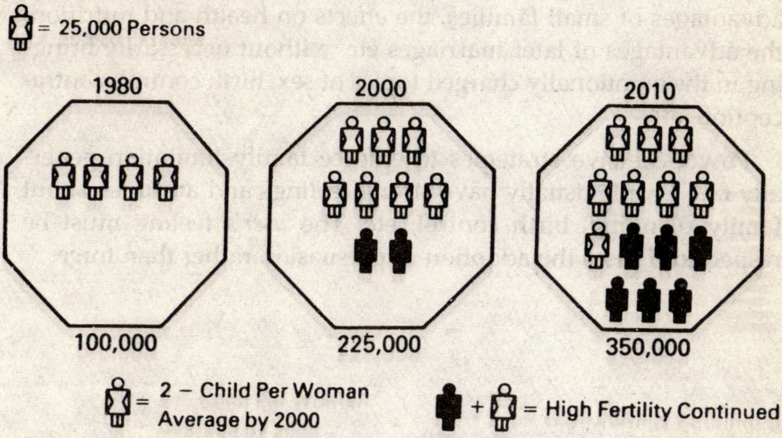

SUMMARY

The introduction of population education into the educational systems of a number of countries is among the most significant curriculum innovations of our time. It was necessitated by the exponential increase in the world's population and its attendant problems—overcrowding, ill-health, shortages of food, housing, water, sanitation and the inability to provide education for ever-increasing numbers. It was believed a solution to the problems of overpopulation lay in the mind rather than the uterus. Hence the introduction of 'population studies' in the school curricula. Population education refers to all the various educational activities dealing with population issues. Its purpose is to aid young people to understand the significance of population factors for their own lives, for their families, for the nation and for the world; to provide insights into the interrelationships between population and development. Population education can be an excellent multi-disciplinary subject, drawing its content from several subject areas and organised around unifying themes such as population dynamics, population growth and its connection with economic, social and health development. One can teach about population dynamics, the problems of overpopulation, the advantages of small families, the effects on health and nutrition, the advantages of later marriages etc. without necessarily bringing in the emotionally charged topics of sex, birth control, contraception, etc.

Power-coercive strategies to enforce family limitation generally fail. People usually have strong feelings and attitudes about family planning, birth control, etc. The *user's* feeling must be respected. Hence the adoption of persuasion rather than force.

21

Health Education

Much of the effort and resources spent on education are often vitiated by the fact that the children are suffering from malnutrition and ill-health. Every month 100,000 children in India die of malnutrition. Severe malnutrition affects 460 million people, and the number suffering from some degree of malnutrition could be as high as half the population of the world—over 2,000 million people. Attendance and performance at school are much reduced by malnutrition and ill-health. A hungry child who has walked miles to school, suffering from guinea worm or tropical ulcers, can hardly be expected to perform with maximum efficiency in school. The intellectual growth of children can be stunted by disease such as bilharsia (schistosomiasis). Eradication of malaria in many parts of Ghana has been attended by a spectacular reduction in school absenteeism. Malnutrition (due to vitamin and mineral deficiencies) leads to poor performance in school. Children suffering from malnutrition suffer apathy, chronic fatigue, lack of concentration, retardation in physical growth and show signs of emotional disturbance. Deficiency of the vitamin, nicotinic acid, causes irritability, loss of memory, insomnia. Deficiencies of riboflavin and Vitamin A cause trachoma which seriously affects vision. Numerous clinical, biochemical, histological and electroencephalogical studies on children confirm that serious malnutrition can lead to mental retardation. Kwashiokor is just one of many diseases, common in many parts of Africa, resulting from malnutrition.

Illness and suffering due to protein deficiency and other forms of malnutrition are often due to ignorance, local customs or superstition. Thus, in spite of a higher level of education than that of other Ugandan tribes the Baganda are remarkably ignorant in nutritional matters and have shown themselves extremely recalcitrant to any suggestion of change. Their cattle are emaciated, being a symbol of wealth and not a product for consumption. Milk is not a food, though it may be given to the sick as a medicine. In other areas children suffer from severe protein deficiency in villages on the banks of rivers teeming with protein-rich fish. There are many food taboos in Africa which unfortunately apply mainly to children.

The Unesco booklet *Education in a Rural Environment* advises:

> Such customs must be fought, but with caution. Care should be taken to avoid showering 'lectures' and ready-made solutions from outside. The people should be helped to see the need to change their ways and to bring about necessary changes themselves instead of relying on the State.

Anything that can be done to break the vicious circle of malnutrition—disease will prove a great boon to countless millions in the Third World. Apart from direct medical treatment, education can play a very significant part in the prevention of malnutrition and debilitating diseases such as bilharzia, hook-worm, and worse. A National Workshop on Primary Education, held in Nigeria, April 26–May 8, 1971, reported as follows:

> Indeed, the proper teaching of Health education would seem so great a priority that there is much to recommend immediate action to implement it in all ciasses.

In the Appendix 1 are given suggestions relating to:—

Pollution Education,
Safety Education,

Drug Education and
Venereal Disease Education.

With a view to educating school children about the dangers of drug addiction the Silliman University Extension Programme in the Philippines is promoting the dissemination of curriculum materials for drug education in all elementary schools of Negroes Oriental and neighbouring provinces. In addition, it trains teachers in a series of in-service seminars on the use of the materials. Its primary objective is preventive education and the conducting of an information drive against drug abuse. It also has a programme for the on-going treatment and counselling of drug abusers.

SUMMARY

Many diseases, malnutrition, ill-health, can all be prevented—if people are told *how*. These are often due to ignorance, and the purpose of Health Education in schools is to dispel such ignorance and instead develop an informed and enlightened school population—especially about pollution, safety, drug addiction and venereal disease.

Questions

1. What aspects, if any, of health education are included in the curricula of the schools in your country?
2. Could such teaching be a) extended, b) improved? Say how and why.

APPENDIX 1

W.H. Southworth, in his *Curriculum Planning and Some Current Health Problems* suggests the following programme of Health Education.

Pollution Education

The rapidly declining quality of the environment...increased environmental pollution...The solution to pollution lies not in attempting to eliminate all pollutants, but, rather, in minimizing the production of pollutants, and in managing the disposal of them.

The *air pollution* problem

The *water pollution* problem—in many countries, drinking water is becoming less and less palatable because of pollutants. The *soil pollution* problem...Man, through poor land management, erosion, pollution, sewerage, seepage, and neglect, can in one day destroy what nature has taken eons to develop.

The *food pollution* problem.

The *noise pollution* problem. Noise in unwanted sound...In some industries and cities the noise levels are not only deafening but also fatiguing.

Implications for Health Teaching

Education about pollution and its control is a legitimate part of health education from the kindergarten through high school. Here are some suggested concepts for various grade levels:

Kindergarten Through Third Grade

1. Our health is affected by our environment.
2. Space affects the way in which we feel and respond.
3. Without clean water and air, life would not continue.
4. Noise has an effect on the way in which we feel and act.
5. Pure food is essential to good health.
6. Many people work to protect our food.
7. Many people work to keep our water and air safe.

8. Garbage and rubbish need to be put into appropriate containers.
9. Each of us can improve his environment.
10. There are living and non-living hazards in the environment.

Grades Four Through Six

1. Human life depends on water, air, and topsoil.
2. Ionizing radiations in the air and soil are a kind of pollution.
3. Disposal of sewage, garbage, and other refuse is an increasing problem.
4. Improper sewage, garbage, and refuse disposal can contribute to the transmission of disease.
5. Our immediate surroundings, including the people in those surroundings, have an effect on us.
6. We are dependent upon many people for safe water, air, and food.
7. Sanitary conditions are improved through the efforts of many concerned groups.
8. Several community organizations and agencies help to abate and control pollution.

Grades Seven Through Nine

1. The health of human beings and lower animals may be impaired by air, water, soil, and food pollution.
2. A small amount of background radiation in our environment is normal.
3. Chemicals are added to water supplies and food for various reasons.
4. The cleanliness, wholesomeness, and safeness of food is maintained in several ways.

5. The wise use of insecticides, pesticides, herbicides, and other such poisons is a complex problem.
6. Public health laws are necessary for good community health.
7. International, national, intermediate, and local health agencies co-operate to abate and control pollution.

Grades Ten Through Twelve

1. The behaviour of man is affected by atmospheric conditions.
2. As man has increasingly triumphed over climatic problems, pestilence, and famine, he has created an environment which introduces new hazards to human health.
3. Many of the present environmental health problems began hundreds of years in the past.
4. Air, water, soil and food pollutants have both direct and indirect effects on health.
5. When ionizing radiations pass through living things, cellular damage may occur.
6. Health science is actively engaged in research which links various kinds of pollution to specific diseases.
7. There is need for the establishment of air, water, and food quality standards in terms of known and suspected effects on what is necessary for the protection of human health and welfare, agriculture and property.
8. The food supply for metropolitan areas presents an increasing number and variety of public health problems.
9. Science and industry are co-operating to solve pollution problems, including noise pollution.
10. Conservation and control of air, water, and soil affect the world community.

11. Communities need co-operative planning to enhance health.
12. Personal health and community health are interwoven with world health.

Implications for School/Community Relations

Pollution, like many other of today's big health problems, is a community affair. It cannot be solved by schools alone. True, schools do have a part in pollution abatement and control; a very important part, that of education. There is, however, a great need for public understanding of the complex problems created by air, water, soil, food, and noise pollution. Life on this planet depends upon intelligent community, national, and world action to minimize the hazards of pollution. Unless some things are done to conserve the air, water, and topsoil and to use them wisely, man may die in his own waste products. Pollution education of today's children and youth may motivate the needed changes in the decades ahead.

Questions for Curriculum Planners

A great many questions about pollution education need exploration by curriculum planners with the help of health authorities, parents, and pupils. Among the questions are these:

- What kinds of pollution are influencing the environment and people in your area?
- What needs to be done about the pollution problem in your area?
- What can an individual or family do about pollution in the immediate environment?
- What curriculum areas lend themselves to pollution education?

In addition to the human suffering caused by accidents, their economic cost is astronomical...The most frequent types of fatal accidents usually involve motor vehicles, falls, burns and drowning. The proportion varies from one country to another.

The spread of electrification, especially in rural areas, the introduction of potent insecticides, the increasing numbers of motor vehicles of all types travelling on roads which were designed for more primitive kinds of traffic are outstanding examples... of increased accident hazards...

The poor, overcrowded home in an old, dilapidated building becomes a special focus of accidents...Where families are in poor economic straits and the mother has to go out to work, young children are apt to be left at home for long periods. Burn accidents—the most serious of all among young children—are especially apt to occur when children are left alone.

The basic aim of safety education is to make children, youths and adults aware of the accident hazards of everyday life and of ways of coping with them...A little thought, time and effort devoted to doing things safely can make the difference between life and death, between fun and misery, between success and failure...

In addition, there are so-called natural and man-made civil disasters such as fires, floods, earthquakes, transportation wrecks, explosion, hurricanes, tornadoes, blizzards, lightning and attack by conventional and nuclear weapons...It is important that people acquire the needed survival understandings, procedures, and skills to meet the problem...Disaster preparedness is a must.

Safety concepts should be taught as an integral part of health education, physical education, science, social studies, reading, arithmetic, language, and art in primary grades.

The safety education programme at secondary school level must be adapted to the maturity and interests of that age group, rather than consist of a repetition of subject matter included in earlier years. Youths at this age are increasingly interested in adventure. They need to be given greater understanding about the causes of accidents and how to prevent them, and they need motivation to accept the challenge of 'playing it safe'. There are those who claim that safety is a discipline with ample content, and that the subject is worthy of its own place in the secondary school curriculum.

Drug Education

Today there is grave concern in many countries of the world about an epidemic upsurge in the use of psychoactive drugs, especially by young people in the population. This drug-taking often leads to dependence...Drugs are two-edged swords; they may save lives as well as wreck lives. Some of the most dangerous and dependence producing drugs are very useful under medical supervision. The acute social domestic consequences of alcoholism are reflected in broken homes, family misery, neglected children, automobile accidents, criminal offences, unemployment and poverty.

The alcoholic is a sick person; he needs understanding by his family, friends and employer; he needs professional treatment and rehabilitation.

The evidence that cigarette smoking greatly increases the incidence of lung cancer is irrefutable. We have simply had the rotten bad luck to have discovered after all these years that the harmful effects are overwhelming.

Implications for Health Teaching

The objectives of drug education are:

- To develop pride in a healthy body and mind;
- To cultivate a wholesome respect for the potential dangers of drugs and household chemicals;
- To help pupils appreciate the medicinal value of drugs, and their interaction within the body;
- To provide factual information about drugs, and to correct misconceptions about them.

In the primary grades attention is focused upon the development of desirable health attitudes and daily practices, rather than specific teaching about drugs.

In the intermediate grades, instruction about alcohol and tobacco is appropriate.

At junior high school level...study of drugs and the ethics of using them for prevention of disease and the maintenance of health.

Venereal Disease Education

Venereal disease continues to be an extremely serious public health problem throughout most of the world. A great majority of the reported cases are in teenagers and young adults.

The 'sex-sell' aimed by advertisers at the teenage market, encourages sexual promiscuity which in turn assures the spread of venereal disease.

There is inadequate sex education and venereal disease education in homes, schools and community agencies.

A complete programme of venereal disease education includes instruction about the nature, spread and consequences of the disease... the treatment, prevention, and all other information needed to produce an informed and enlightened school population. It is a logical part of instruction about communicable diseases.

22

Day Schools

This innovation consisted essentially of an attempt to introduce a measure of practical work into what was, at the time, a traditional, examination-oriented academic curriculum.

Ghana was faced with the problem of a growing number of school leavers who were unable to continue their education further. About 80 percent of the children who completed middle-level education did not continue to secondary education. Moreover, these children were not equipped for their new independence, they had no work skills, and, even if they had, there were no jobs available. The country faced the massive problem of unemployed schools leavers, of joblessness and urban drift.

The Government recognised:

(i) the need to plan towards the solution of the problem of unemployment;

(ii) the need to plan towards effecting a change in the attitudes of school leavers from white collar jobs to more profitable practical vocational occupations;

(iii) the need to train children to acquire the necessary skills that would aid development in rural areas.

The strategy the government decided on was to change the curriculum of the schools from being traditional and academic to one that related work of the school to the conditions young school leavers would face when they left school; in other words, the children would do in school something that would be directly useful to Ghanaian youngsters in a Ghanaian community. Education was to be relevant and indigenous. The existing middle schools were to be replaced by schools—continuation schools—that would provide a more suitable terminal education for school leavers. The continuation classes were to occupy the two years (and later four years) after primary school. The children were to devote a proportion of their school time (up to one-third) doing something that would yield an economic return, such as growing things, making things, providing services. In other words, they would devote this time to practical activities that not only produced tangible (and profitable) results but also involved mastery of productive skills and techniques that would prove useful when the school leavers returned to their communities.

But this was not what the children or their parents wanted. Farming parents did not want an education that would bind their children to a life of toil on the soil. Farming as a future way of life did not appeal. They wanted the time-honoured academic education that would lead to white collar jobs. This was pre-eminently the vocational education that gave access to the most prestigious and best paid jobs. Manual work was regarded with dismay; the 'dirty hands syndrome' applied.

So when the continuation classes started in 1962 with 18 trial schools the circumstances did not bode well for success. However, either by chance or by design, their introduction was timed perfectly. At the time the government had started a national 'feed yourself' campaign. These schools no longer came to be regarded as a job for the educationally unfortunate but as a new means to a very necessary end. Agriculture was no longer despised; agricultural activities not only had quick and tangible results, they now had the stamp of official approval. Education for life was legitimate.

The schools flourished. Village craftsmen were invited to the schools as (paid) specialist tutors. The schools had farms of various kinds including poultry, sheep and staple crops; the school gardens produced vegetables; the specialist craft centres produced sandals, Kente cloth etc; the home science activities included baking, cooking, needlework, the pupils produced goods and services for which they were paid. Most of the activities of the school were self-supporting. The children, teachers and parents were enthusiastic. Community support was abundant. By 1973/74 there were 467 continuation schools.

However, by 1978 these schools were coming to an end. By 1980/81 they no longer existed. Why had they failed? In effect didn't fail. The basic concept of continuation schools was incorporated into a new structure of junior schools. Although this was not state explicitly in the Ministry report setting up the new system of education, the basic idea of continuation is easily recognisable in the statement that the content of the new educational structure aims at a type of curriculum that will make education both *terminal and continuing*. It will be terminal in the sense that it will orientate the pupil psychologically to his immediate environment and provide him with some basic knowledge and necessary skills to earn a living in this environment.

So the idea of continuation schools has proved flexible and adaptable.

One aim of the schools that has not been achieved is the reduction of unemployment. In fact, unemployment has increased, not decreased. But this has been due to causes outside the control of the education system. The faith in the capability of education to solve all individual and social ills is touching, but the problems of unemployment are primarily political, not educational. Curriculum reform is not able to solve the problem of unemployment since the causes of unemployment have very little to do with what is or is not taught in schools. The way to defeat unemployment is to provide jobs. Edwards argues that a larger share of development expenditures should rather be used to create jobs, and less on secondary and higher education. And Mark Blaugh suggests that a more effective way of reducing unemployment is not to expand education but rather put the capital into the direct creation of jobs.

SUMMARY

The continuation day schools were set up in Ghana to introduce more practical work into a traditional, academic curriculum. The country was faced with growing numbers of unemployed school leavers, unable to continue their education and with no jobs to go to. The curriculum was designed to be relevant and indigenous, giving the pupils the practical skills and techniques they would need on returning to their communities—for farming, crafts etc. The schools were later incorporated into the junior schools established in their place.

Questions

1. Do you have something similar to 'continuation classes' in your country?

   What was the specific reason for their being introduced?
2. What are the main reasons for their success or failure?
3. Is the curriculum in your middle/junior schools relevant to the particular circumstances and situation in your country? What alterations, if any, would you make?